Law & Empire in t

**Publication of the Advanced Seminar Series
is made possible by generous support from
The Brown Foundation, Inc., of Houston, Texas.**

**School of American Research
Advanced Seminar Series**

Richard M. Leventhal
General Editor

Law & Empire in the Pacific

Contributors

Donald Brenneis
Department of Anthropology, University of California, Santa Cruz

Jane F. Collier
Department of Cultural and Social Anthropology, Stanford University

Martha Kaplan
Department of Anthropology, Vassar College

John D. Kelly
Department of Anthropology, University of Chicago

Brij V. Lal
Research School for Pacific and Asian Studies, Australian National University

Sally Engle Merry
Department of Anthropology, Wellesley College

Hirokazu Miyazaki
Department of Anthropology, Northwestern University

Jonathan Kamakawiwoʻole Osorio
Center for Hawaiian Studies, University of Hawaiʻi at Manoa

Annelise Riles
School of Law, Northwestern University

Noenoe K. Silva
Department of Political Science, University of Hawai'i at Manoa

Law & Empire in the Pacific

Fiji and Hawai'i

Edited by Sally Engle Merry and Donald Brenneis

School of American Research Press
Santa Fe

James Currey
Oxford

School of American Research Press

Post Office Box 2188
Santa Fe, New Mexico 87504-2188

James Currey Ltd

73 Botley Road
Oxford OX2 0BS

Director: James F. Brooks
Executive Editor: Catherine Cocks
Manuscript Editor: Kate Talbot
Design and Production: Cynthia Welch
Proofreader: Heidi Utz
Indexer: Sylvia Coates
Printer: Maple-Vail Book Group

Library of Congress Cataloging-in-Publication Data:

Law and empire in the Pacific : Fiji and Hawai'i / edited by Sally Engle Merry and
Donald Brenneis ; [contributors, Donald Brenneis...et al.].— 1st ed.
   p. cm. — (Advanced seminar series) Includes bibliographical references and index.
   ISBN 1-930618-24-7 (alk. paper) — ISBN 1-930618-25-5 (pbk. : alk. paper)
   1. Chiefdoms—Hawaii—History. 2. Chiefdoms—Fiji—History. 3.Hawaiians—Government
relations. 4. Fijians—Government relations. 5.Hawaiians—Legal status, laws, etc. 6. Fijians—
Legal status, laws, etc. 7. Law—Hawaii—History. 8. Law—Fiji—History. 9. Hawaii—Colonial
influence. 10. Fiji—Colonial influence. 11. Hawaii—Race relations. 12. Fiji—Race relations.
13. Great Britain—Colonies—Oceania. 14. United States—Territories and possessions.
I. Merry, Sally Engle, 1944– II. Brenneis, Donald Lawrence, 1946– III. Series: School of
American Research advanced seminar series.
GN673.H3 L39 2003
306'.09969–dc22   2003021458

British Library Cataloguing-in-Publication Data available

Cover photo credits: Hawaiian plantation; presidential palace guard, Suva, Fiji
© 2003 by Sally Engle Merry; *Protect Kaho'olawe, May 1977* © 1977 by Edward Greevy;
'Iolani Palace, Honolulu, Hawai'i, courtesy of the Hawai'i State Archives Collection

Contents

CONTENTS

Figures

Acknowledgments

SAR Press thanks Noenoe Silva for her assistance with the Hawaiian words in this volume.

Law & Empire in the Pacific
Fiji and Hawai'i

1

Introduction

Sally Engle Merry and Donald Brenneis

Fiji and Hawai'i, two chains of high volcanic islands at one time controlled by powerful chiefs, lie a few thousand miles apart in the Pacific Ocean. Colonized in the late nineteenth century, both developed a thriving sugar plantation economy based on imported Asian laborers. In each case, colonial officials formed a coalition with the indigenous people and excluded the immigrant sugar workers from land and political power. The workers responded by organizing into labor unions and mobilizing politically to improve their lot. By the end of the colonial era, the indigenous people in both places were more or less outnumbered by the people of other nations who had come to work the land. British and American law and bureaucracy were layered over a system of chiefly authority in both places.

The duration of the colonial period was similar: The British controlled Fiji from 1874 until 1970; the Americans ruled Hawai'i as a colony from 1898 until 1959. Fiji became independent in 1970; Hawai'i became a US state in 1959. Fiji is now independent but economically dependent; Hawai'i is a state but retains a neocolonial economic relationship to the United States. Both are neocolonial, not postcolonial, in the sense that they are nominally self-governing but as economically dependent as they were under colonialism. Native Hawaiians remain in an essentially colonial status within the state of Hawai'i, excluded from their lands and politically subordinated in state politics.

However, ethnic conflicts in these two places varied dramatically during and after colonialism. In the years following direct colonial control, both Fiji and Hawai'i faced ethnic tensions and indigenous nationalism, along with ongoing and unresolved charges of social injustice. In Fiji, ethnic Fijians feared economic domination by the Indo-Fijians, even though ethnic Fijians own the vast bulk of the land in perpetuity. Indo-Fijians were elected to political leadership, but ethnic Fijian–led coups quickly deposed them in the name of indigenous rights and primordial connections to the land. Two coups in 1987 and one in 2000 excluded elected Indo-Fijians from political power and allowed ethnic Fijians to retain political control. However, this came at the price of political stability. Ethnic Fijians now feel economically secondary to the Indo-Fijian community and are seeking affirmative action to equalize their position.

Hawai'i, in contrast, appears to be a successful multiethnic state. The descendants of European and Asian plantation workers, Native Hawaiians, American colonial elites, and mainland US immigrants live in peace under a democratically elected government. Certain immigrant groups have achieved political power and economic affluence. Other immigrants, such as those from the Philippines and the Pacific Islands, are caught at the bottom of the social hierarchy. The indigenous Native Hawaiian people are a dispossessed and largely poor minority struggling to recapture their culture and their control over land. The ongoing but unresolved demands for land and sovereignty in Hawai'i by *Kanaka Maoli*—Native Hawaiians—have fueled an energetic and sometimes angry sovereignty movement since the 1970s. The movement seeks to restore political power to Kanaka Maoli through a range of remedies, from independence to a system of reserves, but there is no consensus within the community about the best path to self-determination.

Although the political turmoil in both places is usually understood as ethnic, the causes are equally economic and political. Many are rooted in the legal and institutional arrangements of land and governance developed during the colonial era. This book explores how the colonial legal legacies of Hawai'i and Fiji contributed to their contemporary political instability and ethnic turmoil. Comparing the ethnic situation in Hawai'i with that of Fiji highlights the impact of colonial legal arrangements on the shape of contemporary ethnic conflict.

Among the most salient differences between these two societies are their sharp contrasts in the legal regulation of land and citizenship. These systems of land and citizenship grew out of different theories of colonial governance. Hawai'i was colonized by Americans who sought to privatize the land, Christianize the Hawaiians, and convert them into free laborers independent of the chiefs. Governance shifted from a system of chieftains to a constitutional monarchy with an elected legislative body. The result was a weakening of the chiefs, the massive loss of land by Native Hawaiians and its purchase by whites in the nineteenth century, and a gradual economic and social marginalization of Hawaiians in the twentieth. By the middle of the twentieth century, most Hawaiians lived in remote villages and poor urban neighborhoods. Following the model of privatized land and capitalist development, the sugar planters imported laborers from China and Japan to plant and harvest the cane. In the 1880s, the increasingly powerful Americans succeeded in excluding them from citizenship. When Hawai'i became a US territory, however, the Hawai'i-born children of the Chinese and Japanese became US citizens with the right to vote. They gradually acquired political power in the twentieth century while Hawaiian political power diminished.

Fiji, on the other hand, was governed by a British regime that sought to protect and isolate the Fijians in villages and to maintain the power of the chiefs and their control over land. The vast majority of the land remained under the control of Fijian villages and chiefs. The white-owned sugar companies imported people from India to work the fields but, like the white planters in Hawai'i, saw the Indians as labor units instead of citizens. They dealt with the demand for political participation by creating a system of separate communal voting for seats designated by ethnic identity. Clearly, Hawai'i and Fiji developed quite disparate colonial systems for allocating land and political power.

This book provides the kind of controlled comparison once popular in anthropology but builds on that approach by analyzing societies in a larger sociopolitical context and more historically than much of the comparative work in the discipline. Like controlled comparison, it seeks to look at differences while holding certain features constant. These two places participated in the same colonial social world, shaped by similar ideologies of race, class, gender, capitalism, and Christianity, and even influenced by the same thinkers, yet each developed a very unique texture of ethnic and political relationships. Similar forms of representation, economic arrangements, and ideologies of rule intersected with one another in different ways in different places. It is precisely the emergence of difference despite these connections and mutual influences that makes the comparison valuable. However, this comparison also draws on world system theory, emphasizing the importance of examining interconnections among societies and their changes over historical time. The comparison is not intended to reveal parallel developments that prove a common evolutionary path toward modernity but to show how the conjunction of similar influences varies in meaning and effect under different historical circumstances.

Indeed, this comparison does not move us toward a metanarrative of colonialism but instead points to complexity and intersections. Christianity, colonialism, capitalism, literacy, privatization of land, and electoral democracy formed quite dissimilar constellations in the two island groups. Hawai'i has a more fluid and less racially divided society than Fiji, although it is by no means free of racism or persisting racial/ethnic inequalities. Fijians have managed to retain their cultural identity and political power more extensively than Native Hawaiians but at the price of alienating the substantial Indo-Fijian population. Whereas Japanese-Americans have become politically and economically powerful in Hawai'i, Indo-Fijians have been less able to translate their economic success into political power. Many of the more educated Indo-Fijians are leaving the country.

The comparison highlights the role played by law, both in allocating control over land and power and in constructing ideologies of difference that render the system coherent and legitimate. Law was a central mechanism in these colonial endeavors, as it is in all colonial projects. It is not often theorized as central to the process of colonialism, nor are its complicated effects usually analyzed in colonial situations. Yet, as the chapters in this book demonstrate, law is critical to shaping colonial relations. Law's effect comes through its capacity to regulate, of course. Its effect also lies in the resources it affords—or denies—communities for their own use in managing conflict and shaping local sociality, an issue of particular consequence in Fiji. Beyond this, its importance can also be clearly seen in the ways law solidifies power through its creation of legal documents and forms. In the latter sense, law produces power through its embodiment in objects, records, archives, briefs, systems of land measurement, and ways of regulating voting that constitute a taken-for-granted world, now transposed into the objects of everyday life and interaction.

Therefore, the comparison of two societies with similar historical situations and locations but dissimilar legal allocations of land and political power illustrates the extent to which legal arrangements affect the shape of social life and social inequalities, particularly among ethnic groups. It also should be clear that, although we use law as a singular noun, our sense of the range of institutions, practices, and effects that fall under this rubric is highly varied, differentially apparent, and at times contradictory. A central theme in the book, indeed, is the complex interplay between patently highly determinate structures and rules and the often indeterminate, unpredictable, and contested ways in which they take shape—and reciprocally shape—ongoing social, economic, and political life in Hawai'i and Fiji.

The chapters in this book examine this comparison from a variety of perspectives, looking both at points of commonality, such as the nature of chiefdoms and their encounters with capitalism or the ideologies that shaped the colonial enterprise, and points of difference, such as the particular arrangements of land that the law allowed in each place. For example, the theories of Henry Maine and J. W. B. Money shaped the British colonial enterprise in India and across the Pacific, as did conceptions of racial labor capacities and white supremacy. Similar ideas formed the plantation racial hierarchy in Hawai'i. The land and labor needs of commercial plantation sugar production were a driving influence in both places.

Land was treated differently, however. Many of the chapters focus on the importance of land for defining identity and belonging, as well as for providing economic security and political power. For both the ethnic Fijians and Kanaka Maoli, attachment to land is fundamental to group and individual life. Yet, these two groups differ enormously in their power to enact that attachment. Whereas Fijians still control much of the land, Kanaka Maoli have been largely dispossessed. Patterns of intermarriage and social contact also varied. The social divide between Indo-Fijians and ethnic Fijians is far deeper than that between Native Hawaiians and immigrant communities. Intermarriage and cultural sharing are pervasive between Kanaka Maoli and immigrant communities, and similarities in social class crosscut ethnic differences. Certain chapters look at movements of resistance among indigenous communities; others focus on the efforts of immigrant groups to construct a sense of belonging.

Our original intention was to use this comparison as a way of appreciating the role of law in colonial histories and the complex ways it defined power and property. However, this comparison led to a second level of analysis, that of the system of colonial knowledge that shaped and justified the kinds of legal, political, and economic relationships that developed. The comparison of Hawai'i and Fiji showed the importance of the kinds of knowledge that colonialism itself produced and that were shared among these and other colonial projects. These include knowledge of race and racial labor capacities, the value of village life, a fantasized homogeneous and consensual village as the prototypical site of indigenous society, and the imagined evolutionary path from status to contract. Other forms of colonial knowledge include the disciplinary systems of plantation agriculture, the value of rule by law, and the importance of naval power in the Pacific. These forms of knowledge are shared among British and Americans in a variety of colonial roles. They derive from and imply practices of knowledge and institutionalized ways of knowing, in which policy, political interest, underlying assumptions, and contemporary academic social science constantly interact. Many of these forms and practices were absorbed by those who were colonized. The image of civilization itself, with its link to modernity, to power, and to Europe, is an important feature of this system of knowledge. The chapters in this book explore the second dimension of law and empire: the systems of meaning and knowledge that colonialism made and that made colonialism.

The focus on systems of knowledge led to a third level of analysis: the impact of systems of knowledge produced by anthropologists themselves as they seek to understand colonialism, law, and other social forms. These forms of knowledge production are not divorced from relations of power, any more than those of the colonial sages were. Moreover, they are not separate from colonial forms of knowledge. For example, the focus on understanding both Fijians and Hawaiians as rural village residents and on reconstructing an authentic Hawaiian or Fijian way of life based on residuals from the past, which characterized much anthropological research in these regions until recently, represents a colonial way of thinking about Fijians and Hawaiians. Analyzing them separately from their colonial histories and from the effects of capitalist sugar production and imported labor also replicates colonial forms of knowledge. Anthropological knowledge is a colonial project in these ways, but also a potentially libratory one. The authors grapple with this question in their chapters.

This book grew out of an advanced seminar held in March 2001 at the School for American Research (SAR) in Santa Fe, New Mexico. The seminar brought together scholars working on Fiji and Hawai'i and scholars working on the anthropology of law and colonialism. The goal was to have equal representation from both regions, although the exigencies of scholarly life and availability made that difficult. There are more chapters on Fiji than Hawai'i, and a better representation of indigenous Hawaiian perspectives than of indigenous Fijian ones, but chapters on both places portray a poignant sense of current crises. Both Noenoe Silva and Brij Lal were unable to attend the seminar but contributed papers. Don Brenneis presented an ethnographically grounded paper concerning Indo-Fijian community life but was unable to provide a chapter for this volume because of other obligations. Certain chapters engage more extensively with theoretical issues in anthropology; others are more focused on the shape of contemporary political struggles. This diversity adds to the book, providing various voices and vantage points for the comparison. The book is intended to be a contribution to Pacific anthropology, as well as a Pacific location for an analysis of the intersections between law and culture over time. Also, it endeavors to address basic questions in anthropology about methods of comparison, the importance of colonial knowledge production, and the nature and consequences of anthropological knowledge production.

We found in our own processes of knowledge production that we were constantly encountering gaps in theoretical orientation and knowledge, divergences in the scale and nature of the analytical "units" we considered, and analytical slippages among our frames of reference that proved enormously productive in breaking our conventional frames and moving our thinking forward. We did not all agree, for example, about the centrality of an analysis of political economy or world historical systems. Some put greater emphasis on political economy and world historical systems, tracing the expansion of the capitalist sugar plantation economy and the ideologies that grounded it. Others focused on its calcified legacy of social knowledge in the domains of bureaucracy and everyday legal regulation. Some examined colonial processes and their legacies at the level of the village or through the micro-social analysis of discourse. The systematic comparison of ideal-typic analysis proved fruitful in considering the changing cultural practices of power and personhood during colonial encounters and for conceptualizing the changing basis for identity in contemporary ethnic struggles. The various approaches built on and amplified one another, slipping from more structural forms of analysis to those more concerned with knowledge production or discourse.

As generally happens in SAR seminars, which involve an intensive week of sharing papers and conversation, a movement occurred within the seminar. We began, as this introduction begins, with the comparison of Hawai'i and Fiji and their colonial experiences. Only as the comparison expanded and deepened did the critical role of transnational colonial knowledges, including the knowledge of law and mechanisms for regulating citizenship and land, emerge as a central problem. Moreover, only as we reflected on this system of knowledge were we forced to examine anthropology's role as another, sometimes related, system of knowledge. Thus, the seminar discussions moved us to foreground questions of knowledge and knowledge production, even though our analysis began from a deep grounding in political economy and world system theory. All these levels of analysis are essential, and we argue that they need to be kept in conversation with one another and not in separate books or branches of anthropology. In these chapters, some stretching takes place among various methods of doing anthropological research, but the effect is complementary, showing in diverse

ways the value of comparing two colonial experiences and the importance of seeing them as part of the same social world.

COMPARING HAWAI'I AND FIJI

Both Fiji and Hawai'i were chiefdoms when the first Europeans
arrived, bringing trade, missionaries, and explorers in the late eighteenth century. The early explorers and traders arriving in Fiji and
Hawai'i encountered many separate chiefdoms at war with one
another, organized according to the logic of chiefdoms that Jane
Collier analyzes in Chapter 2. With the backing of European military
equipment, strategy, and ships, a few chiefs gradually consolidated
power during a period of protracted conflict (Lal 1992:10; Waterhouse
1997). In Hawai'i, the assistance of European ships, guns, and military
expertise enabled Kamehameha to become paramount chief by 1810
(Kamakau 1961), and in Fiji two rival governments were established by
the 1860s (Lal 1992:10). Centralized political control, in both cases,
grew out of a combination of European military technology and chiefly
competition.

As indigenous populations plummeted during the nineteenth century, there were fears that the native population would disappear altogether (Lal 1992:18; Malo 1839). White settlers entered both regions
during this period, seeking to establish commercial agriculture. By
1875, both Hawai'i and Fiji were developing a sugar plantation economy and beginning to scour the world for a docile, hardworking, cheap
labor force. At this point, as Collier describes in Chapter 2, the logic of
chiefdoms encountered the very different logic of capitalism.

The first white settlers in both Hawai'i and Fiji were traders and
emissaries of foreign governments, followed soon by Christian missionaries, sugar planters, and whites working for the government. In both
areas, missionaries sought to convert the population by first converting
its chiefs. Political takeover occurred earlier in Fiji. By 1874, political
instability and warfare in Fiji forced the British to take control by
means of the Deed of Cession, in which the chiefs (especially the paramount chief, Cakobau) ceded control of the islands to Queen Victoria.
As John Kelly describes in Chapter 3, this act served to define and constitute the nation. Sir Arthur Gordon arrived as governor a few months
later. He ruled in conjunction with the Fijian chiefs through the Great

Council of Chiefs, an institution he created. In 1882, the Colonial Sugar Refining Company, an Australian company, was persuaded to operate in Fiji, which it did until 1973 (Lal 1992:13).

In Hawai'i, a major step toward colonial takeover was the 1887 constitution, called the "Bayonet Constitution," which was forced on a reluctant Hawaiian monarch who retained his crown but surrendered effective political power (Osorio 2002). In 1893, a small group of primarily white planters and businessmen engineered a coup with the support of US military forces and overthrew the Hawaiian monarch Queen Lili'uokalani, despite strong protest by Hawaiians (Silva 1997). One concern of the sugar planters was duty-free access to the US market for their crops. Although the United States initially balked at annexation, by 1898 a rising tide of imperialist enthusiasm and the enticement of Pearl Harbor as a mid-Pacific coaling station and naval base overrode hesitations and scruples. Therefore, by the 1880s, a small group of elite white Americans, Britons, Australians, and New Zealanders exercised extensive political and economic control in both Hawai'i and Fiji. They developed separate school systems in both Hawai'i and Fiji, and in Fiji, separate living areas for whites and Fijians (Lal 1992:35).

In collaboration with Fijian and Hawaiian chiefs, the white elites supervised the importation of large numbers of indentured workers for the burgeoning sugar plantations. The Euro/American elites viewed the imported workers very differently than they viewed the indigenous inhabitants. The indentured workers were labor units instead of potential citizens or tribal communities. They were also accorded quite different legal and social statuses. In Fiji, the Fijians were conceptualized by the dominant white elites as possessing a culture, whereas Indians were stripped of their culture so that they could be treated as labor (Kelly 1997). Similarly, in Hawai'i the Americans envisioned the Hawaiians in terms of their culture and Christianity but saw the Chinese, Japanese, Korean, and Filipino laborers as temporary residents tolerated as long as they did the backbreaking work in the cane fields. The whites imagined the Hawaiians as requiring moral reform but thought of the Chinese, the first major group imported as laborers, as "coolies," not extensively targeted for conversion or reform. Those conceptualized as coolies were less often taken to court for adultery and alcohol offenses than Hawaiians, although some practices popular among Chinese, Japanese, and Filipino immigrants, such as gambling, smoking opium, and cockfighting, did receive penal sanctions (see Merry 2000).

Strikes rocked the plantations in the 1920s as the immigrant sugar workers, freed from the constraints of the indenture system in Hawai'i by 1900 and in Fiji by 1920, began to push for better wages and working conditions. In both situations, white planters hired indigenous men as guards to put down the strikes (Beechert 1985; Kelly 1991; Lal 1992:81; Merry 2000). By the 1930s, fear that the growing population of immigrant descendants would dominate the society swept through both Hawai'i and Fiji (Lal 1992:63; Fuchs 1961). In Fiji, the Europeans forged an alliance with the chiefly Fijians against the political aspirations of the Fiji-born Indians, much as the Hawaiians and Americans joined forces against the Asians.

This distinctive tripartite social structure has produced similar crises in Hawai'i and Fiji: unfulfilled aspirations for sovereignty by the indigenous people and enduring inequalities among the various indigenous, colonial, and immigrant groups. In Hawai'i, there are demands for land by Native Hawaiians and ongoing exclusion and racism in the midst of a vision of multicultural harmony. In Fiji, there are the continuing separation of ethnic groups, an enduring sense of alienation by Indo-Fijians, and an ongoing effort to retain political power by indigenous Fijians in the face of diminishing economic hegemony. In 2001, the government proposed an affirmative action program for Fijians in an effort to redress the inequality of ethnic Fijians, compared with Indo-Fijians, in education and professional positions. In Hawai'i, the focus of indigenous activism has been on land rather than on enhancing life chances by education or occupational mobility, the strategies adopted by many Indo-Fijians and Asian Americans. This focus on land seems to have discouraged Fijian and Hawaiian attention to resources such as education.

In 1920, recognizing the devastation experienced by Kanaka Maoli in their loss of lands and sovereignty, the US government set aside approximately 200,000 acres to be developed as Hawaiian Homelands, allowing Hawaiians of 50 percent or greater blood quantum to lease lands for homesteads, farms, and ranches. The goal was to "rehabilitate" the Hawaiians by settling them in rural areas (Kauanui 2002:111).

This small allocation of reserved land through the Hawaiian Homes Commission Act has not satisfied the Native Hawaiian demand for land. Because no money was allocated to administer the Homelands program, much of the land was leased at low rates to sugar plantations in order to generate revenue to prepare the land for allocation. This problem, along with bureaucratic inefficiency, meant that relatively few awards were actually made. By the 1990s, the long list of applicants waiting for land proved an enormous embarrassment to the commission (Faludi 1991). Moreover, its restriction to persons of 50 percent or greater blood quantum has excluded many Hawaiians from this benefit and has created an unwanted distinction within the Hawaiian community. Intriguingly, this policy is based on US policy toward Native Americans in that it relies on a blood quantum definition of identity instead of Hawaiian notions of genealogy. It parallels the British policy in Fiji that envisaged the salvation of the Fijian population as remaining in isolated rural villages (Thomas 1994; Lal 1992). In both cases, as the indigenous peoples faced capitalist transformation in the early twentieth century, the solution was to reimagine them in rural villages close to the land. In Hawai'i, though, little land was to be had.

Critical differences also exist between Fiji and Hawai'i. The British colonial elite protected and controlled the Fijians, envisioning them as a separate race and culture, whereas the Kingdom of Hawai'i, under the influence of American advisors, saw Hawaiians as open to incorporation into the regime of citizenship and the market. Whereas the British colonial government protected Fijian land rights in a paternalist and controlling fashion, the American advisors to the Kingdom of Hawai'i encouraged the privatization of land to make it available for purchase by Native and alien alike. In Fiji, the British colonial government created a separate legal regime for Fijians, one that at the same time codified and created "indigenous law" while incorporating Indo-Fijians immediately into the general, explicitly British-based system. In the Kingdom of Hawai'i, on the other hand, a unitary Anglo-American legal system was established for all its subjects, under the influence of American advisors (see Merry 2000; Osorio, Chapter 8, this volume). The British colonial regime in Fiji was a protectionist system, safeguarding traditional authority and indigenous rights to land despite intrusive colonial policies that left Fijian villages isolated and static

(Thomas 1997:52; Lal 1992 and Chapter 10, this volume). The colonial regime kept its populations separate and guarded the customs, land rights, and political prerogatives of the indigenous Fijians. Colonial governance relied on a system of dual courts and voting by racial group similar to that of other British, French, and Portuguese colonies (Mamdani 1996; Roberts and Mann 1991). Fijians retained clan-based land rights and, at the end of the twentieth century, still controlled more than 80 percent of the land.

In Hawai'i, the US intervention was made under the rubric of a republican and liberal regime instead of a paternalistic and restrictive one. Rather than protect Hawaiian land rights, the Kingdom of Hawai'i privatized land. An 1848 land redistribution scheme, called the *Mahele*, replaced the chiefly authority over land and commoner use-rights with private ownership and in 1850 permitted the purchase of land by foreigners. In a short time, the vast majority of land had passed out of the hands of Hawaiian commoners and chiefs and into those of whites. By the 1850s, the Kingdom of Hawai'i had developed a unitary legal system based on Anglo-American law, fully fifty years before annexation by the United States. Promoted by a small group of resident white lawyers and missionaries, the new constitution, court system, and legal codes relied on American models (Merry 2000).

In Fiji, the British insisted on separate communal voting systems for the Indo-Fijians, allowing Indians and Fijians to vote only for representatives of their own ethnicity to the legislative council (Lal 1992:91–94). Despite efforts to reform the government and demands by Indo-Fijians for a common voting role, the communal compartmentalization of politics has persisted throughout the twentieth century. The constitutions of 1970 and 1990 provided for separate seats for each ethnic group (Lal 2002a:154–155). Annelise Riles (Chapter 7, this volume) notes that these policies have left a legacy of group-ness in Fiji. In Chapter 10, Brij Lal describes how this legacy of ethnic compartmentalism has forged the contemporary political instability in Fiji. In Hawai'i, in contrast, a unified voting system always existed. Although Japanese and Chinese were excluded from citizenship in the United States and, after the American-influenced 1887 constitution, in Hawai'i, their Hawai'i-born children became citizens and acquired the vote, becoming a progressively larger sector of the voting population until Japanese American candidates were finally elected to statewide office in the 1950s, as Sally Engle Merry describes in Chapter 5.

The three coups in Fiji reflect the continuing tension between the ethnic-Fijian and Indo-Fijian segments of the population, based partially on the communalism of the political system. A new constitution promulgated in 1997 sought to develop a more multiracial political system with some open (nonracial) seats (Lal 2002a:165). The government elected in 1999 had an Indo-Fijian prime minister. However, the 2000 coup replaced this democratically elected government with an interim ethnic-Fijian government after a period of terror and violence, a situation Lal describes in Chapter 10. The leaders of the coup and of the interim government were ethnic Fijians. These coups, and the violence accompanying them, have further frayed relations between the two communities and have intensified distrust. As Brij Lal (2002a:148–149) observes, "The fabric of race relations, just beginning to be repaired after years of strain following the coups of a decade earlier, is in tatters. The economy is down, and the best and the brightest are looking for greener pastures. The May coup [2000] and the ensuing mayhem have taken Fiji back by a generation."

Thus, the seeds of the present conflicts were largely sown by the legal arrangements of the British and American colonial empires. The structure of governance in Fiji has produced continuing tension between ethnic Fijians and Indo-Fijians. Hawai'i, in contrast, has had no ethnic coups since 1893. Boundaries among groups are relatively fluid, and overt conflict is minimal. Hawaiian society lacks ethnically based group violence and is marked by a high level of interpersonal sharing and tolerance. The indigenous community did not contest the immigrants' rise to political power with coups, as in Fiji. Indeed, there is a long tradition in social science scholarship of stressing the interethnic harmony of the islands. The myth of multicultural harmony, however, obscures enduring patterns of racism and exclusion, now directed particularly toward people of Hawaiian, Filipino, and Pacific Islander descent. The façade of harmonious multiculturalism conceals long-standing racial discrimination and persisting inequalities, as Jonathan Osorio and Sally Engle Merry discuss in Chapters 8 and 5, respectively. By the end of the twentieth century, certain Asian groups had achieved economic and political dominance in an uneasy alliance with the whites. Native Hawaiians, in contrast, became economically marginal-ized and increasingly powerless. Despite this colonial history, as Noenoe Silva demonstrates in Chapter 4, there is a strong movement to recuperate Hawaiian language and culture from the devastation and legal regulation of the colonial era.

At the end of our seminar, we were intrigued by certain striking similarities in the positions of Indo-Fijians and Native Hawaiians within the neocolonial state. Although the more obvious parallel would be between ethnic Fijians and Native Hawaiians, it is the Indo-Fijians who feel marginalized and vulnerable, as do the Native Hawaiians. The con-temporary legacy of these histories leaves ethnic Fijians struggling to retain paramountcy against the demands of Indo-Fijians for political participation and leaves Native Hawaiians working to achieve a degree of self-determination within a multicultural society in which both the colonial whites and some of the Asian descendants are politically and economically dominant. Neither is able to deal with claims for social justice from important segments of the society. In Fiji, these crises are marked by a series of coups by ethnic Fijians challenging claims to political power by Indo-Fijians. In Hawai'i, they are characterized by the ongoing but unresolved demands for land and sovereignty among Kanaka Maoli. Indo-Fijians and Native Hawaiians face similar patterns of discrimination and marginalization, despite their different political statuses. Both have been excluded from landownership.

The way these crises are defined is critically important because it determines their potential remedies. Imaginable remedies shape the scope and definition of the crises. A crisis based on the alienation of Native Hawaiians from access to the land, for example, demands a quite different response than one based on the failure to provide ade-quate educational and economic opportunities to Native Hawaiians or sufficient valorization of Native Hawaiian culture and language. There is no shared clarity on the definition of the current crises in either place or on the current trajectories imagined as ways of dealing with them. In both societies, however, we found recurrent concerns about land and identity. In both, law was the locus of hope for a more just arrangement.

This form of comparison yielded no simple story of the imposition of colonial law or resistance to it. Instead, it demonstrated varying processes of withdrawal and refusal, along with the appropriation of colonial legal forms by local actors even in the present. For example, the government in Fiji has a history of asserting an authority above the law, a conception adopted by certain contemporary Fijians. John Kelly tells how the first governor, Sir Arthur Gordon, sought to establish himself as not limited by the 1874 Deed of Cession and as superior to his invented Council of Chiefs. Many contemporary Fijians continue to feel above the law, entitled to land by virtue of spiritual claims in the absence of legal rights, as Martha Kaplan describes in Chapter 6. Fijian insurgents in the 2000 coup argued that spiritual connections to the land trumped law. Yet, the Fijian insurgents acquiesced to the legal decisions of the Fijian courts concerning the illegality of their newly formed government. Why did they both resist law and ultimately operate within its framework? It seems likely that NGO (non-government) networks, pressure from Australia and New Zealand, and the need for foreign financial aid influenced them, but there was also acceptance of the forms of colonial legality. Nonetheless, many Fijians insist that the linkage between god, now a Christian god, and land creates a tie more fundamental than that forged by human legal arrangements, as Martha Kaplan argues in Chapter 6.

In contrast, an equivalent challenge to the rule of law has not occurred in Hawai'i. Certain groups in the sovereignty movement claim a special relationship to land, and a few have attempted to make those claims outside the legal institutions of the modern state by land occupations, demonstrations, or refusal to register their cars or accept the authority of state courts. More Hawaiian activists, though, have adopted the forms of modern legality and have pursued relief through the courts, seeking to recover gathering rights in lands defined as private property and access to shorelines and water. Those seeking to establish a self-determining Hawaiian polity generally rely on constitutions and elections. Osorio's comparison of two important sovereignty groups in Chapter 8 shows that both legitimate their claims and structure in terms of law. It is possible that the greater willingness to accept the legality of the colonial state in Hawai'i occurs because the Hawaiian Kingdom adopted these legal forms and practices before the colonial takeover by the United States, not after.

The comparison highlighted the intimate relationship between law and the production of social knowledge, as well as the kinds of possibilities such knowledge affords. Knowledge production was vital to the colonial enterprise. It could be as public and transnational as Maine's theory of law or Money's theory of governance through racial separation, described by Kelly in Chapter 3, or as private and obscure as records of family land transfers that are closed to view by outsiders. It was fundamental to the control of colonial spaces, as in the closure of knowledge through documentary strategies, as Miyazaki describes in Chapter 9. Law's suppression of indigenous practices also produces subversive knowledge. This may take the form of stories and dance. Silva's analysis in Chapter 4 shows that, despite the licensing requirements that, in effect, banned hula in nineteenth-century Hawai'i, the publication of accounts of hula in Hawaiian-language newspapers created an ongoing public record, shaping available and recoverable knowledge. Such a public record contested the legal repression of performative practice while crucially sustaining the narrative knowledge embodied in such performances, as well as the claims that such narratives can support and legitimate. The control of knowledge is fundamental to the control of colonies.

THINKING ABOUT LAW AND COLONIALISM

As a great deal of scholarship in the anthropology of law indicates, laws are given life through social practices and their embeddedness in consciousness. The introduction of any new system of law constructs new conceptions of rights and regulations that are carried in individual consciousness and manifested in everyday practices. Law is embodied both in discourses and texts and in documents, practices, and forms. Annelise Riles (Chapter 7, this volume) distinguishes between the expressive dimensions of law (its capacity to construct meanings) and its instrumental dimensions. The latter refers to the technicalities, formalities, documents, and ways of doing things that in their mundane everyday-ness obscure their significance. These two genres of the law shift continually between each other; neither alone provides an adequate account of what law does. The law is in many ways indeterminate, with its tendency to hide, to sink into the everyday, to obscure itself in taken-for-granted practices. At the same time, it incorporates explicit rules that govern shifting and ambiguous relationships, such as those governing ownership of land or rights to political participation.

Law mediates relationships between people, relationships between people and land, and relationships among groups defined by their relations to land. It defines identities such as citizen and alien and crystallizes these identities and relationships through the production of documents and technical legal formalities. It is notable for the complexity of what it accomplishes, not all of which is intended. As these chapters indicate, the shifting meaning of identity and the role of law in defining that identity compose a facet of the expansion of global capitalism and its structures for allocating land, labor, and taxation. Law is a critical point of articulation between global structures such as capitalism and symbolic, representational practices of everyday life. Citizenship, nationality, genealogy, and indigeneity emerge as important competing identities, often derived from legal definitions of personhood, as Merry describes. Laws define citizenship while they exclude immigrants, indentured laborers, or other groups from full entitlement to political participation, land ownership, or other social benefits. The law creates spaces unregulated by law and populations living outside its definitions. In both Hawai'i and Fiji, for example, immigrant laborers from Asia were denied full citizenship and rights of political participation by a legal regime that defined them as permanent outsiders.

This system, however, is a change from an earlier one, in which social identities and benefits were allocated through genealogy instead of law, as Jane Collier describes in Chapter 2. In both Hawai'i and Fiji, the indigenous population was organized around forms of inclusion and exclusion based on the structure of chiefdoms and descent; immigrant settlers and colonial overlords created new patterns structured by capitalism and the colonial state. For example, Miyazaki (Chapter 9, this volume) describes the use of petitions and narratives of ancestry and migration by ethnic Fijians to make claims to land, claims involving the production of self-knowledge of the group. Because these claims are framed in terms of genealogy, ancestry, and migration patterns, these ways of defining the self are being incorporated within law. In Hawai'i, as Merry demonstrates in Chapter 5, discourses of identity in the nineteenth century were based largely on country of origin or Hawaiian ancestry, but in the mid-twentieth century a new definition of identity as "local" emerged, emphasizing social class, connections to the land, and long-term residence instead of nationality. More recently, local identity has fractured into indigenous peoples and Asian Americans as international law moves toward recognizing the human rights of indigenous peoples.

Law is always aspirational as well as exclusionary. The law brought by the American and British colonizing powers offered social justice to the populations it encompassed. It proclaimed equality before the law and security of land ownership. The law always encompasses a vision of the just society. These aspirations offer both substantive justice and technical, procedural fairness through the production and certification of records, land arrangements, petitions, and other techniques that provide certainty in the relationships law governs. Beliefs in fairness through law are evidenced by practices such as nineteenth-century petitions written by Hawaiian commoners protesting the growing power of white advisors to the Kingdom government (Osorio, Chapter 8, this volume) and the massive petition campaign protesting US annexation (Silva, Chapter 4, this volume, and 1997). The passage of laws more favorable to union organizing encouraged a series of strikes by plantation workers during the early twentieth century.

In the contemporary period, law has been central to indigenous people's efforts to assert claims to status, property, power, inclusion, or recognition. The indigenous peoples of Hawai'i and Fiji, long defined as citizens, are adopting international legal definitions of themselves as indigenous peoples with rights to self-determination. Ethnic Fijians mobilized the language of indigenous rights to justify the 2000 coup, and many Hawaiian sovereignty groups make claims to indigenous rights to self-determination. Osorio's comparison of approaches to sovereignty in Chapter 8 shows that the definition of the citizen as defined by law in the Hawaiian Kingdom is one possible basis for claiming a sovereign state in the present.

Law is historically produced and negotiated through ongoing practice, yet it has the capacity to become fixed and produce longer- or shorter-term consequences. It draws strength from the fiction of its fixity. Law gives the appearance of fixity to these relationships, although it has a kaleidoscopic capacity to rearrange them. This volume reveals the variety of points of fixing, showing that these are never unequivocal and are always subject to reaction, renegotiation, and the very diverse responses of individuals and communities. For instance, law makes property, especially in the sense that liberal capitalism defines land as property in terms of utter specifiability. However, even such designation of land as property is never fully fixed and is subject to contestation. For example, the Fijian kin group described by Martha Kaplan in Chapter 6 contests the legal specification of land ownership and constructs its own ideology of ownership and rights to land. She argues that the people in this region see their relationship to land in terms of Christianity and their ritual connections and have not allowed one hundred years of legal dispossession to alienate them from this sense of ownership of the land. Certain groups within the Hawaiian sovereignty movement make claims to land stewardship separate from ownership. Thus, law in its instrumental sense, in Riles' terms, is engaged in producing land as property through various documentary forms that create a fixity and permanence to these relationships, particularly when claimants cannot get access to land records (Miyazaki, Chapter 9, this volume). On the other hand, competing discourses challenge this legal fixing of land as property. For example, the concept of usufruct is an important alternative to the legal regulation of property ownership. (For a provocative refiguring of the question of usufruct instead of ownership as a basis for making rights arguments, see the essays in Zerner 2003.)

Law articulates relationships among individuals and between individuals and the state with apparent clarity, but at the same time it erases and conceals relationships. As a discourse, it shifts the way relationships are understood, sometimes naturalizing them or even rendering them unworthy of thought at all. In both Hawai'i and Fiji, the construction of the indigenous people as legal subjects and of immigrant laborers as labor units underscored the contrasting legal status and social belonging of the two groups. This legal construction of difference was naturalized, though, by discourses of race and innate labor capacities.

The focus of this volume is primarily on such relatively explicit loci of legal effects as land title, group identity, and citizenship. The absence of law—those structured gaps shaped by, among other things, colonial notions of justiciability, culture, and the prerequisites of orderly social life—can be equally consequential. Don Brenneis's seminar paper, for example, was framed explicitly in these terms: Colonial law did not afford a resource for rural Indo-Fijian communities, given their de facto legal invisibility, and, in so doing, was instrumental in dampening the possibilities of formal, local political life for them. Law is always inherently partial. It can never, despite its framers' best efforts, encompass all its potential uses nor meet the needs of all those under its influence. The systematic partiality of those sites, communities, and activities that it defines, constrains, and sustains may well indeed mirror the partiality of its makers vis-à-vis different groups and their interests. Law neither controls nor serves all parts of a society equally. The negotiation of land ownership and identity at the core of many of our discussions provides revelatory cases for understanding such partiality. Riles' consideration of the complexities of freehold tenure for Part-European families in Chapter 7 is an especially rich instance. It also demonstrates, as do other chapters, the ways in which legal forms and documents define kinship and relatedness (for comparison, see Marcus 1992 on the legal constitution of Galveston dynasties). Lal's reflections on the coups in Fiji in Chapter 10 emphasize how law's construction of differences in political participation and land ownership fueled discontent and political instability.

Chapter 9 (Miyazaki) and Brenneis's conference paper perhaps attend most closely to the gaps inherent in a law-centered analysis. Miyazaki does so, in large part, by examining the hopeful practices—new genres, new textual strategies, and the refiguring of imagined archival resources—of claimants in a century-long land debate. His materials and analysis point dramatically to the indeterminacy inherent within legal frameworks, indeed, within any cultural practice. Perhaps central to this is the nonrecognition of these hopeful claims, petitions, and queries by administrative interlocutors; not being part of the conversation critically cuts off the use of law as resource. Similarly, Brenneis suggests a continuing role for local-level ethnography, especially for showing how micro-level discursive analysis might provide a way to illuminate lived legal experience in postcolonial sites in ways that a top-down examination might not. In the vacuum provided by the colonial—and then postcolonial—state's reluctance to intervene in or provide remedies for managing local-level disputes deemed most consequential by Indo-Fijian villagers, colonial law constrained and limited community formation through its absence, its unresponsiveness. Absent formal legal proceedings and records of consequential local events, collaboratively constructed oral accounts became indispensable in providing licit, public reference accounts in light of which subsequent behavior might be appraised and sanctioned. His paper also points to complementary local histories of colonial experience through ongoing resonances, both thematic and performative, in local practice. In this, it shares critical elements with Silva's examination in Chapter 4 of the newspaper rendering of hula narratives, in which the formal prohibition on traditional performance practice and the rise in Hawaiian-language literacy made both possible and necessary new forms for maintaining legally and socially consequential stories. She describes how the retelling of hula narratives occurred at the same time that the law prohibited the performance of hula. Thus, the newspaper publication of these prohibited dances moved into a gap in legal regulation. The stories celebrate identity through genealogy and the connection with the sacred and retell more conventional stories of male power and migration in reverse. Both Miyazaki and Brenneis present accounts of law as promise unfulfilled, a necessary complement to the more activist, constructivist, repressive visions figuring elsewhere.

We sought through these discussions to recenter law in social theory. Although the social anthropology of the early and mid-twentieth centuries imagined law as a fundamental and determinative aspect of social relationships, the field has moved away from viewing law as central to the constitution of social life. Yet, law is a fundamental terrain for the creation of social life and for articulating a vision of social justice. By examining the complex, contradictory processes of colonialism and postcolonialism through the lens of legal arrangements, this seminar recuperated law as a core concern for the anthropological analysis of the production of social life.

PRODUCING COLONIAL KNOWLEDGE

Law, both in the sense of systems of meaning and technologies for specifying the relations of persons to land and property, forms a fundamental feature of the system of knowledge on which colonialism depends. For example, the agreements that made the indenture system possible were the result of bilateral negotiations between the colonial governments of India and Fiji, negotiations that could not have occurred without the assumption of consonant, if not wholly shared, legal frameworks in both colonies. The movement of officials from one colonial setting to another fostered the translocal reach of colonial legal arrangements, illustrated in Gordon's career. As Kelly shows, Gordon sought to preserve Fijian village life in a way that some considered anthropological, but he was also influenced by anthropological theories of the nature of custom and village law developed by Maine and by racialized understandings of capacity and action deployed by Money.

In law, as in other domains of governance, colonial officials drew analogies with other experiences of rule in the wider empire, whether over the British possessions or the American governance of Native Americans. Clearly, a body of theoretical understandings of law, community governance, and colonial rule spread across the British Empire. Strategies in one area were transplanted to other areas. The transfer of persons and ideas also crossed imperial boundaries. Hawai'i and Fiji are historically connected in a chain of colonial experiments with governance and rule, even though one was American and the other British.

Colonial expansion fed on the ideology of the rule of law that linked imperial governance to assertions of rationality and civilization. Law was seen as fundamental to civilization and as a way of controlling "natural" greed, the Hobbesian war of every man against every man, as Collier (Chapter 2, this volume) argues. It was typically described as a gift from "civilized" nations to despotic societies (see Fitzpatrick 1992). It included technologies such as the Torrens System that Riles (Chapter 7, this volume) describes for giving fixed titles to land through documentation. This system locked ownership into a system of colonial knowledge that was full and complete in itself, freed from the contingency of specifying linkages between particular lands and a series of owners. The process of surveying fixed land ownership in both Hawai'i and Fiji in terms of a different system of knowledge from use or local knowledge of shrines or trees.

Indeed, the colonial claim that law is a sign of civilization and rationality has an enduring legacy in postcolonial states. It is noteworthy that postcolonial states do not walk away from the law of the colonial era. These colonial legal legacies of institutions and practices provide a matrix in which consciousness, identity, and life chances take shape. They provide discursive resources central to the notion of sovereignty, to the claiming of position and power in a postcolonial world, as they did in the colonial one.

The benefits of the rule of law were often rhetorically opposed to allegedly despotic regimes such as chiefdoms. Yet, the rule of law simply encodes different ideas about how power is achieved and exercised. Jane Collier (Chapter 2, this volume) analyzes the power relations embedded in the structure of chiefdoms and shows how this logic of power contrasts with that of capitalism. In chiefdoms, power is a product of genealogical closeness to the senior line of the conical clan and is concentrated in persons. This godly power allows its possessor to dispense fertility in exchange for inferiors' gifts produced by the land. In contrast, according to the cultural logic of capitalist societies, all people are equal. Inequality is explained on the basis of "natural" differences such as gender and race instead of genealogical descent or godly power. Such logical contradictions between chiefdoms and capitalism shaped the colonial encounter. Because Westerners did not understand the system of genealogy and exchange that regulated chiefdoms, they assumed that chiefly rule was despotic. Because they misinterpreted *kapus* (chiefly regulations that marked and reinforced social hierarchies) as law, they expected chiefs to pass other laws and enforce them. Therefore, Collier argues, at the intersection between chiefdoms and expanding colonial states, the two quite disparate cultural logics defining persons and power caused considerable misunderstanding and hostility. As the chapters in this book demonstrate, such encounters shaped the way law was established in the colonial state.

To understand the intersections between chiefdoms and the expanding colonial state, the authors have examined such varied legal locations as bureaucracy and its regulations, documents, specifications of citizenship and nation, courts, enforcement mechanisms, and forms of governance and knowledge production defining relations between groups and land. Some of these are encoded in legal systems; some are not. These studies demonstrate the intimate relationship between law and the colonial production of social knowledge. We were particularly interested in the possibilities that such knowledge affords. This included bureaucracies that close off knowledge, as Miyazaki (Chapter 9, this volume) describes, structures imported from outside that open knowledge, such as the union movements in Hawai'i discussed by Merry (Chapter 5, this volume), and mechanisms that preserve knowledge, such as the newspaper stories Silva (Chapter 4, this volume) examines from nineteenth-century Hawai'i.

PRODUCING ANTHROPOLOGICAL KNOWLEDGE

One conclusion of our discussions was the obvious permeability of colonial and anthropological forms of knowledge. Anthropology produced colonial knowledge, and colonial experience contributed to the anthropological body of knowledge. Maine contributed to both fields. Indeed, anthropological concepts of groups have taken on a reified identity in colonial and contemporary political discourse. Primary among these notions of group are the village and the "culture." The rural village, the primary object of anthropological scrutiny, was an artifact of colonial policy for Fijians. In marked contrast, after the fulfillment of their indenture contracts, Indian immigrants lived, as do their descendents, in "settlements" defined only in cartographic, not administrative, terms; settlements were not "villages." In large part, this had to do with the colonial assumption that the Indians were purely labor and not to be understood or administered in cultural, or even specifically social, terms. The largely landless and increasingly urbanized Hawaiians were understood anthropologically, until recently, only in their isolated villages and through a reconstruction of their past. This form of analysis ignored the ways colonialism shaped these villages, effacing its impact. This contributed to seeing Hawaiians as a residual, vanishing community, a position currently challenged by the dynamic sovereignty movement that draws on urban Kanaka Maoli as well as rural villagers.

In both areas, the immigrant laborers were not considered a serious subject of anthropological inquiry until quite recently, nor have white elites elicited much anthropological attention. Only the indigenous peoples were understood in terms of culture, and only those groups currently serve as the objects of tourist attention. Those designated, protected colonial subjects, envisaged as living pristine lives in rural villages, whether protected by chiefly authority in Fiji or ensconced in rehabilitative rural homeland areas in Hawai'i, became the centerpiece of anthropological understandings of both places. Anthropological knowledge, like colonial knowledge, remained within the boundaries of racially circumscribed communities, rarely attempting to examine the intersections among them. Moreover, like colonial policy, it also fixed its subjects in time, as timeless embodiments of a stalled evolution. In Fiji, this understanding shaped policies that restricted Fijians to village life and discouraged them from participating in the wider society. Yet, the categories of kinship by which lands were assigned to Fijians inaccurately imagined kinship as more fixed and less flexible than it was in practice.

On the other hand, Miyazaki (Chapter 9, this volume) argues that parallels exist between the Fijian creation of indeterminacy as an achievement in the production of knowledge and the anthropological insistence on indeterminacy. He argues that indeterminacy, as well as determinacy, can be the product of carefully developed strategies, whether for Fijians making claims to land and kinship status or anthropologists asserting the limitations of knowledge. He concludes that anthropology needs less a dialogic framework than an analysis of the work this dialogic framework does in both Fijian and anthropological knowledge production.

The seminar discussions also revealed the analytical potential of core anthropological approaches such as controlled comparison and the value of concepts refigured to incorporate a much stronger sense of history, power, and social inequality. The discussions reflected our efforts to move beyond conventional anthropological categories and at the same time recuperate older topics such as land, kinship, and chiefdoms. Some examined sites that were familiar, such as villages or world systems, and others considered archives of land ownership and practices of record keeping. The seminar discussions and papers considered the power and danger of cultural representations and moved toward a more comprehensive theory that recognizes the relatively solidified structure of power that law represents and the critical role of practices in shaping that structure. Therefore, this volume offers a range of strategies for bridging the often intractable divide between macro theory and the particulars of social practice in context.

A final point to consider in this regard is that different kinds of anthropological knowledge speak to and from different kinds of legal and policy interests. In both Fiji and Hawai'i, the assumed fixity of legal forms and categorizations has also shaped the points at which both activist and anthropological knowledge can speak to issues of control, domination, and resistance. Some kinds of data are likely to make a difference; others are not. The knowledge sustained and understood through newspaper accounts of hula, for example, might not have standing in an independent Hawaiian court or in its territorial and state successors, no matter how much that knowledge underpins local values and understandings of relatedness, ownership, and rights. Yet, Silva (Chapter 4, this volume) powerfully demonstrates how hula narratives help to recover from the extensive loss of language, cultural understandings, and history produced by colonialism.

In other postcolonial contexts, however, where such assumed fixity of ownership or social identity was not put into practice for specific historical reasons, such traditionalized accounts are now taken as crucial evidence of ongoing relationships to and rights to land and other resources. The central role of oral narratives and ancillary visual and musical "mappings" of the territorial linkages of Australian Aboriginal kin groups in recent land rights cases is a particularly marked example. The standing accorded such materials is made possible by the absence of formal legal documents, such as treaties, in the conquest history of Australia. Similarly, several Southeast Asian cases documented in Zerner (2003) argue for the standing of local performance traditions in determining at least usufructory rights to previously unmapped territory. Fiji and Hawai'i offer many contrasts, but they do not exhaust the complex possibilities.

AN OVERVIEW OF THE BOOK

The collection begins with Jane Collier's ideal-typic analysis contrasting the cultural logics of chiefdoms and those of liberal capitalism in Chapter 2. These models differ in the ways in which they conceptualize the authority of the leader over his or her subjects and the nature of status and personhood. In a chiefdom, a chief acquires power through rule over people, which shifts under the influence of capitalism to a greater importance to rule over land. Possessing goods shows that a chief can incorporate the power of others and indicates his mana, whereas the same control over goods in liberal capitalism provides resources for competition among contenders for power. This analysis elegantly outlines the differences in the structures and logics of the two systems and then examines what happens when they collide.

In Chapter 2, Collier traces the transition from one ideal type to the other and the conversions and misrecognitions along the way, a process characteristic of nineteenth-century imperialism in the Pacific, as elsewhere.

In Chapter 3, John Kelly examines the historical figure of Sir Arthur Gordon, the first governor of Fiji, and his strategies of establishing colonial rule for the British. Kelly demonstrates the linkages between what happened in Fiji in the 1870s and other areas of the Pacific by tracing Gordon's past assignments in New Brunswick, Mauritius, and Trinidad and the influence of translocal theorists such as Sir Henry Maine and J. W. B. Money, theoretician of colonial rule in Java, on his administrative practice. Chapter 3 demonstrates the importance of conceptions of law giving and authority for the creation of the land arrangements and taxation structures that shape Fijian society today. Kelly argues cogently that, despite Gordon's commitment to Maine's notion that village governance depends on a separate sphere of custom, his policies in Fiji were influenced more by Money's theory advocating racial separation between Europeans, indigenous people, and the surprisingly culture-less space for "intermediate races," such as the Indians in Fiji. Kelly's historical account of the founding of the Fijian colonial state describes the legal arrangements undergirding the land arrangements of the contemporary state that have contributed to the coups and instability of the postcolonial period.

In Chapter 4, Noenoe Silva offers an analysis of hula narratives in the context of nineteenth-century missionaries' efforts to regulate this artistic expression. She shows how its performance had many meanings besides the sexualized ones imposed by white outsiders and that both its performance and its retelling in Hawaiian-language newspapers represented potent forms of resistance to efforts to extinguish the Hawaiian language and culture. Silva depicts multiple layers of resistance to this effort to curtail hula. Within the narrative itself, women are described as powerful and sexually desiring rather than as docile and sexually constrained, the mission ideal. The production of the hula story itself opposes missionary concerns about the immorality of the dance and its role in distracting Hawaiians from labor. It challenges missionaries' understanding of women's status by portraying women as powerful and filled with desire. A central feature of the current Hawaiian cultural renaissance is the recuperation of hula and the expansion of its repertoires and performers. However, tourism has made the dance into a commodity and an erotic entertainment. The legal constraint on hula of the nineteenth century was perhaps a less severe threat to hula than its contemporary appropriation as a tourist spectacle. Silva describes the struggle over the meaning of hula in a colonizing context in which the law endeavors to extinguish the practice, by banning or requiring a license, and commodification subverts its meanings and distorts its performances.

In Chapter 5, Sally Engle Merry's exposition of contemporary ethnicity in Hawai'i locates the origins of ethnic identities in the shifting historical relationships among groups and the changing legal definitions of citizenship and political participation in the nineteenth and twentieth centuries. Rather than present these identities as uniform or coherent, she demonstrates their multiplicity and historical malleability. Contemporary ethnic conflicts are products of histories of exclusion and domination and reflect struggles for power and position and shifting alliances among contemporary groups. For example, Native Hawaiians are now using indigenous rights language from the international human rights system to claim a new status as indigenous and to distinguish themselves from other residents of the islands, with whom they made common cause as "locals" in the past. With legal changes in access to citizenship and the birth of a second and third generation on the islands, Asian immigrants in Hawai'i are no longer imagined as dangerous aliens but as co-participants with whites in the governance of the islands. This historical change left the Native Hawaiians abandoned by their erstwhile allies and set the stage for the rights of a sovereignty movement based on indigenous instead of "local" claims and entitlements.

In Chapter 6, Martha Kaplan examines how contemporary ethnicity in Fiji is structured by the colonial legacy of Gordon and his institutional policies and by the way Fijians have appropriated and redefined that legacy through their actions in contemporary events. Kaplan's analysis shows how the people of the region she studied assert ownership of land in a way that articulates spiritual/religious/ritual understandings with those of the law. Although they lack formal legal entitlement to the land, their understanding of their relationship to the land melds the logics of investment, rights, and Christian promise. She sees this pattern also in ethnic-Fijian claims underlying the 2000 coup led by George Speight. These ideas can be traced back to Money and his conception of racial separation and difference more than to Maine and his notion of separate legal spheres for villagers and states. In this situation, law appears as one of several resources available for constructing social action and group identity, along with linkages to the land, often spiritually understood. This conjunction of land ownership based on the assertion of legal authority and the production of documents with processes of asserting ownership based on religious authenticity and residence on the land, as in chiefdom polities, is quite parallel to Gordon's approaches. Thus, in their appropriation of legality, along with other forms of authority, Fijians build on the colonial legal legacy, a strategy that shapes the future of the law in Fiji.

In Chapter 7, Annelise Riles points to two distinct genres of law whose interplay and oscillation may explain the current interest in recentering law in anthropological analysis. She argues that law can be seen both as an expressive genre that creates groups and meanings and as objects that are part of the trivial minutiae of life yet have clear instrumental effects. These objects represent the materiality of law in the form of documents, titles, survey maps, registry books, or other things. Riles argues that it is important to see how law acts in the world, not just through its normative regulation but also in the myriad practices and objectified forms by which it regulates social life. Her insistence on the importance of documents and bureaucratic forms helped to move the seminar toward recognizing the importance of analyzing the production and maintenance of social knowledge through such legal objects. The focus on law and its documentary presence enables a new way of moving between the material and symbolic, of recognizing the co-presence of each and its relationship to the other.

In Chapter 8, Jon Osorio contrasts two competing models for sovereignty, each drawing on notions of law, land, descent, ethnicity, and citizenship in very different ways. Apparently straightforward claims to land and sovereignty take different forms, based on the logic of race/ethnicity or citizenship. He shows that law represents one way of forming a sovereign Hawaiian state and that race/ethnicity represents another. Ka Lāhui advocates Hawaiian sovereignty by means of a nation of citizens with a constitution and government. Membership depends on genealogy and ethnicity: on descent from a Hawaiian ancestor. Another sovereignty organization roots its claims on the existence of the Kingdom of Hawai'i as a legal entity in the nineteenth century and on genealogical descent from its citizens. Citizenship in the Kingdom was awarded on the basis of loyalty, not race, so the contemporary nation is not all of Hawaiian descent. This segment of the sovereignty movement argues that the Kingdom was never legally extinguished and that the contemporary Hawaiian Kingdom should be reinstated and should include as citizens all descendants of those who were citizens of the nineteenth-century Kingdom.

In Chapter 9, Hirokazu Miyazaki foregrounds the closure of knowledge by the colonial state through the mundane practices of record keeping, an analysis that complements Riles's insistence on attention to the bureaucratic practices of knowledge production. At the same time, Miyazaki shows the efforts to contest that closure and the multiplicity of textual devices used for the contest. For example, he talks about the use of appendixes and questions—technologies of knowledge adapted from the bureaucratic state. At the same time, he describes other strategies in this legal terrain, such as the technique of telling stories of migration and descent, knowledge strategies derived from the divergent conceptions of identity and power. These strategies are rooted in the structure of chiefdoms, a structure illuminated by Collier's analysis in Chapter 2.

In Chapter 10, Brij Lal closes the volume with his reflections on the current state of crisis in Fiji. As a historian and a principal architect of Fiji's non-racial constitution, challenged by the 2000 coup, he writes with a sense of tragedy about the current ethnic conflict in Fiji. His analysis foregrounds the themes in the rest of the chapters: the significance of inequalities in the allocation of land and the enduring legacy of a political system based on race. He describes the sustained efforts by Indo-Fijian politicians to eliminate the system of voting by racial group and to replace it with a common roll. Moreover, he notes how the issue of unequal access to land between ethnic Fijians and Indo-Fijians remains a space of contention. Lal sees the dilemmas for both groups and attributes the tragedy to the nation's inability to overcome the racial compartmentalization of land and politics that colonialism has produced. As ethnic Fijians insist on a special relationship to land, Indo-Fijians insist on justice. The dilemma is painful, and the future offers only the continued out-migration of those Indo-Fijians who have the means to emigrate.

CONCLUSION

This discussion of the individual chapters returns us to the question of law as an actant, as Riles puts it, drawing on Latour—as a more indeterminate and occasionally irrelevant frame of meaning than is often assumed and perhaps more relevant as a technology of documents and papers than as a set of rules. It also shows the multiplicity of manifestations of law, from identity and consciousness to modes of asserting authority to divide land, to titles and rules about access to them. These chapters show how law mediates identity by the way land is allocated and political power delineated. This includes the arrangements of political power that give some the rights to allocate land, as well as notions of alien races and indigenous owners that confer legitimacy on particular arrangements. Those who create laws claim authority to regulate the distribution of resources and possess the combination of symbolic authority and documentation technology that meet in this moment of social creation. Law provides frames of meaning, ways of creating identities and connections. In conjunction with other processes, law bridges the divide that has been created within anthropology between symbolic and material forms of power. Finally, examining law within the colonial process reveals the linkages between colonial and anthropological forms of knowledge.

2

A Chief Does Not Rule Land; He Rules People (Luganda Proverb)

Jane F. Collier

In this chapter, I briefly develop ideal-typic models of two political-economic systems—chiefdoms and liberal capitalism—to suggest commonalties in how the people of Hawai'i and Fiji experienced the role of law in transforming chiefs' rule over people into rule over land.[1] Ideal-typic models are necessarily abstract: "It is probably seldom if ever that a real phenomenon can be found which corresponds exactly to one of these ideally constructed pure types" (Weber 1947:110).[2] Nevertheless, models that suggest what "rational" people would do and say in identi-fied circumstances "can be used to aid in the understanding of action"(Weber 1947:111).[3] My project is, therefore, to develop brief ideal-typic models of the two cultural traditions that encountered and interacted with each other in eighteenth- and nineteenth-century Fiji and Hawai'i. I supplement my model of chiefdoms with a model of lib-eral capitalism for three reasons. First, the bearers of liberal capitalism were important actors in the history of Polynesia. Second, most of the knowledge we have about chiefdoms is filtered through lenses worn by Westerners. Third, my own understanding of chiefdoms (and of liberal capitalism) is shaped by the cultural conceptions available to me. I am, after all, writing in English.

Although I follow Max Weber in developing models to understand what "rational" people might say and do, my models are neither equilibrium systems nor logically integrated. At their core are contradictions. Rather than take maximizing economic man as my prototype for rationality, I imagine an ordinary person who simply hopes for respect and attention from valued others. Following the analytic strategy Michelle Rosaldo and I (Collier and Rosaldo 1981) proposed for understanding similarities in the gender conceptions of people living in "simple" societies of foragers and hunter-horticulturalists, I focus on the organization of social inequality. I assume that "inequalities in status and privilege determine the goals people fight for, their motives for politics, and the conditions they seek to explain....People celebrate those very self-images that they use when creating relationships, promoting cooperation or conflict, articulating desires and claims" (Collier and Rosaldo 1981:276). I therefore explore the complex relationship between how elites justify their privileges and how people get ahead.

In this chapter, I use my models to understand conceptual oppositions, for example, the one between foreign conquerors and people of the land that recurs in descriptions of chiefdoms and the one between politics and law that people in liberal capitalist societies seem to assert continually, despite (or because of) the difficulty of maintaining it. Similarly, I use my models to make sense of reported behaviors, such as chiefs adopting Christianity but later backsliding and colonizers imposing law on conquered peoples even though their efforts produce the disorder that impositions of law are supposed to prevent. Finally, at the end of this chapter, I use the models to suggest critical turning points in the (never completed) process of turning chiefs who rule people into chiefs who rule land.

CHIEFDOMS

The cultural logic—and illogic—of a chiefdom political economy is best revealed by starting with an imaginary conical clan in which everyone is unequal and ranked on the basis of seniority. Parents outrank children, and within sibling sets, older siblings outrank younger ones. It is also best to imagine a male bias in which younger brothers found junior descent lines (fig. 2.1). This pyramidal ranking is justified

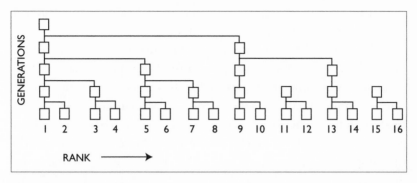

FIGURE 2.1

An imaginary conical clan.

by a religious ideology that posits a slowly dissipating power of the gods who created all life. Although this power disperses with each succeeding generation, it remains most concentrated in the senior line, slowly becoming less and less concentrated as genealogical distance from the senior line increases.

Next, one needs to imagine an economic system based on two types of estates, or relationships to land: usufruct and estates of administration (Gluckman 1965b). Usufruct is the right to take products from the land but not to grant similar rights to others. Estates of administration include the right to grant rights to others, and these typically occur in nested hierarchies in which all but the lowest-ranking estate include the right to grant estates of administration, as well as usufruct, to other people. This nested hierarchy of estates of administration correlates with the political-religious hierarchy because estate holders do not grant rights in the western sense but do provide fertility—the sacred power that makes land and people productive. The highest-ranking person, who concentrates the most godly power, bestows fertility on the largest amount of land by performing rituals for it—and so on down the line, as those with lesser power fertilize ever-smaller tracts. In return for these fertility rituals, subordinates obey their benefactors, typically through offering labor and foodstuffs. Ongoing exchanges of labor and agricultural products from inferiors to superiors, of fertility rituals from superiors to inferiors, and of manufactured items (often textiles) as status-appropriate offerings from inferiors to superiors and as status-validating gifts from superiors to inferiors constitute the political-religious-economic hierarchy of chiefdoms.

However, it is common knowledge that few, if any, chiefdoms conform to the model of a conical clan. Most observers comment that status is achieved rather than ascribed by birth. As a result, the conical clan is best imagined not as a structure but as a cultural model for the kinds of statuses a person can achieve and, most importantly, for how a person obtains these. In chiefdoms, people achieve a status by publicly fulfilling the obligations associated with it, which means obeying immediate superiors, "fertilizing" immediate inferiors, and exchanging status-appropriate manufactured items with both superiors and inferiors. Because the most important status-validating exchanges take place in public, chiefdoms appear to be "theatre states" in which ceremonies mobilizing vast numbers of people and great quantities of wealth objects are "not means to political ends, but...the ends themselves" (Geertz 1980:13). The "gift exchanges with rigid protocol" that occurred during the rare gathering of precolonial Fijian chiefs were political acts, despite France's argument to the contrary, as quoted by Kelly in Chapter 3 (n. 11).

Genealogical manipulation is the primary means for mobilizing the people and goods needed for performing ceremonies (see Comaroff 1978). Chiefdom genealogies can always be manipulated because endogamy within the conical clan enables people to trace descent through females as well as males, a practice made easier by the fact that females also embody godly power. The imaginary conical clan of clear-cut descent lines thus contains a contradiction at its core. Moreover, marriage in chiefdoms is always ambiguous. It is not an event but a process. Marriages exist only to the extent that they are validated through ongoing exchanges, and they may be renegotiated even after the principals die. Moreover, the ambiguous quality of marriage is reinforced by the fact that stable pairings coexist with, and often blend into, practices that Westerners label as polygyny, concubinage, adultery, and fornication. Even generational distinctions within the conical clan can be overcome through adoption, ghost marriage, and the omission of ancestors. Because every individual enjoys several options for rewriting his or her genealogy, no one is without competitors for status, even as each person's version of a genealogy affects the opportunities of others. As a result, those who are most successful at mobilizing the crowds and goods necessary to perform status-validating ceremonies tend to be those who can rewrite genealogies in such a way as to benefit more people than would be benefited by a rival's genealogical manipulation. Typically, successful claimants for higher status produce family histories that raise the genealogical status of large and growing lineage segments and diminish the status of lineage segments that are losing population.

This brief description of how chiefdoms work suggests explanations for certain features of chiefdoms that have often been noted. First, chiefdoms commonly have three competing descent lines at the top of the system (for example, see Kaplan, Chapter 6, and Miyazaki, Chapter 9, this volume). This tripartite structure appears puzzling because the conical clan model posits but a single chief at the apex of the genealogical pyramid. The existence of both superior and inferior lines, however, is doubly determined. Within chiefdoms, three top lines are continually produced and reproduced because claimants to chiefly status are never without competitors and because claims to status are validated through exchanging goods and services with both superiors and inferiors. As a result, some person or group has to perform the ceremonies that confer chiefly status on a successful contender, even as some person or group must be the immediate recipient of chiefly fertility. Moreover, the cultural logic of chiefdoms encourages sitting chiefs to recognize someone as superior because this logic immobilizes the person who embodies the concentration of godly power. Were the embodiment of concentrated power to move, that power would appear dispersed rather than centered.[4] By recognizing and immobilizing a superior, a chief acquires the ability to act. Frequently, a chief's sister is cast in the role of sacred and immobilized superior, and the chief's wife is cast as the immediate subordinate who receives his fertility. Because sisters and wives have—and create—kin, their descent lines can all too easily be mapped onto competing lineages of superior chief makers and inferior (but potentially competitive) chiefs' allies.

Another commonly noted feature of chiefdoms is their tendency to celebrate conceptual oppositions, such as sacred-profane, male-female, superior-inferior, active-passive, or sea-land, as in Polynesia (Kaplan, Chapter 6, this volume). Chiefdoms provide a paradise for followers of

Levi-Strauss who enjoy analyzing dualistic ritual systems. That chiefdoms, which inevitably produce and reproduce three competing descent lines, should celebrate dualisms might seem strange. Again, such dualisms are multiply determined. The cultural logic of ever-dispersing godly power casts concentrating power, particularly through combining conceptual opposites, as a world-preserving act.[5] Dualisms ripe for uniting must be continually reproduced, a process helped by the fact that the cultural logic of chiefdoms continually collapses tripartite divisions into dualisms through rendering centers invisible. Centers are both conceptual and practical voids because a person's status is publicly validated through exchanges of goods and services with superiors and inferiors rather than in terms of what that person is or does. It is also true that individuals in chiefdoms achieve higher status by collapsing two potentially opposing descent lines into one. People have good reason to talk about dualisms instead of tripartite divisions. Many writers who analyze chiefdoms observe that chiefs (or men who aspire to higher status) try to marry into the lines established by their father's siblings in order to collapse the distinction between sisters and wives.[6] Although this strategy does have the effect of converting potential superiors (father's sisters' descendants) and competitors (father's brothers' descendants) into inferiors and allies (wife's kin), it also immobilizes potentially disloyal allies by "sacralizing" them and converting them into future chief makers. Similarly, both superiors and inferiors benefit by collapsing the center into one or the other side, converting three into two. Superiors secure their superiority by collapsing centers into inferiors, even as inferiors who collapse centers into superiors rise in status by reducing two superior lines to one.

A common conceptual opposition produced in chiefdoms is the one between conquering foreign chiefs and conquered people of the land, which was often imagined as a sea-land opposition in Polynesia. This widespread, foreign chiefs–local subordinates dualism is multiply determined. First, chiefs are often foreign conquerors because warfare is endemic. Chiefdoms are forever expanding and contracting as successful warriors conquer previously independent groups and as previously subordinate groups secede or rebel.[7] However, chiefs have another reason to cast themselves as foreign conquerors. By doing so, they rid themselves of problematic superiors. Not only can a conquering chief portray himself as self-made, freeing himself from obligations to chief makers, but he can also recognize as superior someone who poses no threat, such as an unmarried sister. A chief's successors have even better reasons for maintaining the distinction between foreign and local because over time the distinction tends to blur. Conquering chiefs commonly marry women of the land, giving the women's kin an opportunity to define themselves as relatives and valued allies rather than as conquered slaves. Also, chiefs commonly marry at least some of their daughters into local lineages, giving daughters' husbands' kin an opportunity to cast themselves as chief makers to their mother's brothers' sons. As a result, successors to conquering chiefs who hope to keep local rivals at bay have good reason to stress the distinction between superior foreigners and inferior locals. At the same time, local people have good reason to stress their ties to the land, for by claiming to embody local sources of godly power, they not only establish themselves as allies and potential chief makers to foreign usurpers but also keep alive the possibility of secession (see Kaplan, Chapter 6, this volume, and 1995).

Another common conceptual opposition is the territorial one between centers and peripheries. Many observers have pointed out that people in chiefdoms frequently imagine political power as concentrated in ceremonial centers, gradually becoming weaker as distance from a center increases. Whereas chiefly centers tend to appear permanent, marked by palaces and temples, peripheries appear unclear and fluctuating as the diminishing power of one chiefly center gradually fades into the increasing power of a neighboring one.[8] Not surprisingly, centers tend to be located in fertile valleys and the peripheries of mountainous or otherwise inhospitable regions. If peripheries are imagined as power vacuums, they are also experienced as locations where untamed powers can emerge. Chiefly centers are always trying to absorb the potentially disruptive powers of peripheries, commonly by seeking to concentrate people and deities in central locations. Chiefs who manage to expand their territorial control, for example, may move whole populations from peripheries to centers or, at least, move local deities into central temples. Such moves reflect practical, as well as conceptual, concerns. Conquering chiefs have good reason to fear peripheral powers because populations far from chiefly centers enjoy the best opportunities for seceding, either to establish egalitarian relationships or to set up chiefly centers of their own.

Finally, observers commonly note that people in chiefdoms have a different understanding of the self than people raised in the western tradition. Whereas the West has long posited a distinction between I and Me, imagining the body or self as a resource that the will (or the I) may use for good or ill, people in chiefdoms are often portrayed as lacking this distinction. Rather than view the body as a bounded entity housing a soul or will, chiefdom peoples frequently perceive body boundaries as permeable and appear to lack a sense of personal responsibility. Because people in chiefdoms come to know the self through the ongoing exchanges that establish their relationships with others, they tend to think of themselves less in terms of who they are "inside" than in terms of the effects they produce on those around them. They aspire to concentrate in their persons the godly powers that attract gifts and services from others even as they fear that their powers will flow away, leaving chaos and confusion. Just as the western bounded self with a conscience reflects a religious tradition that has long imagined God as having granted humans the free will to seek or disdain His salvation, chiefdom peoples' efforts to concentrate godly powers reflect the religious ideology of gradually dispersing mana. For people living in chiefdoms, concentrations of power create peace and prosperity, and power vacuums are manifested in conflict and loss.[9]

LIBERAL CAPITALISM

The liberal-capitalist equivalent of the conical clan in chiefdoms is best imagined as the society envisioned by some of its founding fathers: Hobbes, Locke, and Rousseau. Despite differences among these political philosophers, they all imagined a society made up of equal men whose equality consisted of no man owing anything—either political submission or economic debts—to any other man. They owed nothing because each man was imagined as self-provisioning—able to provide all his own needs by working land that he himself had appropriated from Nature. This equality was justified by a religious ideology positing a creator God who gave the Earth and its resources to all men in common and who endowed all men with the reason necessary to subsist and to understand God's order.

Although all men are equal, they are also selfish and competitive. As a result, equal men must form a government if they are to forestall the warre of each against all. Each man must surrender a measure of his God-given independence to create a sovereign capable of guaranteeing the security of persons and property, for it is only by creating a sovereign capable of punishing those who infringe upon the rights of others that men can be assured of enjoying the fruits of their own labors. This imagined society of equal men also requires a free market. Because men inevitably need goods that they themselves cannot produce, they require a forum in which they can exchange products they do not need for ones they do need. Hobbes, Locke, and Rousseau imagined both the republican political system and the free market as based on contracts in which men freely consent to exchange some of their God-given independence and self-acquired products to obtain the security and goods they need to survive and prosper.

Everyone knows, of course, that this imagined society of equal, independent men never existed and can never exist. Privately held property creates a contradiction at the core of liberal capitalism, just as endogamy creates one within the conical clan.[10] However, just as the conical clan provides people in chiefdoms with a cultural model for the kinds of statuses a person can occupy, the cultural model of social contract provides us (me included) with a model of what we can hope to achieve. We all want autonomy in the sense that we want to acquire enough private property to support ourselves and be able to recognize and honor only those debts and obligations we freely choose. We also want a world in which others fulfill their obligations toward us because they, like us, freely choose to do so. Even Marx embraced this ideal of liberal capitalism. He, too, wanted a society in which men were free from want and could decide for themselves which activities and affiliations to pursue.

Social contract theory also provides us with a model for how to go about achieving the desired status of autonomy. Just as the conical clan encourages people in chiefdoms to imagine that they realize desired statuses by publicly exchanging the goods and services that define their position in relation to superiors and inferiors, those of us who live within liberal capitalism typically believe that we realize valued autonomy by acquiring, through our own efforts, the human and material capital that enables us to engage in equal and consensual exchanges with others. For most of us, our paychecks, along with receipts from sales, dividend checks, and profit margins, testify to our earning power. They symbolize our ability to pay our own way without having to accept handouts from anyone. Moreover, social contract theory suggests that the more human and material capital we acquire, the more contracts we can negotiate with others and the more pleasures we can enjoy.

Finally, the liberal-capitalist equivalent of genealogical manipulation in chiefdoms is the manipulation of exchanges to make them appear equal and consensual. Marx, of course, is famous for explaining how and why so many men became willing to sell their labor to capitalists in return for wages that were lower than the price capitalists received when selling laborers' products on the market. The spread of private property in land, which deprived many peasants of their means of subsistence, left them nothing to sell but their labor. The job market created by competition among these landless laborers ensured that workers (and those who employed them) understood workers' wages not only as freely chosen but also as achieved on the open market. As Marx's analysis reveals, the most effective strategy for casting unequal exchanges as equal is to limit the options of those who are disadvantaged, making it appear that they freely choose the obligations they assume.[11] Land plays a crucial role in this process. Whereas people in chiefdoms get ahead by giving land and fertility to potential followers, people in liberal-capitalist societies get ahead by holding land as private property, depriving others of the right to use it, creating a pool of workers who own nothing but their labor power.[12]

Because liberal capitalism works by making unequal exchanges appear equal, equality is a forever contested term. Actually, the contest is less often about equality—which can be a vacant term, much like the invisible center in chiefdoms—than about equality's presumed opposite: exploitation. Endless debates occur over whether the options of some person or group have been unfairly limited, forcing them to consent to contracts they would never have accepted if they had been free to do otherwise. This unending, and essentially irresolvable, debate over exploitation suggests explanations for certain recurring features of liberal-capitalist society, including the fact that Westerners who write about chiefdoms tend to spill vast amounts of ink trying to answer the question of why commoners work for and give their products to chiefs.[13] The point, of course, is not that it is wrong to ask whether commoners in chiefdoms are exploited by their chiefs but rather to recognize that this question is ours, not theirs.[14]

This question is ours because answers to it have consequences for us (but not for people in chiefdoms, at least not until chiefs start to rule land instead of people). Within liberal-capitalist society, those who portray some person or group as forced by limited life chances to accept an exchange that benefits the other party are issuing a call for action. They want the exploiters punished and/or the laws changed to prevent such exploitation in the future. As a result, those who favor keeping things as they are must produce arguments that portray disadvantaged parties as freely choosing the exchange that harms them. Advocates of the status quo have a couple options. They can portray disadvantaged people as having a different hierarchy of values than those who argue that the exchange is unequal, continually reproducing the idea of cultural differences, or they can argue that the options of disadvantaged people are limited not by human action but by natural processes humans are powerless to change. As many authors have recognized, racism and sexism, which rely on assumptions of biological inferiority, are not antithetical to liberalism but are continually produced by it.

Many authors have also observed that the capitalist world system created by European expansion since the sixteenth century tended to foster regimes of coerced labor in peripheral regions at the same time that apparently free labor came to dominate in the core (for example, Wallerstein 1974; Wolf 1982). Whereas sixteenth-century European colonizers often justified coerced labor as reflecting conquerors' god-given right to extract labor and tribute from conquered peoples, later colonizers, particularly during the nineteenth and early twentieth centuries, preferred to imagine that conquered peoples consented to work for and/or pay taxes to their colonizers. On the one hand, colonizers used ideas of racial and cultural difference to justify educating "savages" to comply with contractual obligations. They passed laws creating customary jurisdictions, discouraging miscegenation and the movement of peoples, and limiting subject peoples' access to the linguistic and legal skills that would enable them to challenge coerced labor regimes in European courts (Mamdani 1996). On the other hand, colonizers drew on ideas of human similarity, that is, acultural, "economic man," to justify imposing penal sanctions on debt peons, indentured laborers, and sharecroppers who failed to honor the contracts they (or their ancestors) had supposedly signed.

A commonly noted feature of liberal-capitalist societies is the conceptual distinction that people make between law and politics. Fitzpatrick (1992), for example, has observed that Westerners continue to imagine law as transcendental and unchanging, even though everyone knows that existing laws reflect the outcomes of particular political conflicts.[15] This conceptual distinction between law and politics is multiply determined. First, law must be distinguished from politics if the pursuit of individual self-interest is to make sense. There have to be laws to define what may be achieved and how. Games must have rules that define prizes and permissible moves. More importantly, the unending and irresolvable debates over whether exchanges are forced or consensual cast the distinction between law and politics as both necessary and impossible to maintain. Both sides in the debate must treat law as if it could guarantee the equality that enables equal exchanges, even as they must argue over whether existing laws reflect unfair political maneuverings. Just as those who would maintain the status quo must portray cultural or natural differences, instead of law, as responsible for inequalities in wealth, power, and prestige, those who would argue that exchanges are exploitative must assert that existing laws unfairly limit the options of disadvantaged groups. They have to argue that those with political power have used their power unfairly, either to pass laws that benefit their own interests or to prevent the passage of laws that might allow disadvantaged persons and groups to compete on a more equal footing. Given that the distinction between law and politics must be maintained even as it is always contested, people in liberal-capitalist societies commonly try to immobilize law by writing it down in code books, constitutions, and legal forms and by establishing separate institutions—courts and document registries—to administer it. Nevertheless, the distinction keeps blurring, as should be obvious to those of us who watched the Supreme Court appoint a president in 2000.

Another commonly noted conceptual opposition of liberal-capitalist societies is that between nature and culture. Although Westerners seem to discover this opposition wherever they go, I believe that its imagined universalism owes more to the concerns of the observers than to those of the observed. Not only does the idea of man-made law inevitably construct its imagined opposite (laws not made by men[16]), but also practical politics in liberal-capitalist societies continually reproduce the nature-culture opposition. As noted earlier, the most effective strategy available to those who support the status quo is to argue that apparently unequal exchanges are really equal because the limited options experienced by disadvantaged individuals and groups are imposed on them by Nature (or God) rather than by human action. Therefore, we are condemned to endless, and irresolvable, nature-nurture debates, along with endless scientific efforts to determine which differences among humans are due to our genes instead of our histories.

Practical politics in liberal-capitalist societies also tend to reproduce the supposedly universal opposition between private and public spheres, albeit less as a spatial one—between inside and outside or between encompassed and encompassing arenas—than as one between two forms of regulation. In liberal-capitalist societies, private spheres are supposedly regulated by natural laws, and public spheres are regulated by man-made ones. Given the unending debates over whether observed inequalities reflect natural or human laws, the distinction between private and public is forever contested, even as it must be constantly maintained. This distinction is particularly controversial when the private is imagined as the home or the economy, because both of these supposedly natural spheres are created and regulated by human laws. Continual vigilance and work are required to make homes and markets appear governed by laws beyond human control. Locke and Rousseau, for example, took special care to distinguish the domestic from the public, arguing that within the domestic sphere, natural differences of age, sex, ability, and situation foster mutual cooperation, whereas the public realm is regulated by the laws that equal, competitive men enact to protect their homes and private properties from encroachment by others. Similarly, we witness endless efforts to cast economics as a science—to discover the mathematical laws that govern the free market and therefore should be allowed to work their magic without interference from meddling humans.

Finally, people engaged in practical pursuits continually reproduce

47

the I/Me distinction that is central to the self in western thought. Market capitalism requires that subjects be differentiated from objects—that humans who transact be distinguished from the properties they own and exchange—even though this distinction is impossible to maintain.[17] This liberal-capitalist I/Me distinction differs slightly from the religious distinction between soul and body that Europeans inherited from the past. Because the laws of liberal capitalism supposedly make all men equal, people tend to experience the Me less as flesh to be mortified in the hope of heavenly bliss than as a resource to be used for achieving success on Earth in this life. Differences in bodily equipment and material circumstances, which supposedly have little effect on a soul's chance of salvation, take on special meaning. Our bodies are ourselves (as a feminist classic proclaims), even as our genetic and cultural heritages become resources to be deployed for advantage (or used to explain why others unfairly discriminate against us). The I/Me distinction is so central to our thinking and so inscribed in the English language that we have a hard time imagining other ways of experiencing the self.

CHIEFDOMS IN THE COLONIAL ENCOUNTER

The encounter between chiefdoms and western imperialism commonly produced a novel dilemma for chiefdoms: the coincidence of concentrated power and declining fertility. Within the cultural logic of chiefdoms, such a coincidence cannot occur because concentrations of power are supposed to have the effect of promoting peace and prosperity among the population. The existence of peace and prosperity testifies to the existence of concentrated power. However, western imperialism brought both political centralization and demographic disaster. Western guns encouraged political centralization by enabling one chief to defeat many rivals. Guns, along with newly introduced diseases, also decimated local populations (Merry, Chapter 5, this volume). People living in chiefdoms faced the breakdown of their conceptual system even as their bodies suffered. Their familiar conceptual system offered no explanation or understanding of what was happening to them. Western imperialists, in contrast, did not experience a similar conceptual breakdown. Although they inevitably argued over whether they were responsible for the terrible fate that overtook colonized peoples, Westerners could do so by drawing on familiar conceptual oppositions between natural and humanly imposed disasters.

Many of those who write the history of chiefdoms have noted that chiefs often converted to Christianity before their subjects did, as occurred in both Fiji and Hawai'i (see Kaplan, Chapter 6, and Merry, Chapter 5, this volume). Chiefly conversion may seem surprising, given that chiefs appear to benefit from maintaining the pagan religion that legitimates their power, but conversion makes good sense within the cultural logic of chiefdoms. As already discussed, chiefs are supposed to concentrate power within their persons. They usually take over the deities of peoples they conquer. It makes sense that Fijian and Hawaiian chiefs ingested the Christian God, whose "body and blood" the missionaries so generously offered, and gave missionaries land on which to construct Christian churches and schools. Moreover, chiefs have to encompass rival deities if they are to avoid the dispersal of power that causes conflict and death. The demographic disasters experienced by newly encountered chiefdoms must have propelled chiefs to embrace Christianity. Even though chiefs eagerly converted, they inevitably backslid. In contrast to Christian missionaries, who could maintain the fiction of a unitary God because they lived in societies where inequalities were negotiated in terms of unequal opportunities instead of competing deities, chiefs (and their people) had to keep reproducing multiple deities for incorporation into single power centers. Chiefs who converted to Christianity had to honor the old gods even as they joined missionaries in worshiping the One God of Christianity.

The cultural logic of chiefdoms also required chiefs to obtain other items Westerners valued. Although it may be true that chiefs competed with one another through conspicuous consumption, as some observers have suggested, chiefs—at least newly encountered ones— were not the possessive individuals imagined by neoclassical economists. Rather than acquire goods to compete with rivals for market advantage or political power, chiefs sought goods to incorporate sources of power they did not yet embody. The cultural logic of chiefdoms suggests that if Westerners valued items such as gold, fine cloth, or mahogany furniture, these items must be powerful. As a result, a chief who aspired to concentrate power in his person had to bring such items into his domain. Chiefs who succeeded in acquiring large quantities of western luxury goods may have triumphed over potential rivals, but not because they controlled more economic resources than their competitors. They triumphed because they appeared to concentrate more power in their persons. As several authors have recognized, the acquisition of luxury items was not a means to an end, but the end itself.

Finally, the cultural logic of chiefdoms suggests a different interpretation for chiefs' apparent exploitation of commoners' labor condemned by many western observers. When chiefs in Hawai'i, for example, sent commoners out to collect the sandalwood that chiefs needed to trade for western luxury items, both the commoners and their chiefs may well have had a different understanding of what they were doing than western missionaries and traders. Given that the people of Hawai'i were experiencing a demographic disaster, commoners may well have wanted their chiefs to acquire all the western powers chiefs could buy. As long as Westerners controlled powerful items such as ships, books, and furniture, power would remain dispersed and people would suffer. Only by incorporating western powers could chiefs concentrate power and bring prosperity again. This strategy, of course, failed. Westerners continued to arrive, and their supply of valuables was inexhaustible. As a result, the people of Hawai'i finally changed strategies. Rather than urge chiefs to incorporate western powers, they urged chiefs to throw out the foreigners (Sahlins 1992:129; Osorio, Chapter 8, this volume). This switch in strategy, however, probably signaled people's abandonment of chiefdom cultural logic. Westerners are the ones who think that power accrues to those who collect things while disposing of people. Cargo cults are a product of the western imagination, not of the peoples Westerners conquered (Kaplan 1995).

THE IMPOSITION OF LAW

When Westerners encountered and conquered chiefdoms, they commonly overlooked the chiefdom equivalent of western law. They misunderstood how people resolved their conflicts. They failed to see the social processes and cultural concepts through which people in chiefdoms negotiated their obligations to one another. Because genealogical relations supposedly determine obligations in chiefdoms, the crucial question facing those involved in a conflict is not whether someone violated a rule but how the conflicting parties are related to one another. Also, because people in chiefdoms live in a world where relationships are known by the exchanges that constitute them, people refer to past gifts of goods and services to determine the relationship between parties and their future obligations to one another (Gluckman 1965a). For example, when people in chiefdoms face a problem that Westerners might view as theft, they are often less concerned with who took what or whether the object belonged to the victim than with discussing past exchanges to decide whether the relationship between the parties is one in which the person who suffered the loss has the obligation to provide the taker with the object. If discussion of past exchanges convinces people that the victim has no kinship obligations to the thief, people might punish the thief by showering that person with goods (and ridicule). Such an outcome—which Westerners would interpret as rewarding rather than punishing a thief—makes sense, given the cultural logic of chiefdoms. Because people demonstrate concentrated power (and high rank) by giving things to inferiors, a person who is forced to accept goods from another becomes a genealogical subordinate who owes obedience in return.[18]

Westerners who encountered chiefdoms also "found" law where it did not exist. They frequently misinterpreted the taboos chiefs put on resources (to reserve these for ceremonies) as instances of law. Why this occurred is easy to understand. For Westerners, chiefly taboos were the closest thing in their experience to the western idea of law as rules imposed by a sovereign. This misinterpretation, however, had at least two serious consequences. First, it enabled Westerners to cast chiefs as exploiters of their peoples, as fickle tyrants who appropriated public resources for private gain. Gordon, for example, apparently thought that Fijian chiefs sometimes imposed levies "merely to gratify idle longings" (Kelly, Chapter 3, this volume). Second, Westerners who interpreted taboos as laws expected chiefs to have the power (and legitimacy) to impose other laws, such as laws banning adultery or imposing house taxes. As a result, when Westerners began to rule through chiefs—which they usually did, given the practicalities of maintaining order—Westerners expected chiefs to pass laws and see that they were enforced. To the degree that Westerners succeeded in turning fertile chiefs into law-giving sovereigns, they transformed the social world of chiefdom peoples.

Among the first laws western colonizers pressed chiefs to pass and enforce were laws designed to facilitate the expansion of liberal capitalism by creating responsible individuals and private properties. Almost immediately, for example, the colonizers required chiefs to regulate family relationships and sexual affairs (Merry, Chapter 5, this volume, and 2000; Kelly, Chapter 3, this volume; Silva, Chapter 4, this volume; Osorio, Chapter 8, this volume). Although observers of the colonial process often blame Christian missionaries for laws banning polygyny, adultery, and fornication, colonial officials and traders also had a stake in distinguishing legal marriage from other sexual liaisons. Colonizers wanted to distinguish legitimate heirs from illegitimate contenders to ensure the orderly transmission of property and office that Westerners treat as the basis of social order. Colonizers, for example, had a vested interest in replacing lengthy interregnums—during which contenders for chiefly status vied with one another by sponsoring lavish ceremonies—with the orderly and immediate inheritance of chiefly authority (and responsibilities). Colonizers also wanted to take over the role of appointing chiefs, replacing former chief makers. Ironically, colonizers often recognized as chiefs people who would not have been contenders without colonial interference. For example, colonizers often took chiefly hierarchies at face value and treated the most sacred person as the highest chief, thus conferring chiefly status on women or children whose role had been to embody the concentrated but immobilized power that enabled chiefs to act. (It is also true, of course, that Westerners may have preferred appointing women and children, thinking them easier to manipulate than the wily men and women who had achieved high status through astute manipulation of genealogies. It is also true that wily chiefs may have preferred providing colonizers with powerless substitutes rather than submitting themselves to foreign authority.)

At the same time, colonizers tried to ensure the orderly transmission of property and status by legalizing inheritance. As discussed earlier, people in chiefdoms commonly validated their genealogical positions by exchanging gifts with superiors and inferiors. As a result, the estate of a deceased person appeared to revert to that person's superior because it was the superior who appointed the successor by conferring the estate on the winning contender. Westerners often misinterpreted this practice, however, assuming that voracious and unprincipled superiors appropriated the property of deceased subordinates to pass it on to their cronies and allies, depriving legitimate heirs in the process. To ensure the orderly transmission of property (and contractual obligations), Westerners tended to require that estates be inventoried so that legitimate heirs could be assured of receiving all the property they were due. Although lists of the goods and lands held by important people serve as invaluable resources for historians of chiefdoms under colonialism, such lists mark the disruption of a chiefdom cultural order. When heirs fought in western courts using written documents (inventories, wills, deeds, certificates of marriage and birth), they created a social world in which wealth and power accrued to people who denied, rather than fulfilled, their obligations to others. Greed replaced generosity as the route to social and economic success.

In addition to laws creating identifiable subjects and fungible objects, colonizers also required chiefs to pass laws allowing the collection of taxes. After all, if people in the colonizers' home countries had to pay for the government services they received, colonized peoples should do the same. Moreover, chiefdoms already appeared to have taxation systems in place. As previously noted, chiefs received regular gifts from subordinates because subordinates validated their claims to genealogical status by continually fulfilling obligations to superiors and inferiors. Subordinates' gifts to chiefs could easily be misperceived as taxes imposed by rulers on their subjects. As a result, colonizers had few qualms about requiring chiefs to regularize the collection of taxes, both to prevent chiefs from exploiting their hapless subjects and to ensure an orderly source of revenue for financing government functions. In situations of indirect rule, colonial officials often required chiefs to turn over tax revenues to representatives of the colonial government, who then paid chiefs a salary for their work. Such a practice, of course, broke the bonds uniting chiefs with their people, by making chiefs dependent on the good will of colonial officials rather than on the good will of their subordinates. The transformation of gifts into taxes also marked the transformation of chiefs who ruled people into chiefs who ruled land, because colonial officials commonly delimited the territories within which chiefs were required to collect taxes and enforce laws. As Kaplan (Chapter 6, this volume) describes for Fiji, colonial officials installed chiefs as rulers of districts, creating a top-down system of rule over territories.

Although colonizers who required chiefs to collect taxes were often surprised when commoners showered their chiefs with gifts without asking for favors in return (because what Westerner would pay more taxes than required by law), colonizers and tax-collecting chiefs more often faced resistance from commoners. Commoners had many reasons to resent the transformation of gifts into taxes. Not least was the fact that taxes, unlike gifts, were no longer used to put on the ceremonies that ensured fertility for people and land. Rather than restore the fertility of people whose numbers were rapidly declining because of guns and new diseases, colonizers and their client chiefs tended to use taxes for things that harmed commoners, such as salaries for chiefs, judges, and policemen. At a time of demographic disaster, commoners particularly resented the policemen who were charged with enforcing tax laws and with bringing criminals to "justice."

The colonizers who promoted western-style courts probably thought that they were offering native peoples the most important benefit of civilization. Sir Arthur Gordon, for example, told Fijians that "you must know that laws are necessary; a country without laws would be in a pitiable condition" (quoted by Kelly, Chapter 3, this volume). However, people in chiefdoms suffered when courts became punitive instead of conciliatory. Because Westerners misunderstood the rewards that accrue to problem solvers in chiefdoms (where those who help others to settle their disputes validate the genealogical relationships that determine people's obligations to one another), colonizers required judges and policemen to be paid for their services. In the western imagination, law enforcement is a thankless task no one would perform unless paid to do so. As a result, the western-style courts established by colonizers usually required payments from those who used them, such as filing fees from litigants and fines from wrongdoers. Western-style courts thus appeared to emphasize punitive sanctions instead of the restitutive ones common in chiefdoms, in which exchanges of gifts affirm the relationship between the parties established by the hearing. Moreover, the western belief that people who violate the law must be punished—both to reform the wrongdoer and to serve as an example to others—led colonizers to establish jails for punishing offenders. Prisons had a particularly devastating effect on the chiefdom peoples confined to them, because wrongdoers who were locked away could not engage in the exchanges of goods and services that established them as social beings. When imprisoned "natives" languished and died, colonial officials had a hard time understanding why their prisons failed to have the salutary effect expected by Westerners, whose understanding of the I/Me distinction led them to believe that prisons should encourage offenders to assume personal responsibility for their actions.

Observers of the colonizing process in chiefdoms have noted that as courts became more punitive, the number of cases brought by individuals declined and the number of cases brought by policemen increased. Once started on the route to punitiveness, courts became more punitive, confined to handling cases in which individuals were accused of breaking laws passed and enforced by governing authorities. The courts' increasing punitiveness, however, had an unintended and ironic effect. As ordinary people found that their leaders had been transformed from mediators promoting reconciliation into judges imposing fines and prison sentences, they began settling their interpersonal conflicts in family conclaves, where respected elders could help disputants sort out and repair their kinship relations (Merry, Chapter 5, this volume). The imposition of western courts, paradoxically, encouraged the creation of forums in which the cultural logic of chiefdoms could survive and flourish. As Merry and Brenneis observe in the introduction, the absence of formal law, whether caused by a lack of state oversight, as in Indo-Fijian communities, or by people's avoidance of punitive courts, can have a powerful effect on local life by encouraging people to create their own ways of handling conflicts.

In colonized chiefdoms, the respected elders who presided over family conclaves commonly handled disputes by analyzing genealogies to determine how people were related to one another and what their mutual obligations should therefore be. By appearing to focus on family matters, such conclaves tended to avoid interference from colonizing officials, who, as Westerners, imagined that private homes should be regulated by natural bonds of obligation rather than by man-made laws. The private nature of family conclaves, however, had another effect. Because the family conclave–punitive court contrast meshed so well with the liberal-capitalist conceptual opposition between private and public spheres, the existence of family conclaves tended to reinforce visions of the ethnic contrast between the colonized and the colonizers as one between nature and culture. Depending on who was speaking for what purpose, colonized peoples could be cast either as animalistic and childlike in contrast to civilized and rational colonizers or as helpful, generous, and cooperative in contrast to selfish, greedy, and competitive Westerners (see Osorio, Chapter 8, and Merry, Chapter 5, this volume).

I suspect that legal histories of the colonial encounter between liberal capitalism and chiefdoms can be written in terms of the expansion and contraction of family conclaves. Over time, most high chiefs either died out or merged into the class of western property owners, but lesser folk in chiefdoms commonly contracted and expanded their sphere of influence as pressures from the capitalist world system waxed and waned. When western pressure is extreme, family conclaves are probably small affairs, but when western pressures relax—as they do during world economic recessions or when investment opportunities are more promising elsewhere—family-type conclaves can expand to encompass whole communities. In the latter situation, people often take back their local courts, converting them from primarily punitive forums into forums where people can negotiate their relationships with one another. Westerners commonly understand such forums as applying customary law, reinforcing the distinction between positive and customary law that anthropologists have helped to reify.

Finally, people's resort to family conclaves to handle interpersonal disputes has the unintended consequence of preserving chiefdom religious beliefs in the face of considerable pressure from monotheistic world religions such as Christianity. To the degree that genealogical relationships determine people's obligations, ceremonies (and the exchange of gifts and services necessary to put on these ceremonies) appear to be less about people's individual relationship with God than about their relationships with one another. Christian pastors, for example, are often horrified to discover that chiefdom peoples continue to worship ancestor gods and local deities simultaneously with Jesus and the saints, as occurs in Fiji (see Kaplan, Chapter 6, this volume, and 1995). Similarly, pastors who view souls as distinct from bodies are often appalled to realize that supposedly Christian people perceive baptism not as a rite to ensure the salvation of a human soul but as a rite to center and concentrate the weak and dispersed power of a newborn.

CONCLUSION

In summary, colonizers from liberal-capitalist societies may have succeeded in transforming chiefs who ruled people into chiefs who rule land, but they simultaneously encouraged the creation of a realm where customary beliefs and practices could survive and flourish. Such customary realms, however, may be disappearing today as the latest wave of capitalist expansion fosters land-titling schemes and literacy. When people find their life chances determined more by the written documents they possess than by the gifts they exchange with kin, the cultural logic of chiefdoms may fade from people's memories. Lest I be too gloomy, however, I should end by noting that chiefdom cultural logic has revealed a remarkable capacity for survival. The people who invoke it may yet give those of us who live within liberal capitalism an alternative vision of human possibilities.

Acknowledgments

This chapter was a paper prepared for discussion at the advanced seminar "Law and Empire in the Pacific: Intersections of Culture and Legality" held at the School of American Research, Santa Fe, New Mexico, March 18–22, 2001, and has benefited from the comments and suggestions of conference participants, as well as from comments by Saba Mahmood, Bill Maurer, Sally Merry, and George Collier. The generalizations I make about chiefdoms are primarily based on readings about "native kingdoms" in Africa, Southeast Asia, the Americas, and the Pacific, which I did in the 1980s when co-teaching two graduate seminars on chiefdoms, first with Michelle Z. Rosaldo, then with Donald Donham. These readings included a fascinating paper on the Tikopia by Allison Tom. My speculations about conflict management procedures in chiefdoms are also based on my own research among the highland Maya of Chiapas, Mexico (Collier 1973), although my understanding of what I observed in Chiapas has been enriched by reading Max Gluckman's (1955, 1965a and b) analysis of Barotse legal concepts and procedures.

Notes

1. The idea that chiefs rule land rather than people is drawn from a Luganda proverb quoted in Fallers 1969: "A chief does not rule land; he rules people."

2. Ideal-typic models are, of course, fictional constructs, but they can be useful if they illuminate historical relationships and processes that previously appeared problematic. Ironically, they can be even more useful if they are wrong, for only by raising previously unasked questions do new answers become possible. This spirit of exploration animates my offering of the two ideal-typic models presented in this chapter.

3. Benedict Anderson (1972:1–2), in his influential article "The Idea of Power in Javanese Culture," justifies his attempt to provide a systematic analysis of traditional Javanese political conceptions by observing that the absence of a systematic exposition has "hampered the analysis and evaluation of the influence of such conceptions on contemporary political behavior. The tendency has been to select discrete elements from traditional culture and correlate them in an arbitrary and ad hoc manner with particular aspects of present day politics." Because anthropologists have already developed sophisticated analyses of chiefdoms (Adams 1966; Fried 1967; Goldman 1970; Service 1975; Ortner 1981), I cannot borrow Anderson's principal justification for the systematic analyses I develop in this chapter. However, I do follow him in recognizing that systematic analyses provide useful tools for helping us to understand historical and contemporary behavior.

4. Sacred chiefs, for example, are frequently depicted on monuments as sitting immobilized in the lotus position.

5. Anderson (1972:15), writing about the "idea of power in Javanese culture," describes this as the "unity-in-opposites formula of Power."

6. The cultural logic of concentrating ever-dispersing power also casts brother-sister marriage as a prestigious act, for it reunites the dispersing godly power of parents. By this logic, the marriage of brother-sister twins is even more potent.

7. Chiefdoms commonly occur in bands of big and little chiefdoms, with no-man's land and some apparently "egalitarian" groups in between.

8. Anderson (1972:28–29) contrasts the meaning of frontiers in traditional Southeast Asian kingdoms with that in modern states, observing that for the modern state, sovereignty is even across the entire territory but ends abruptly at the frontier, where the (supposedly) complete sovereignty of another state begins.

9. Westerners, such as I, find it difficult to talk or write about the concept of

self in chiefdoms because English requires active subjects of verbs. I find it hard to imagine—and to describe—a social world in which people are experienced not in terms of their actions but in terms of the effects they produce.

10. Not only does privately held property inevitably create inequality among supposedly equal men, but also, obviously, no human society can be composed solely of healthy adult men. The equal male property owners imagined by Hobbes, Locke, and Rousseau had wives (or mothers or sisters) to keep their homes, children to obey their commands, and servants to take care of their properties.

11. For example, many people experience the marriage contract as an equal exchange of female services for masculine support because women's lack of access to land, along with the reluctance of capitalist employers to hire mothers who must bring their young children to work with them, cast female homemakers as condemned by Nature to need the support of male breadwinners.

12. Within liberal-capitalist societies, land plays a political role as well as an economic one. Those who aspire to self-government must control a territory to govern. They must be able to exclude aliens from the territory (even if they must resort to ethnic cleansing to do so).

13. For example, the archaeologists and social anthropologists who attended the 1988 School of American Research advanced seminar on chiefdoms asked the question, What do the bosses do to gain and extend power (Earle 1991:5)? Not surprisingly, seminar participants came up with three strategies bosses could use to deprive people of the resources they need to survive, putting commoners in the position of having to obey chiefly commands or suffer dire consequences.

14. My earlier discussion of how chiefdoms work also suggests an answer to the question of why commoners work for and give gifts to chiefs. My answer, however, evades (hopefully) the issue of exploitation.

15. This modern myth of law as transcendental has a historical origin. Under the absolute monarchies that social contract philosophers sought to overthrow, law was transcendental: It reflected the will of God, who appointed kings to enforce His laws on Earth. When social contract theorists argued that equal men must pass the laws that govern them, they blurred the formerly clear (if always problematic) distinction between divine law and human desire. People living within liberal-capitalist societies had to find another way to maintain the crucial distinction between law and politics. This they commonly did by producing constitutions and law codes that supposedly reflected the common good and were (somewhat) immune to self-interested political maneuvering.

16. This conceptual opposition between man-made laws and laws not made by men existed under absolute monarchies but was not very important. All the laws that mattered emanated from the Mind of God. When men wrested from God the right to make their own laws, they left God in charge of all that humans did not regulate. Latour (1993) observed that man-made laws and the scientific method were created together. When Hobbes argued that men of reason must make the laws that govern them, Boyle simultaneously argued that men of reason, through coming together to observe an experiment, could ascertain the laws God established to regulate natural processes.

17. Children provide a good example of the difficulty in maintaining the subject/object distinction required by capitalist markets. Children belong to the parents who produced them, even as they are subjects in their own right.

18. Westerners frequently portray chiefdoms as recognizing collective instead of individual liability, as holding an entire kin group responsible for the harm done by one of its members. Such a portrayal misses the fact that conflicts between kin groups provide opportunities for (re)ordering relationships within kin groups. The kin group member who takes responsibility for providing the goods required to compensate the victim of a wrong establishes superiority over, and the right to demand services from, the person who committed the wrong. Exchanges of compensation, like exchanges of gifts, give people opportunities to (re)negotiate genealogical relationships.

3

Gordon Was No Amateur

Imperial Legal Strategies
in the Colonization of Fiji

John D. Kelly

Grumblers might construe into tyranny and injustice the course
Her Majesty's Government has determined to pursue.

—*Sir Arthur Gordon, speech to settlers, September 2, 1875*

In Fiji, colonial inheritances have been nurtured into sad new
flowers possible orenly in the soils of postcolonial predicament. Voting
rights are "racially" demarcated and unevenly distributed. Almost all
land is reserved as the inalienable property of legally demarcated clans
of one ethnic group, the ethnic Fijians. Ethnic Fijians also monopolize
the military. In Fiji, a Great Council of Chiefs wields a strange form of
paramountcy, not only over ethnic Fijians but also, increasingly, over
everyone else, across multiple coups and constitutions. The constitutive
nature of law and some particular problems posed by inherited colonial legal schemes for ex-colony nation-states can be illuminated by
study of Fiji.

Nation-states have different architectural problems when built
amid the ruins of empire, and with imperial materials. However, there
is more to the omnipresence of colonial legal legacy in Fiji's current
crisis than uncleared detritus, more than old codes ill-fit to new circumstances, old devices ill-suited to new applications. In postcolonial
Fiji, active efforts have been made to sustain and enhance colonial legal
legacies. These legacies include specific legal instruments, a field of

objects (offices, titles, deeds, registers of ownership) that can, in turn, be considered actants in Latour's sense (Latour 1988:159ff; see also Riles, Chapter 7, and Merry and Brenneis, the introduction, this volume). This chapter explains the origins of several legal legacies. But it also pursue matters of the spirit of the law, as well as its embodied letters. In addition to specific objects that are actants, historically born to complex lives of their own, in Fiji a particular kind of top-down, specifically colonial, legal subjectivity has never really died. In Fiji, a repeatedly reinvigorated tradition of colonial lawgiving asymmetrically organizes the rights and privileges of ethnic groups. Embedded within what appears to be ethnic conflict is a contest between the inherited tradition of colonial lawgiving and constitutional, democratic structures of legality. Reinvoked powers of lawgiving paramountcy repeatedly challenge democratic, constitutional orders and are challenged by them.

Leaving to other chapters in this volume (Merry and Brenneis's introduction, Miyazaki's Chapter 9, and especially Kaplan's Chapter 6) the fuller description of current crises in Fiji, this chapter re-examines imperial legal strategies in the colonization of Fiji, in particular, the sources of legal strategy for Fiji's famous first governor, Sir Arthur Gordon. Thereby we pursue the logic and limits of some specifically colonial and postcolonial modes of lawmaking. Above all, we seek to understand, in its particular local efflorescence, the commitment to racism and authoritarianism that is not merely part of the letter of Fiji's inherited law but also a spirit that still haunts lawmaking there.

The story is often told that Gordon was an amateur anthropologist, applying the evolutionary models of his day. His reading in anthropology, the rest of his education and experience, and the larger British imperial context of the onset of Crown rule in Fiji all merit our attention. First, let us clarify that Gordon was no amateur.

GORDON AND FIJI

Gordon was above all a governor, and not a novice. Fiji was his fourth post as governor (after New Brunswick, Trinidad, and Mauritius). In Fiji, he began the project of codifying customary law of ethnic Fijians. He instituted a system of taxation for ethnic Fijians in kind rather than in cash, slowing the entry of a cash economy into the villages. He invented and inaugurated the Great Council of Chiefs. And his land commissions established the rigid land tenure system that makes 83 percent of the land in the islands the unalienable property of ethnic-Fijian *mataqali,* named patrilineal clans.

Gordon also negotiated a fundamental reorganization of Fiji's industrial landscape. He persuaded Australia's leading sugar producer, the Colonial Sugar Refining Company (CSR), to make major investments in Fiji. By the early twentieth century, CSR would take over all of Fiji's sugar refining, much of its sugar growing, and thereby more than half its cash economy. And, in perhaps the biggest change he engineered, Gordon arranged with India a government-managed scheme to bring large numbers of indentured laborers for Fiji sugar plantations. In the twentieth century, Indo-Fijians became half of Fiji's population.

Gordon looks a little different if we start with indenture. Gordon was an experienced governor of indenture plantation colonies and much more than that. He was famous in empire for his reforms of law and improvements of social relations in both Trinidad and Mauritius. In Trinidad, he arranged a multifaceted new deal for ex-slaves and "time-expired" indentured laborers from India, granting them deeded title to surveyed, good agricultural land in new planned townships in exchange for guaranteed tax payments. He lured the alienated out of the inaccessible regions of the land and made them visible, legible, productive, revenue-producing subjects of the colonial state. In Mauritius, Gordon was sent to break down the power of a Francophone planter class in a colonial backwater taken by the British from the French just as the Suez Canal was set to destroy its position as a port on the sea route to India. While there, vilified by the French Creole press, he forced the reforms ending the "vagrant hunts" that had virtually enslaved time-expired "coolies." He prosecuted violent planters and took other steps to bring the plantation regime under the control of colonial law.

Gordon was sent to Fiji to clean up an anarchic, troubled plantation economy. The new colony's cotton plantations, boomed up by fools, had collapsed at the conclusion of the American Civil War, and many of the cotton boom's white settlers were rambunctiously fading into highly ungenteel poverty. Fiji's retrenchment as a sugar economy was severely undercapitalized. Fiji's planters were dependent for labor on the outrageously immoral, already fatally criticized system of "black-birding," rounding up Islanders for labor on distant islands. And its sugar industry was already outflanked by an extant, very well-organized, productive Australian system. Gordon was an expert on South Asian indentured labor and knew how to run a plantation economy and society efficiently.

Depictions of Gordon as amateur anthropologist focus on colonial law and order as a matter of relations between ethnic Fijians, European settlers, and the incoming British government. One hears less about amateur anthropology when the topic is Fiji's plantation lines, where suicide rates among workers were high, where more than half the children born were dead before age eight. In stories of amateur, applied anthropology, one hears far more about unalienable land rights than about the extraordinary alienation experienced by the people indentured on Fiji's plantations, the people Fiji's Europeans called "coolies." I have written elsewhere about the culture of grace in alienation that developed in indentured labor plantation colonies in the British Empire, a culture that came to tell the story of indentured migration in parallel with the Ramayana as a narrative of unfair exile.[1] Here, let us stay focused on Gordon. The story of an instituted anthropology does not explain the paradox in Fiji's legal planning: deep concern for supporting indigenous or ethnic-Fijian custom and protecting ethnic Fijians against exploitation versus ready willingness to exploit South Asian migrants as plantation laborers.

The paradox in Gordon's planning lasted well beyond his own term of office. Of course, a myriad of other influences, global and local, also made changes in the course of Fijian law, but it exaggerates little to focus on Gordon's administration not only for what Peter France called "the charter of the land" but also a charter of most everything else. It is startling to recognize that this incongruity was part of Gordon's planning from the beginning of his rule in Fiji.

THE CHARTER OF THE LAND, AND THE CHARTER OF EVERYTHING ELSE: TWO INAUGURAL SPEECHES

Gordon managed his first months in Fiji carefully and expertly. As he wrote his wife three days after arrival, "I am thoroughly in my element" (1897:125). The day he landed in Fiji, June 25, 1875, Gordon announced that he carried the Royal Charter of the Colony and his Commission under the Great Seal as first governor. However, for weeks he did not read them publicly or assume office as governor. For two months, Gordon traveled, conducted correspondence, and received a large stream of visitors. He organized the many officers he brought with him (who had served him in Trinidad, Mauritius, and elsewhere), took stock of local talent,[2] organized the medical fight against a major measles epidemic, and laid his plans within his own growing network of loyal counsel. Finally, on September 1, 1875, he was ready. He read the Charter and his Commission, assumed authority, assembled his Legislative Council, and had it pass four crucial pieces of legislation that day.[3]

Of these, one troubled him more than the others, the one concerning land. Before leaving Sydney on the way to Fiji, he had advertisements published in Sydney, Auckland, and Melbourne calling for submission to him of all private land title claims in anticipation of a Titles Commission. By mid-August he was happy with the pile of claims he was gathering for review, but his formal instructions from Lord Carnarvon, Secretary of State for the Colonies, contained a contradiction. They called for him to announce "that the Queen has the full power of disposing of the whole of the land in such manner as to Her Majesty may seem fit, having due regard to such interests as she may deem to deserve recognition under Article 4" of this Deed of Cession (Gordon 1897:168). Gordon and his legal advisors, the Attorney-General and the Chief-Justice, intensely disliked this instruction. None of them were connected with the drafting of Fiji's Deed of Cession, a conveyance of sovereignty arranged the year before by Hercules Robinson, then lieutenant governor of New South Wales. Robinson had been sent by Disraeli's newly elected and more imperially minded government to reconsider King Cakobau's repeated offers of cession of Fiji. In classic frontier fashion, Robinson had exceeded his brief from London to investigate the possibility of annexation and arrange appropriate terms. He presented the center with a document, a Deed of Cession, already signed by many "native Chiefs," including a large group assembled on October 10, 1974, for ceremonies that variously and multiply marked conveyance of sovereignty.[4]

Gordon did not want to recognize this Deed of Cession as the foundation of his own sovereign power. To acknowledge it as a source of land law, he argued, could lead to disaster. It could undermine his "full power" to dispose "the whole of the land," by subjecting his authority to that of law courts. If the Deed of Cession was recognized by the new governor as the source of land law, then the Deed of Cession's recognition of "private rights to landed property already acquired previous to cession" would cause these rights to exist legally (compare Gordon's private note of July 6 concerning royal and private lands, quoted in note 2). Worse, the foundation and limits to their existence could not properly be determined by "the decision of the Crown," that is, by the governor, because they would fall beyond the domain of his authority. Horror of horrors (to Gordon, and this is crucial), if so constituted, "they can only be determined by a court of law" (Gordon [1897:168–169] to Carnarvon, explaining his plans, August 21, 1875). Gordon, scarred by his endless battles with the Mauritian settlers, had no hope of justice for the natives from local courts. He insisted that "fraud upon the unfortunate natives will be sanctioned under the colour of law...the association of the enforcement of these claims with the establishment of British rule would preclude all hope of conciliating or benefiting the native race" (1897:168–169). To Gordon, it was an easy choice, between respecting the Deed of Cession and carrying out Carnarvon's instruction to declare the Queen's absolute power over lands. The former would, in the natives' interests, have to give way to the latter. He wrote to Carnarvon, "It is my intention to introduce and pass a declaratory Ordinance, couched as nearly as may be in the terms of your Lordship's despatch, and asserting the Queen's rights as therein stated" (1897:168–169).

It took New Zealand courts of law from 1840 to the Prendergast decision of 1879 to determine that the Treaty of Waitangi was "a simple nullity." Gordon set aside the Deed of Cession as a foundation for sovereignty less than a year after it was signed. Parts of the Deed of Cession were returned into the language of land law as Gordon proceeded, bound up in controversies especially over settlers' rights to land obtained in "bona fide" transactions, recognized as valid by Article IV of the deed. It strikes me as very important to understanding the actual constitution of law in early colonial Fiji, however, to see that the Deed of Cession is a legal zombie, killed dead, especially with respect to land law, by Gordon at the outset and then brought back to life when and as it aided him and his successors in their administrative work. To be clear, he had to kill it, precisely to keep land claims out of court.[5] This principle, preventing courts of law from delimiting his lawmaking authority, was also the foundation of his fourth and final ordinance the day he assumed rule. This prohibited for twelve months "any action, suit, or proceeding in any Law Court of the Colony in respect of any claim or cause of action between Europeans and Natives accused prior to the passing of this Ordinance…all such claims shall be arbitrated upon by a Commission" (Gordon 1897:175). Systematically, Gordon shifted authority over "native affairs" away from courts of law and into his administration.

On September 11, 1875, Gordon spoke formally for the first time as Governor of Fiji to an assembled group of Fijian chiefs. Actually, Carew delivered the speech as his spokesperson, at Bau, on the day Gordon received the homage of the chiefs and the chiefs who were appointed provincial heads took oaths and received "their staves of office."[6] On September 2, 1875, more than a week earlier and only one day following his public reading of the Royal Charter, Gordon spoke to assembled settlers.[7] Examining these speeches and comparing them, we can observe two things: how much of Gordon's planning was already firm in his mind at the outset of his governorship and how wide a disjuncture had already set in between the "native" and plantation portions of his domain.

Both speeches began with the same key point, that on September 1, 1875, Gordon had read his Commission and had thereby become Governor of Fiji. To the assembled chiefs, Gordon added that "you have acknowledged me after the custom of Fiji to-day as ruler of the country; you have promised to obey me in all matters." (His meeting had begun with a ritual drinking of *yaqona;* see note 6.) He then announced the purpose of his meeting: to clarify "what customs shall be lawful and what forbidden." An unprecedented form of order, rule of law, was to come with British rule. "In former times nothing was stable, but the foundation of the building we are now about to erect shall be firm and strong." Everyone had to obey laws, even the chiefs, Gordon told them. But he also sought to reassure: "All that I tell you shall be perfectly true. The ownership of your own lands is with you, it shall not be taken from you; but if you wish to give away or sell land, it shall be decided by me whether or not it be sold. I remember the words of the Vunivalu [that is, Cakobau] at the time Fiji was offered to Great Britain. He said, 'We are being eaten up daily'; now I have come to prevent this." Gordon reviewed the history of offers of cession, the first offer in the 1850s, which was refused, and the second in 1874. The Queen accepted "unwillingly" because "in her all-loving heart" she "believed it would be right to do so, remembering the words of the Vunivalu." The Queen "disliked much" that her subjects had come to Fiji "without law and order, and each doing what seemed good to him," and she had accepted "the offer of annexation" so that "you should be cared for and led into the proper path." Gordon promised to make "all necessary laws for you the natives, and also laws relating solely to the whites....Any useful native customs shall be retained, but improper customs let them be given up: nevertheless I do not intend to make sudden changes."

The necessity of law was the key theme: "You must know that laws are necessary; a country without laws would be in a pitiable condition." Gordon spoke against murder, cannibalism, compelled marriage, and adultery and asked the chiefs to assist in making new laws work. "Also, I do not intend to detract from the respect due to the Chiefs by the lower orders. I believe it to be a most proper thing that we should all of us pay due respect to those above us; let the people continue to pay respect to their Chiefs." From here, Gordon turned to matters of taxation. Because laws would now govern taxation, chiefs could no longer levy outside their districts or levy "merely to gratify idle longings." Such things were "tambu sara" (most strictly prohibited). Gordon described the taxes he planned to administer. There would be "district plantations" where "I alone shall then decide what shall be planted." The government would be offered all the produce, valued at prices fixed by the government, but when sufficient tax payment was realized, the surplus would belong to the "owners" of the district plantation.

Concluding, Gordon admonished the chiefs to obey the magistrates he appointed, to avoid jealousies and rivalries among themselves, to encourage activity and industry, and to communicate with him always about injustices. He encouraged respect and attendance to schools, religion, and the Vunivalu. And he warned the chiefs about "some whites in Fiji with whom it is quite impossible that I could associate...be good enough not to associate with them yourselves; decide now whether you will lean on me, or lean on them; decide at once."

On September 2, nine days before, Gordon spoke to the meeting of settlers. He omitted several themes he emphasized before the chiefs and added several, in a speech twice as long. Gordon began by insisting that he would speak plainly, desiring "utmost freedom of intercourse" between officials and settlers. He then assured them that he would not hesitate to use the "very large powers" he had been granted. He had no preconceived plans and was slowly gathering facts. However, "there are some things so plainly wanted that I cannot hesitate at once to declare them. We want capital invested in the Colony; we want a cheap, abundant, and certain supply of labour; we want means of communication; we want justice to be readily and speedily administered; we want some facilities for education; and lastly (though, perhaps, that interests me more nearly and specially than you) we want revenue. Now, as to capital, it is clear that will not be invested in the Colony until there is good security for its investment, that is to say, until the land titles are settled, and a steady supply of labor provided for." Gordon discussed labor before land. He already had sheets of paper by the door for attendees to answer two questions: "Is it in your opinion desirable that the Government should undertake the conduct and management of the immigration of labour?" and "Is it in your opinion desirable that efforts should be made to effect the introduction of immigrant labour from India?" He devoted nearly a thousand words to the reasons why he should get affirmative responses to both questions. Government management would enable financing, security, efficiency, and guarantees against abuses. India's supply of "coolies" was "practically boundless," wage rates established and reliable (versus the decreasing supply and increasing cost of so-called Polynesian labor from other Pacific island groups), and Indians' commitments were longer, five years' indenture and five more in the colony versus three years only for Polynesians.

Before turning to land, Gordon addressed several other topics: government debts (soon to be paid), communication and transportation ("The roadmaker is the first civiliser"), education (soon, after roads), representation on the Legislative Council (elections were forbidden by his instructions to establish a Crown Colony, but he set out paper for each settler to note down four appropriate names and the location of the capital (advice requested). Then he turned to land. Gordon read verbatim his instruction on land from Carnarvon.[8] He explained his plan, already literally enacted, to take advantage of the "technicality" that all land had passed to the Crown. His government would "obviate the necessity for tedious lawsuits" and their "technical legal decisions, not always in accord with substantial justice." Instead of "a labyrinth of legal forms," Fiji would have "a well-chosen Commission" and all land tenure claims would be "fairly and promptly" settled. Gordon was aware that his plan was something that "grumblers might construe into tyranny and injustice," but he was certain that it was not.

Gordon turned to other questions, such as Cakobau government debts, poverty among the settlers, and his intention to forego half his salary and spend the rest entirely in Fiji. Finally, he addressed gossip that he was "a friend of the blacks": "My sympathy for the coloured races is strong; but my sympathy for my own race is stronger." He had the warmest sympathy for those whose hardship, privation, and toil had "laid the foundations of civilisation." His months in Fiji had taught him that Fiji's reputation for drunkenness and dawdling was overstated, that "there were in the community men of education, probity, kindness, and enterprise who would do credit to any state. With this expression of opinion I will bring my address to a close."

GORDON'S STRATEGIES, AND MINE
FOR FINDING THEM

The Deed of Cession did not describe a Fiji in need of capital. It did not call for a cheap, abundant, and certain supply of labor. It did not call for an infrastructure of communication and transportation or a new system of administration of justice. It did not see want of security of investment as the primary problem from which all others stemmed. It certainly did not call for investment policy to drive land policy. To the settlers, Gordon specifically denied that his land policy followed from sympathy for "the blacks." To the chiefs, he spoke of the Queen's all-loving heart. He described Fiji's annexation as something she did not want, a duty, not an ambition. He described a Queen heeding words of the Vunivalu, come to care for Fiji's chiefs and people, protecting them from Europeans otherwise without law and order. Can this add up?

Gordon told the chiefs that "the ownership of your own lands is with you, it shall not be taken from you." Nine days before, he told the settlers that "the land has, strictly speaking, all passed to the Queen."

Here, our historical ethnography reaches a moment not of impasse but of abundance. We could push backward or forward, globally or locally, into Gordon's biography, Fiji's quotidian transformations, or imperial tides and fashions. And we could adopt several strategies for reading and aligning the two Gordon texts. We could find one to be more important, closer to truth or reality. For example, a Fijian nationalist might find dialogue between chiefs and administrators to be the central axis of Fiji's history. A student of "the world system" might suppose that plans for capital address reality, while insistence on respect for rank is merely ideology.

Alternatively, we could read both documents skeptically. Roko Tuis take their staffs of office and agree to respect magistrate courts that will regulate custom. Settlers cast virtual votes on government-controlled Indian indenture just after hearing Gordon enumerate the advantages, with as little personal experience to guide their commitment. Of course, Gordon "in his element" is manipulating the situation. However, I prefer a third approach, in the mode of the anti-ironies of Bruno Latour: In both speeches, Gordon is telling the truth. In parts, we have simply not yet hit upon the hermeneutics that resolve apparent contradictions and mediate larger paradoxes in his plans. But more fully in Latourian mode, the path I will take from here, interpreting Gordon's words and deeds, is the most irreductive. My premise is that the immanent truths of Fiji's colonial order were, themselves, still coming into alignment, alignments that would have to accommodate many disparate elements internal and external to Fiji, alignments that Gordon in his element was already rapidly making, forcing some connections and blocking others.[9]

We can see Gordon here, framing policy choices for Fiji's economy, contrasting the tokens of Polynesian and Indian labor. Aware of abolitionist protest movements against blackbirding, as well as supply trends, and believing in government management as a check against abuses, he pushed hard for a government-regulated monopoly of labor supply and for immigration from India. He had no patience for advocates of new, private blackbirding companies or for schemes that would make ethnic Fijians into plantation labor. However, he offered his settlers the prospect of government-run schemes of both Polynesian and Indian labor, to allow supply and demand and planter preferences in allotment to do some of his work for him. If a labor supply had been found that better served the security of investment in Fiji, one can picture him adapting his plans to it.

The evidence cannot sustain an account of Gordon as bumbling or in any sense an amateur as an administrator.[10] The question we will push further is whether, and how, Gordon already had a framework, an overall plan, even a blueprint, that connected the disparities of nascent colonial Fiji into one overall order when he assumed governorship, and if he did, whether it relied on amateur anthropology. We can already say a few things about his virtual blueprint, including its blank spaces. By the time of his speech to the chiefs, Gordon had already made extraordinary commitments to ethnic-Fijian ranks, rights, and distinction. They are extraordinary not merely on a globally comparative basis but also in light of what he did not know, and did not have, when he made these commitments. Before September 1875, there was no Great Council of Chiefs. Gordon was in the process of inventing it. He appointed *Rokos* and *Bulis* to administer provinces and districts in a scheme he was adapting from the Cakobau government, but he also gathered them into a "council." Before this, Fijian chiefship had no collective order or entitivity beyond individual installations, either from the bottom up to specific titles or in the novel government bureaucracy.[11] In September 1875, Gordon's intention to sort out Fijian customs, and codify some while forbidding others, was established and announced. But it was not yet begun. Most importantly, the land was reserved from sale, except on his approval, long before any idea reached him about the specifics of Fijian custom over landownership and sale. It would not be until early 1880 that missionary Lorimer Fison would provide him with the spectacular principle that mataqalis, not chiefs, were the owners of land, with ownership rights inalienable. As has been well described (Legge 1958; Chapman 1964; France 1969), Fison had imagined his views a challenge to Gordon's chiefs-centric scheme and was most surprised by the alacrity with which Gordon embraced them. Fison's approach was a challenge, to the extent that the Gordon of 1875 clearly envisioned chiefs as the landowners: "The ownership of your own lands is with you."

Therefore, Gordon in his blueprint must have had reasons to insist on (semi!) inalienable Fijian ownership of lands long before he had specific customary principles (and, in effect, Fison's anthropology) to back it up. From Fison, he was highly pleased to gain useful content in custom for the forms he already needed. On multiple levels, Gordon had already insisted on separating ethnic-Fijian transactions from European courts of law long before he could claim any sophisticated ethnography of Fijian exchange customs.

To understand why, let us begin with the person, in the context of empire, who found himself so perfectly fit for the complexities of organizing the highly troubled new colony. How much of all this was just Gordon's aristocratic taste, dislike of the crude world of the emergent industrial bourgeoisie, a nostalgia for the present of empire in a world going ineluctably capitalist? A lot. Gordon's distaste for white colonial settlers long preceded his grotesque run-ins with the white press and public in Mauritius. His first governorship, in New Brunswick, was largely a failure because he disdained local society; the locals resented Gordon's concern to keep his daughter out of their company. Contrarian nostalgia is definitely part of the mix in Gordon's motives: Preparing to go to Fiji, Gordon visited a retired, declining family friend and sponsor named Gladstone (yes, *the* Gladstone), who did not oppose the Fiji mission but urged Gordon to write biographies of ecclesiastical figures. They discussed the bad time coming, in which "money is the sole power worshipped," and with Lord Acton discussed religious questions, especially Gladstone's concerns about Roman Catholic threats to civil rights and religious peace in the empire. On the way, Gordon stopped by the tomb of Warren Hastings, one-time governor of Bengal, the famous/notorious touchstone of Orientalist colonial policy (in the original sense of respect for Oriental law and statecraft; see Trautmann 1997). Gordon (1897:13–14) was appalled that his tomb was marked by "a mere urn—tasteless and mean. I looked on the tomb of that great governor with a sympathetic interest."

Gordon's political career began well. At age twenty-three, he took up the post of private secretary to his father, Lord Aberdeen, who had just become the successor to Gladstone as Prime Minister of Great Britain. Yet, what I have called his nostalgia for the imperial present was already established by then. While studying for holy orders (on his father's advice) at Wells College, Cambridge, he became aware as he wrote in his diary and to his friends of a longing for a different destiny. He wrote a dialogue between Ego and Alter Ego, in which the Alter Ego observed, "Thou wouldst have *thy will* the law to others &…it is most bitter *to thee* to renounce the attempt." Two years before, just after his twentieth birthday, he wrote about his ambivalence over leaving school to pursue a career as a "statesman." He was aware that many noble geniuses came to failure and ruin in "this lawyer-ridden country." "Shall we oppose ourselves to the current of the world and sink in the attempt? Shall we turn and head it? Or shall we in some distant corner of the globe attempt to *re-create* what we cannot restore?" (Chapman 1964:6–9).

Gordon clearly had a longing for the job of lawgiving, thus his sense of being in his element in Fiji, the perfect job for *"me."*[12] His estimation of the importance of Fijian hierarchy also came long before his knowledge of any byways of its rituals, customs, and cultural principles. In fact, as Kaplan has documented extensively, neither Gordon nor most of his successors had an adequate appreciation of the land-sea logic of Fijian politics, with the consequence that they transformed a system with bottom-up moments as well as top-down encompassment into a system more wholly and overdeterminantly (in church, in empire, and in chiefship) top-down in its installations (Kaplan 1989a and b, 1995; on land-sea, see also Hocart and Sahlins, especially Hocart 1936 and Sahlins 1985). Out to experience in empire his fantasy of an aristocratic power to make will into law (a fantasy possibly conjoining nineteenth-century romances of aristocratic will with nineteenth-century romances of legal positivity), Gordon got his chance in Fiji. He designed all the really important legal machinery—over labor immigration, land, native affairs—with controls in his own hands.

Two objections, however, limit the precision of this somewhat infantilizing interpretation. First, granting that we see here reasons for Gordon's confidence and pleasure, and factors contributing to his blueprint, we still need to know more than Gordon's motives to know his agency. Second, elements of his strategies, or blueprint, are specifically not entailed by this nostalgia.

As with any powerful agent, Gordon really is an agent in the strict sense: He is an actant on behalf of very much larger entities. His creativity has historical bite precisely as it aligns, allies, and otherwise shapes relations of realities much beyond himself. It is no falsehood that he deployed the will of the Queen, and more particularly that of her Colonial Office, as he established his terms of government. Knowing what he wished to do helps us understand his agency, especially when we also understand that his attitudes were no secret in London. It was well known by the 1870s that he was a failure as governor in a democratic and white settler colony, that he flourished in Crown Colonies where he could command more. In fact, the way his Trinidad governorship demonstrated his capacity to command settlers and resettle "blacks," to use his indecorous but London-recognizable trope, was crucial to his appointment to Mauritius, where London wanted more government control over the settlers and better law for plantations and the ex-plantation population. His mixed success in Mauritius did not dissuade London from settling on him for Fiji. In fact, he was told by Sir Robert Herbert on behalf of Lord Carnarvon that they thought Gordon "in many ways qualified to make the best of that very queer bargain which appears almost certain to be forced upon us" (quoted in Chapman 1964:157), this conveyance of rule, creating a new colony where revenue was going to be an extreme problem, the economy difficult, and native affairs potentially volatile. Herbert knew his audience when he wrote to persuade Gordon that "nothing but a despotism is thought of…if John Bull chooses to incur the cost, much good can be done in Fiji; and you are the man to do it" (quoted in Chapman 1964:157). Why was John Bull (that is, Britain) willing?

Second, consider Gordon's concern for capital and security of investment, a major part of his blueprint perhaps reconcilable with but certainly not entailed in his nostalgia for an aristocratic imperium. As Robinson and Gallagher long ago pointed out, the British Empire in the nineteenth century had a long gap in the establishment of new colonies, an early period of successive expansions ending with New Zealand, a long middle period without new colonizations, marked also by violence, perhaps marked in public apprehension by the Zulu wars, the Maori wars, and most importantly the Mutiny in India, and then a late-century return to empire-building, marked especially by the "scramble for Africa." This third phase began in 1874—with the reluctant acceptance of Fiji! However, the pattern, argued Fieldhouse

(1984), was capable of more consistent assessment than an idea of shifting public ethical discourses alone would allow. Local factors were always pertinent, and the pattern was one of shifting real opportunities for investment. Put into the history of enterprises seeking and finding real returns, Fieldhouse argued, the pattern made substantial sense. We need not make the colonial world a simple function of investment markets to ask about their influence, also.[13]

Though he was no champion of settlers, Gordon was no opponent to large-scale companies. He sent J. B. Thurston, among others, to play a very complex shell game with Australian sugar companies, starting in the middle of their ranks. Making, breaking, and using deals to pressure the bigger fish, finally he could almost blackmail the CSR, the biggest fish in the Australian lake of sugar capital, into committing major resources to Fiji. Gordon well understood what it would take—land and labor guarantees—to make Fiji not merely vaguely attractive to abstract capital but also actually acceptable to very-well-organized capital financing. He was avid, not merely sanguine, to guarantee CSR dominance that verged on monopoly and by the 1920s was realized as monopoly/monopsony. Gordon did not complete his negotiations with CSR until well into the writing of his mataqali-centered land laws, and London was perturbed that he sponsored major land leases and sales to CSR of supposedly customarily inalienable lands. However, Gordon had envisioned his own power to alienate the reserved lands for matters of real public interest from the outset and was only tactically concerned about justifying the move. He knew that the highly conservative, anti-competitive CSR would be pleased that the rest of Fiji's land would not be readily available to rival sugar millers. And he was not at all sorry to set up an anti-competitive, top-down capitalism in Fiji. Gordon wrote casually to his wife about the inevitability of the ruin of undercapitalized "first-comers" and was not the least nostalgic in his certainty that Fiji's economy required "a new set of men."[14] As we fine-tune our sense of this part of his strategies, then, his dislike of settlers was not, as he assured them, a dislike of whites or even a simply anti-money nostalgia for aristocratic life. His sense of class could accommodate future as well as past elites; while he liked gentlemen, he was ready to accept a new, financial class of them. We need to know more about the dislike, even fear, of competition in his blueprint.

Gordon was as ready, even anxious, to hem in local markets by way of preference to dominant joint-stock companies as he was to hem in local contracts to a tightly bounded civil realm of contract law. The two, of course, must be connected, but how? One could also ask, by whom?

HENRY MAINE, OR THE "NATURE" OF COLONIAL LAW

Was it the influence of Henry Maine? Gordon is connected to Maine by many who focus on Gordon's alleged amateur anthropology. Gordon read Maine. Gordon's biographer, Chapman, does not mention this, let alone rely on it. Other scholars of Fiji have deduced this and relied on it largely, perhaps entirely, from a reference in the Stanmore papers. In a letter, Gordon offered his copy of a book by Maine to Fison on March 3, 1880, the day before Fison's mataqali lecture. Possibly, France (1969:124) starts the trend, writing that Gordon "kept a copy of Maine's *Lectures on the Early History of Institutions* with him in Fiji," citing this letter. Following France, the claim inflates, for example in Riles 1997a:128: "Gordon is well-known to have viewed himself as an amateur ethnologist and to have carried a copy of Henry Maine's *Lectures on the Early History of Institutions* with him on his expeditions." Now, 1880 is not 1875. This particular book was not published until 1875, the year Gordon arrived in Fiji. Perhaps Sir Arthur picked up his copy hot off the press just before he got on the boat. It is perhaps possible. We know that he did acquire a copy sometime.[15]

Let us suppose that Gordon had a wide-ranging, lucid understanding of Maine's scholarly corpus, achieved while Gordon governed hither and yon and Maine produced his major texts—*Ancient Law* in 1861 (Gordon was beginning in New Brunswick) and *Village Communities in the East and West* in 1871 (Gordon was in his second year in Mauritius). Gordon's Trinidadian reforms could perhaps have been influenced by *Ancient Law*. What would he have learned there?

Ancient Law, in particular, is often remembered among evolutionary models for anthropology and sociology and is usually reduced to one general model, status to contract. Read in the context of rising, late nineteenth-century evolutionary materialisms, Marxist, Darwinian, and archaeological, Maine is often presented as weakened by overinfluence of philological comparative models, which lacked robust mechanisms for describing forces of evolutionary change. His evolution lacked natural law, dialectical law, something like that. To read Maine as a bad evolutionary anthropologist and to read Gordon as an amateur anthropologist will cause us to miss what Gordon, a lawmaker and governor with an interest in Rome, might find reading Maine, a radical critic of the history of study of Roman law. We might miss what Gordon, with a fundamentally philological education, might find in Maine, the theorist of comparative methods. We would almost certainly neglect what Gordon, an inheritor not merely of aristocratic title but also the Whig re-evaluation of the (to the Whigs, progressive and vital) role of aristocracy in history, might find in Maine, the pre-eminent Whiggish critic of political economy.

To make a long story short (see also Kaplan and Kelly forthcoming), Maine argued that political economists misapprehended both "law" and "nature." They misunderstood the intrinsically customary and historical basis of human regulatory rules. They did not know that the idea of "natural law," a concept which distorted the regularities studied in physical sciences, was actually an invention of Roman jurists who were amending a doctrine of Law of Nations, itself devised to govern events and transactions that extended beyond the domain of civil law regulated by the explicit civil code. Latin *nat-* is, of course, the etymological source of both *nature* and *nation* (*native* as well), all things that grow themselves. As contracts increased in number and kind, judges had problems they could solve by resort to an increasingly abstract and ethically principled "Law of Nature."

Ancient Law, in short, was a treatise about law. If Gordon read it, it was probably law and lawmaking that he thought about. Maine was less interested in understanding laws—especially "natural laws"—of material evolution than the dilemmas of jurisprudence and the fatal errors that followed from taking political economists' advice on how to resolve them. Their laws of nature were, in fact, the historic artifacts of a complex, civilized society. The guardians of civilization, those with the perspective on progress in history that only gentlemen could attain (the Whig perspective here), needed to keep at bay the political economists' crude, mistaken apprehensions that markets and contracts were natural.

If we read the book Gordon definitely read, *Lectures on the Early History of Institutions,* what do we find? Above all, we find a principled, comparative, and historically founded attack on John Austin's "positive" theory of sovereignty. Austin had argued that jurisprudence could be a science, if it stripped away all metaphysical error, and started by defining law as the enforced commands of a sovereign. Austin sought to expunge from facts of law all but the realities of enforced human will. Maine insisted that this doomed the analysis of all prior forms of sovereignty and occluded their real legacies. Using a comparative method based on those in philology, Maine was certain that he could assign each system he studied a relative place in one chronology. Although he attended to Indo-European linkages of legal systems (thus, an Aryan lineage), he had no interest in tracking divergences or multiple families of developed legal traditions.[16] After all, he found two general types of organized political society. "In the more ancient of these, the great bulk of men derive their rules of life from the customs of their village or city, but they occasionally, though most implicitly, obey the commands of an absolute ruler who takes taxes from them but never legislates. In the other, and the one with which we are most familiar, the Sovereign is ever more actively legislating on principles of his own, while local custom and idea are ever hastening to decay" (Maine 1987 [1875]:392). When the one system was overlaid by the other, for whatever reason, "the force at the back of law comes therefore to be a purely coercive force to a degree quite unknown in societies of the more primitive type" (Maine 1987 [1875]:393). The imposition of the only form of sovereignty recognized as such by Austin was bound to be a traumatic historic event, especially under colonial conditions.

If they knew what they were doing, makers of colonial law therefore had definite problems to address. In Maine's terms, the idea that the Deed of Cession could be a cession of sovereignty is a confusion of these two types of law. The kind of law Gordon was planning, and thus the kind of sovereignty he would exercise, was unprecedented.[17] Gordon would have to deal with this unevenness as a whole, as well as all the details. Addressing the impact on the "natives" of this force of civilized contract law was, from Maine's point of view, a core problem in colonial lawmaking. About how to do it, Maine was largely implicit, especially in the book Gordon read. He offered no blueprints or even direct advice. Nevertheless, his diagnoses clearly helped change imperial legislating, and not just in Fiji.

MAINE, THE MUTINY, AND J. W. B. MONEY

Maine was not only a theorist of comparative jurisprudence. In the wake of the publishing of *Ancient Law,* Maine was appointed Law Member of the Council of the Governor-General of India, the post originally invented for Macaulay. In India, Maine had the job, for almost a decade, of backtracking and rerouting from Macaulay's ambitious plan to write a new, positive civil and criminal code. Maine had to deal with the Mutiny.

We turn now to some dynamics, and dialogics, of actual lawmaking in the British Empire. It is not an accident that New Zealand was the last colony of the first expansionist phase of the British imperial nineteenth century. While much about the Treaty of Waitangi is decried, and rightly, for its haste and some outright fraud involved in translating conceptions of sovereignty, critics more commonly attribute the Crown's motives to general colonialism than inquire into its timing. Momentous was the East India Charter Reform of 1833, a document with far more impact on the Pacific than is generally realized. Before this reform, New Zealand, Fiji, and the Pacific were all territories more or less belonging, so far as the British were concerned, to the British East India Company. However, it was proving impossible for the Crown to regulate the company, which Macaulay described as a new kind of leviathan, a monster undreamed of (see Kelly 1999). Smith's *Wealth of Nations* (1961 [1776]), especially in the bulky historical parts few students are assigned any longer, insisted on the destruction of the East India Company monopolies that restrained trade. Led by Macaulay, in 1833 Parliament reformed the company in many ways. Two dimensions matter to us.

First, the monopoly in trade was broken. The Pacific was no longer a private company domain, of use mostly to supply the China trade, a use that dwindled anyway with the exhaustion of sandalwood and *beche de mer* and with the rise of opium gardens in India. This led rapidly to new investment efforts, such as the wacky Polynesia Company for Fiji, but from a market point of view, most spectacularly to the Wakefield plan for scientific colonization of New Zealand. The New Zealand Company soaked up an extraordinarily large investment capital, demanded a royal charter, and set off to colonize New Zealand. Precisely to forestall a new, Raj-style, unmanageable joint-stock company sovereign in its colony, the Crown moved quickly to take legal control of New Zealand's land, via the rushed, incoherent Waitangi treaty. To forestall the company, the Crown would dole out the parcels and insure the equities. The results were chaos. Investors lost their shirts, the colony was swamped with white settlers, and as much as the Maori wars cost the Crown, the complex moral invectives concerning both settlers and Maori probably cost more. It was easy for the British government to conclude that further Pacific colonizing ventures were unnecessary (because nowhere else was capital so rashly speculative on a large scale) and inadvisable in light of the costs. Even though the chiefs in Fiji were getting into trouble with small-time swindlers and others, London, burdened by Maori war, wanted nothing to do with Fiji—until the cotton boom and bust and the growing, untrustworthy Polynesia Company made Fiji a much bigger problem.

Second, in the 1833 charter debate (see especially Macaulay 1910 [1833]), India was again diagnosed as needing legal reform, a new code of law. As Barney Cohn (1989) has documented, this project was recurrent through the years of company rule.[18] By the 1930s, the Macaulays of Parliament offered a new diagnosis, fortified by the theories of Bentham and Austin, and in Macaulay's case, in addition, with a fine Whiggish sensibility that a shelf of his library was worth more than the entire civilization of India. The problems of India lay in the chaos caused by the company's incomplete acceptance of its own sovereignty. India, with its complexities, needed a law code to be written for it, not found within it. In the wake of his stirring call for a new code in his speech on the 1833 reform bill, Macaulay himself was made the Law Member of the Council of India and chaired the commission that proposed a uniform civil code for India.

If Macaulay's code was an index of the self-confidence of British rule in the 1850s, beyond criminal law its details were never ironed out to the point that it could be installed as actual law. In the wake of the Mutiny in 1857, the plan for a uniform civil code became part of the problem in the next round of diagnoses of the problems in British rule. Scholars of the Mutiny, or Rebellion, of 1857 discuss among many things whether any widespread anti-British uprising actually took place. What was clear, and traumatic to the colonial British, was that the sepoys, or soldiers, of their army had rebelled against them. Wars with enemies and with noble savages they had understood, but this was a rejection from the ranks thought most loyal and best connected to colonial civilization. The trauma was widespread in administrative circles, and the idea of imposing an entire legal code written by Austinian principles was dead (for at least a century; it has gained new life in recent decades in India). A few unpopular critics suggested that the roots of British trouble in India lay in the structure of government and the poverty caused by high British taxes and the export of capital. Henry Maine provided an entirely different perspective that proved vastly more popular. The errors of the Company's quests for law, in the past, had been that it was aiming to find the Rome of India, the drafters of real civil law for a place that had never had it beyond elite fragments. The errors of the Macaulay era had presumed India nothing but a despotism. In fact, beneath the elites and their courtly letters, India had always had, and still had, the customary legal systems of the village communities. These were what the impositions of British law, especially the draconian force of its impositions of taxation and enforcement of economic contracts, had catastrophically and ignorantly disrupted. What India needed, then, was respect for more levels of customary law than had ever been noticed before.[19] Maine had a substantial impact on policy in India and elsewhere in the empire.[20]

Was Gordon's Fiji plan an example of applied Maine? Several lines of his blueprint might be more sharply defined in Mainean light. His connection of markets, contracts, and courts of law as phenomena, his insistence on distancing them from the world of ethnic Fijians (before he had access to detailed information about Fijian ways and means) might well embody a Maine-informed common sense as much or more than an aristocratic good taste—too primitive for contract, inevitably status. Also, at another level of remove, we might sense in Gordon a Mainean common sense about political economy, an interest in crafting the place and boundaries of economic institutions, instead of an ineluctability to their nature and an inevitability of their laws, even a Mainean common sense about what might be called the locality of civil societies and the local, subordinate scope of courts of law. In other words, Gordon might have gleaned the principle from Maine that, as Maine (1869) once minuted as Law Member in India, "The legal question in this case is quite distinct from the political question, and altogether subordinate to it."[21] The case concerned the trial of "European British subjects" under jurisdiction assumed by Travancore State, a "native" or "princely" state. In 1869, Maine (1869:400–401) minuted that even though no British or British Indian legislature had legal power to legislate away Travancore jusrisdiction, Britain's power to annex was indisputable and its executive should not hesitate to mount irresistible pressure to teach, "without denying its abstract right to try Europeans," that "Native States ought not to try European British subjects." In Gordon, one might observe similarity in both substance and style of legal reasoning. In substance, Gordon also sought to keep separate legal systems for separate legal types. In style of reasoning, and in premises, the similarity is subtler but, I think, profound: A certain very Whiggish and particularly imperial position is presumed to be held by both writer and reader as agents. It is, in short, a position above the law. Maine not only respected Montesquieu but also retained a surprising amount of Montesquieu's genre, writing to a timelessly magisterial audience, an audience of magistrates, lawmakers, and law managers, moving from an education in Roman experience to an experience of empires of their own.

Clearly, Gordon fits into Bayly's image (1991) of a general stream of transformation of British colonial administrators away from Macaulayism and toward indirect rule. Yet, elements of Gordon's strategies do not follow as applied Maine, especially the disjuncture in Gordon's affections. Gordon looks more Mainean, just as he looked like the amateur anthropologist, the more we focus on his relation with the ethnic Fijians. But where is any concern for the customary law of the so-called coolies? Where is the concern for effects of contracts or courts of law on them? Whence his confidence that the force of contract law would not devastate the immigrants, or his lack of concern that they might be devastated? Remembering that the Indian indentured laborers, under direct government management, were a major part of Gordon's plan, we find a magisterial Gordon as anxious to sustain his control over their immigration and regulation as he is to sustain his control over native affairs—still not content to let private market relations manage their migration and discipline but sanguine that fairness would follow if all was kept visible and legible to his state. It is known that Gordon placed the indentured Indians at a higher level of social evolution than the Fijians (Kaplan 1989a and b) but still well below the Europeans—and one sees no effort to measure the impact of contracts. Why?

Another mystery will lead us directly to the solution. There is nothing particularly Mainean about the taxation system Gordon announced to the chiefs on September 11. When Maine was India's Law Member, he confronted proposals for reforms for Punjab in the 1860s. He was critical of an effort to reform land tenure and taxation by universalization of a principle thought by Mr. Prinsep to be native. Maine argued that the indistinctness of principles of land tenure in Punjab was a result of generations of rapacious government followed by years of British confusion. In the tenor of Montesquieu, Maine (1866:339) concluded, "I can see no rule to follow, except to abide by actual arrangements, whether founded or not on an original misconstruction of Native usage. I say, *Let us stand even by our mistakes. It is better than perpetual meddling.*" There is none of this Montesquieu conservatism in Gordon's taxation scheme, his payments in kind to the governor's order of crops, chosen by the governor to be grown on "district plantations." Where, exactly, did that come from?

Astonishingly, Gordon has told us. In 1897, Gordon published a "private and confidential" volume of his Fiji papers and wrote an introduction to the chapter including his first speech to the chiefs. This introduction focuses on his theory of governance and incorporates passages from his 1879 taxation paper, much in accord with Maine.[22] However, there were also things from another vat, such as the view that "the most enlightened views and the most liberal legislation can be neutralised by the social aversion between discordant races which may accompany a full concession of political rights, and which renders their practical exercise impossible" (Gordon 1879:9, 1897:197).

It was not Henry Maine informing Arthur Gordon about the natural social aversion of races, nor was it Henry Maine describing taxes in kind to him. It was J. W. B. Money. Gordon (1897:196) named Money, not Maine, as the theorist behind his tax policy, connected to his entire native policy: "On my voyage out I had roughly outlined to myself a plan founded on the culture system of Java, as described in Money's interesting volumes, *How to Govern A Colony*, but differing from that system in many essential particulars, more especially in this: that in Java any surplus produce became property of the Government, whereas in my opinion all but a fixed amount ought to remain the property of the cultivator, and in my scheme accordingly did remain so. With this was connected my whole scheme of native policy, with respect to which it is necessary to say a few words." Gordon's opponents in Fiji correctly identified his taxation-in-kind scheme as one related to the Dutch "culture" system in Java (Chapman 1964:168), but Fiji scholars have done less with Gordon's claimed connection to Money.[23] Money was no Maine. But his text is well worth reading for those seeking to understand Gordon in Fiji.

J. W. B. MONEY AND HOW TO MAKE RACE THE ORGANIZING PRINCIPLE OF A COLONY

J. W. B. Money was a bureaucrat in Bengal who described the government of Java precisely in order to understand why India had had a Mutiny while Indonesia was so peaceful. His two-volume book was saturated with anxieties about the Mutiny, endlessly concerned to portray a Java in which peoples high and low, local, European, and other, all get along (its subtitle, *Showing a Practical Solution of the Questions Now Affecting British India*). Affection and disaffection, the necessity for a colony to manage the former carefully and the absence of the latter in Java, were discussed almost endlessly. Money (1861b:53) wrote, for a pertinent example, about "our hated courts of justice." In Oude (in India), "nearly the entire aristocracy joined the rebellion, but it was to preserve their estates, their dignities, and their feudal power, and to escape our inevitable if not heavy taxation, our revenue and civil decree land sales, and our hated courts of justice" (1861b:53). Money (1861b:57) wrote of the "Dissimilarity of English and Native Ideas" about court-decreed land sales. It was not enough that the tax laws in India were based on Hindoo and Mahomedan rules. The solution, insisted Money, was not courts run by Native laws, but courts run by supervised Natives, above all, with "consideration for the personal dignity of High Natives...to which the Natives are most sensitive, and which is utterly ignored by our officials, as apparently opposed to our English principle of equality before the law" (1861b:3). Gordon (1897:196ff) emphasized this theme of Money, not Maine, in his explanations of his "scheme of native policy."[24]

How does this solution generate taxation in kind, with land guaranteed against seizure, for either Money or Gordon? The race concept comes in again in the description of the dangers lurking in systems of exchange and taxation, because "the state of society in India makes other motives more powerful than the ordinary principles of political economy" (Money 1861a:148).[25] The cultures, meaning the agricultural production systems, of India were introduced "on the theory of free bargaining" that worked so well "among homogeneous races like the people of Europe" (1861a:140). But "strong races" like the Englishmen were honest, energetic, determined not to be cheated, and prepared to employ violence. "The Native, like most weak races, is apparently submissive and docile, but really obstinate in his prejudices and in his determined avoidance of new modes of labour," grasping, without foresight, "using deceit and lying in all its forms to get some temporary advantage from the stronger race, and afterwards to evade the bargain" (1861a:141). Inevitably, "leaving these two races to uncontrolled action on each other naturally leads to violence on one side to secure benefits or rights, which deceit on the other side is called in to evade or deny. Our Indian Government, instead of recognizing the fact of European supremacy, and modifying the relations between the races so as to protect the Native from force and the European from fraud, has generally left these relations uncontrolled to settle themselves on the ordinary principles of political economy" (1861a:141). There was no Maine-style subtlety here, no querying whether the rules of political economy presuppose conceptions of production, exchange, or value that might not fit "Native" culture. Here, racial character was Native deceitfulness creating fraud, European determination resorting to force when contract fails. Money therefore advocated his version of the Dutch culture system precisely "to protect the Native from force, and the European from fraud." Government would fix the rules, choose the crops, and via Native chiefs, supervise the growing. The Europeans buying the produce from government gain "large opportunity" and government assistance, despite restriction against direct dealings with the Natives. Meanwhile, "the Native was required to assist in developing the resources of the soil…but was secured large profits for so doing…regulated by fixed rules plainly beneficial to him" (1861a:113).

The key features of Money's system should by now be clear.

Pervading "the entire colonial policy of the Dutch," as he recounted it, was "an unchangeable rule, to which no exceptions are allowed," that competition was to be prevented, especially competition between Natives and others (Money 1861b:233). The "High Natives" cared more about honor, rank, status, and power than about wealth and should have their ranks scrupulously maintained and recognized. The "low Natives" wished mostly for security, to be guaranteed by their natural rulers, the High Natives. The Europeans came in pursuit of wealth and did not need to compete with the Natives for rank, just as the Natives needed to sustain rank, not augment wealth. The system abounded in hierarchies, implicit and explicit, to be marked above all by asymmetrical affection: "respectful on one side and kind on the other," Natives respectful to all Europeans, and the Europeans kind to all Natives (Money 1861a:39).

And what about people neither Native nor European? Money planned, in passing, for "intermediate races" also necessary to maintain the colony of Europeans and Natives. The "classes of Europeans and Natives, properly so called, nearly monopolize all power, and share with the intermediate races the other benefits of the country" (Money 1861b:234). While Europeans would fill the top tiers of government proper, Natives of rank would exclude all others from "the subordinate government of their fellow-countrymen." For "half-castes," said to almost universally emulate their European fathers, not their Native mothers, Money prescribed "subordinate offices of the state" (1861b:235). "Chinamen" and other "foreign Orientals," however, were "practically excluded from power, and confined to the pursuit of wealth," mostly living in and around the city centers, "combining industrious habits as artisans with the universal trade of usury" (1861b:235–236).

> With this exception, Europeans and Natives in Java have such lines of ambition, of power, and of prosperity marked out for each, as best suit the respective ideas of each race, and the station in life of each individual, but the palpable distinction of European and Native is recognized and acted on in every line of life, so as to avoid collision and consequent ill-will. Different duties, ranks, and advantages are allotted and strictly preserved to each. The Native has ample

fields of employment and ambition open to him, from
which he is not ousted by the European's superior knowledge and power, while the European's pride of colour, conquest and civilization is not irritated by the native galling his
kibe. Each race has its allotted sphere, and it is as impossible
for the Native to be a contractor, a planter, a resident, a secretary, or a controleur, as it is for the European to be a
regent, a member of the landraad, a wedana, a mantrie, or a
village chief.

This separate employment in distinct lines best suited to
the natural capacity of each people, and the consequent
absence of competition between races of unequal powers, is
a far greater advantage to the Native than any mere theoretical equality…nature will assert her rights, and [in the case
of European-educated Natives] the friction of necessity or
danger generally reveals the Oriental substance under the
European varnish. (Money 1861b:236–237)

Again, we are far from Maine. Maine's elegant critique of the legal
foundations of things thought natural in political economy and
jurisprudence is replaced by assertion of stark racial natures under-
neath all social varnishes—but where are we with respect to Gordon?

Gordon clearly went farther than Money in his desire to protect his
natives from labor for any kind of planters. There and elsewhere in his
efforts to insulate Fijians from the market, he might well reflect Maine's
concern for the social alienation attendant on money transactions.
However, on many other points we have pondered, we find Money's
blueprint in Gordon's hands. Gordon's Fiji, at least as clearly as
Money's fantasy Java, gave each race "its allotted sphere."[26] It made
organizing principles out of minimizing competition, maximizing security for low natives, and recognizing and reifying rank for high natives.
And it made great use of "intermediate races" to fill the positions
unsuited to either the natives or the Europeans. To the so-called
coolies, too, it would appear that Gordon sought to offer security with
his governmental supervision of the system he knew well. His successors
in CSR and government took steps somewhat akin to his in Trinidad
when they arranged ten- and five-acre land leases for the time-expired,

trading a measure of security for visibility. In Fiji, though, it was actively ensured all along that power would reside first of all on that asymmetric axis between Europeans and natives. The "intermediate races" would have no chiefs, as little customary law as possible, and no honour system of their own (see also Kelly 1989). Indenture was brutal in this colony, with so much tropical forest to clear and so much social space already filled.

GORDON, RACISM, COLONIAL LAWMAKING, AND THE DEED OF CESSION

Gordon wrote his wife on June 29, 1875, his fifth day in Fiji, that "old Thakombau...made me his personal feudal submission in proper style" by presenting "an immense root of kava" (1897:127–128).[27] Thus, June 29, 1875, can be added to the list of candidates for the date of segmentation of actual sovereignty in Fiji, along with the September 1874 chiefs' resolution to Robinson and the October 10, 1874, signing of Robinson's Deed of Cession. Gordon himself clearly preferred September 1, 1875. In both the letter and the spirit of the law, Gordon specifically rejected founding the ordinances he had passed that day on the timing or substance of the Deed of Cession, especially the laws requiring commission inquiries into land and other transactions. He wrote to his Chief-Justice on August 26, 1875, criticizing a land law draft that mentioned the Deed of Cession in its preamble: "Was the cession made by the Chiefs? Could they cede? The charter says 'Chiefs and people.' It is true the cession was accepted as 'unconditional,' but was it really so? Was it at the time, or is it now, held to have been so by those who were immediate parties to the deed? All these are questions which it might be necessary to touch, if the mention of them were essential to the enacting clauses. But is it so?" (Gordon 1897:172–173). In fact, Gordon insisted, the law of a Crown Colony could begin with what "must be admitted without dispute by all," the will and pleasure of the Queen. "As to the Queen's order to appoint a Commission, there can be no dispute," so that is where law should begin. Therefore, "the *period* should not, I think, be the *Cession,* but the erection of the Fiji Islands into a Colony by Her Majesty's letters patent under the Great Seal" (1897:172–173).

Much has been made of the Deed of Cession in the history of Fiji's politics. At least since debates in the aftermath of World War II, it has been made the charter and foundation stone of paramount rights in Fiji for ethnic Fijians. However, Gordon had nothing to do with its drafting and did not respect it as a foundation for law. The irony is clear. No doubt, an extraordinarily large proportion of what is taken to be the legacy of the Deed of Cession in Fiji has its actual roots in theories and histories of imperial legal practice very distant from anything indigenous to Fiji. Gordon's decision to make his meeting with the Rokos and Bulis into a formal Great Council of Chiefs, for example, has more to do with Money's theory of race management than any echo of the Deed. And only Money's theory gives us principles—anti-competition, pro-security and -stability, careful governmental intercession to keep market freedoms from disrupting race relations—that apply equally in the Fiji of plantation lines and the Fiji of tax gardens.

Henry Rutz (1995) pointed out brilliantly that the mainstream of ethnic-Fijian politics, before and after the coups of 1987, actually justified the power of chiefship with reference to the British Royalty. By the 1980s, the story of the Deed of Cession became a top-down charter for chiefship, a story of recognition and devolution, chiefs recognized by the British as real, native leaders, supplanting the bottom-up story of installation of chiefs by people of the land. At least by the coups of 2000 and thereafter, more radical claims have gained ascendance, not only a sensibility that the chiefs of Cession had sovereign standing and powers before Cession but that they gave it conditionally and retained rights to take Fiji back. However, what is actually sought is not a pre-Gordon Eden but Gordon's powers to replant the gardens. Renewed commitments to racism and authoritarianism in Fiji do not all trace from and to Gordon, of course. But Gordon's insistence on an authoritarian center unchecked in its pursuit of race management has cast a long shadow in Fiji's history. J. W. B. Money was a major source for the racism that lurks, too often unconfronted, within Fiji's claims to be a culturally sensitive state. Maine's contribution was, if anything, to be a particularly moral, culturally sensitive source for justification of the authoritarian position, the position above the law, which is perhaps Gordon's most dangerous legacy for Fiji. The world has provided Fiji with alternative blueprints, notably constitutional law. But in the wake of every coup so far, a lawgiving position above the law has been assumed, inhabited, and nurtured by the Gordon-invented Great Council of Chiefs, using stories of the Deed of Cession to hide their roots in specifically colonial legal organization.

Notes

1. Among other developments, there emerged among Indo-Fijians what Brenneis has elegantly called "tender egalitarianism" and a valorization (partially in response to ethnic-Fijian celebrations of *mana*) of the goal of *shanti*, or peace, especially among Fiji Hindus. On the history of Indo-Fijian culture, see Gillion 1962; Kelly 1991, 1995a and b, 1998, 2000b; Kelly and Kaplan 2001; Lal 1992, 2000a; Sanadhya 1991.

2. Here are some samples. July 2: Mrs. Blair and Captain Beatson, "Feeble, foolish and knavish"; Joske, "Sugar planter—from Suva—flabby and feeble—but this is only the son"; Chalmers, "Of Goro—was secretary to Ratu Savenaca—sensible but limited—*very* limited"; Rupert Ryder, "Rather favorable to Indian labour. Wants to talk of sugar and cacao. A good sort, I think. A gentleman" (Gordon 1897:128–129). The raging measles epidemic that would kill a quarter of the indigenous population (and would soon cause London to cut his government's capital grant by one-third) dominated Gordon's attention, and he was particularly impressed by Carew's work on it "among the Kai Colos," whose divisions Carew described. "Told him of my schemes—Mem. to get him to define the boundary of excepted district" (July 6) (1897:135). Whether the reference was to schemes to combat measles, schemes for interior government, or schemes for land and tax policy more generally is not entirely clear. However, the prospect that Gordon was plotting districts of government for "his scheme" with Carew this early is intriguing, especially in combination with a different note from the same day regarding Mitchell: "Wants to know the distinction between royal and private lands. I don't suppose either exist. Wants to prentice young Fijians to labour. *mē genoito* [in Greek characters: "May this not happen"]" (1897:135). Across these months, in interviews with planters, the correlation was robust between approval for Indian immigration and gaining Gordon's respect. Two more examples: "Otway— Irishman from Nandi in Vanua Levu. Wants Senior's place. In favour of Coolie immigration, and thinks nothing can be done till the present race of planters is cleared off, himself included" (1897:153). "Lee, Planter, Namena—Bad sort. Wants to transfer some labour. Thinks 'though New Hebrides men are dying out, there are plenty of islands to the north not properly worked up yet.' Wants to set up what would be virtually a Slave Trade Company" (1897:153).

3. These were "an Ordinance to confirm certain Laws, Ordinances, Proclamations, and Regulations enacted, issued, or made by the Residential Government of the Fiji Islands prior to the Proclamation of the Royal Charter under the Great Seal of the United Kingdom making such Islands into a British Colony, and for indemnifying all persons who may have acted under any of the said Laws, Ordinances, Proclamations, Regulations, or any part thereof." "An Ordinance to continue temporarily certain Laws, Ordinances, Proclamations, and Regulations adopted, enacted, or made prior to the Proclamation of the Royal Charter, etc." "An Ordinance to prohibit the maintenance of suits in respect to present existing claims to land in the Law Courts of the Colony." "An Ordinance to provide the adjudication of certain claims between divers Europeans and natives in the Colony of Fiji" (Gordon 1897:174–175). Notice that the first two specifically named the Proclamation of the Royal Charter under the Great Seal, not the Deed of Cession, as the point of inception of British sovereignty.

4. Here we follow Derrick's account (1950:248–250): At Levuka, on October 10, 1874, in the Council Room of King Cakobau's 1871-founded government, Hercules Robinson and his party of British officials, civil and military, were received by Cakobau, the ministers of his government, and other high chiefs. David Wilkinson acted as translator, first reading the resolution presented by Cakobau and other chiefs to Hercules Robinson in late September: "We give Fiji unreservedly to the Queen of Britain, that she may rule us justly and affectionately, and that we may live in peace and prosperity." He then read a Fijian translation of the Deed of Cession prepared by Robinson, and then the chiefs present signed two English-language copies. Robinson signed and sealed both, handing one to Cakobau, who then, through his Chief Secretary Thurston, offered another gift. "Before finally ceding his country to Her Majesty the Queen," Thurston began (remarkably enough, in light of what was already, literally, signed and sealed), the King had a gift for Queen Victoria. He handed over the King's "old and favourite war-club" and a message for the Queen, both of which Robinson promised to transmit. Outside, Robinson declared Fiji a possession and dependency of the British Crown, the flag of the Cakobau Government was lowered, and a Royal Standard was raised. The warships fired twenty-one guns, a guard of honor presented arms as a band played the National Anthem, and cheers were given for Her Majesty and for Hercules Robinson. Robinson then led cheers for Cakobau. "The ceremony ended with general handshaking and congratulations," and "immediately" a proclamation was issued declaring Fiji a British possession and dependency. For fuller discussion of these events, including De Ricci's

account of them, see Kaplan and Kelly forthcoming; see also note 17.

5. See Chapman (1964:202–211) for a narrative of Gordon's successful struggles in Fiji and London to keep the determination of titles to European-owned lands in the hands of his administration and out of courts of law. Gordon traveled to London in 1878, in part, to arrange the legislation that would keep the land title distribution in Crown hands, successfully overcoming objections from the Crown legal officers who felt that courts should be able to hear cases based on the terms of the deed and that the deed should limit the competence of Fiji's legislature and executive, not the other way around. See also Riles 1995, an examination of efforts by unsatisfied claimants to mount a case against Gordon's land laws as a matter of international law.

6. These staves were "very long stout poles of *vesi* headed and ornamented with whale's tooth ivory. Each took the oath with his hands in mine, seated in the attitude of respect before me, and then, while still holding their hands, I delivered to each a short but grave admonition" (Gordon 1897:209). They were given, after oaths of allegiance, by Gordon to ten *Roko Tuis*, heads of provinces. Earlier in this ceremony, before these oaths and Gordon's speech, Gordon had drunk yaqona prepared by the chiefs present. Cakobau, Gordon noted, had been anxious to have all other chiefs *tama* in subordination to Gordon after Cakobau himself had in the week of Gordon's arrival, but Gordon had delayed this, also, to ensure its subordination to his own installation of Crown authority. See note 27 and the comments on sovereignty concluding this chapter. In this ceremony, Gordon accepted yaqona from the 200 assembled chiefs and drank: "As I began to drink, at Cakobau's signal and himself leading, the assembly raised the hand-clapping and shouts which imply acknowledgement of superior rank and position, and on their cessation, as I ceased to drink, I was much struck by the sudden momentary buzz of suppressed but excited conversation, which contrasted strongly with the silence observed both before and subsequently….Cakobau seemed much relieved and in better spirits when the whole affair was over…the significance in the eyes of the native population of the public act of homage rendered, not only, as on my first arrival, by Cakobau himself, on behalf of others, but by all the assembled Chiefs, can hardly be overrated" (1897:215). There is some confusion in Gordon's papers about the date of this ceremony. His day note describing it is labeled September 10 (1897:209), but he claims in his dispatch to Carnarvon on September 20 that the ceremony and speech took place on "the 11th instant" (1897:214). I suspect the latter date is accurate, not only because he cited it in the formal document but also because his papers include dispatches written on

September 10, therefore less likely to be a day he spent in long ceremonies. All quotations from his speech of this day come from Gordon 1897:210–213.

7. He wrote to his wife, "To-day I had my settlers' meeting—a *very great* success, you will be glad to hear. I have no time for particulars. I forget whether I told you in my last letter to bring some sofas" (Gordon 1897:176). All quotations from this speech come from Gordon (1897:177–184).

8. This is what Gordon said:

> I will read to you *verbatim* the instructions I have received from the Imperial Government on this point. Lord Carnarvon says: "It should be declared that the whole of the land within the limits of Fiji, whether in the occupation of, or reputed or claimed to have been, prior to the cession of the Islands, the property of either Europeans or natives, as well as all waste and unclaimed land, has by virtue of the instrument which ceded to her Majesty the "possession of, and full sovereignty and dominion over, the whole of the Islands," become absolutely and unreservedly transferred to the Crown, and that the Queen has full power of disposing of the whole of the land in such manner as to Her Majesty may seem fit, having due regard to such interests as she may deem to deserve recognition under Article 4 of that instrument. With the view of disturbing as little as possible existing tenures and occupations, and of maintaining (as far as practicable, and with such modifications only as justice and good policy may in any case appear to demand) all contracts honestly entered into before the cession, the Colonial Government, to which the rights of the Crown are delegated on that behalf, should forthwith require all Europeans claiming to have acquired land by purchase to give satisfactory evidence of the transactions with the natives on which they rely as establishing their title; and if the land appears to have been acquired fairly, and at a fair price, should issue to the persons accepted, after due inquiry, as owners, a Crown grant in fee simple of the land to which they may appear entitled, subject to any conditions as to further payments and charges, or otherwise, as may appear just. Henceforth all dealings in land between Europeans and natives shall not only be invalid and not recognisable by any court of law, but shall be expressly forbidden by enactment. Whenever any European desires to purchase any native lands, his application must be addressed to the Colonial Government, which, if it think fit to sanction such purchase, shall itself acquire the land, and fix the price at which it shall be granted by the Crown to the applicant…" The object of these instructions is to settle the claims in the speediest, cheapest, and most equitable manner. Advantage has therefore been taken of the technicality that the land has, strictly speaking, all passed to the Queen, in order to obviate the

necessity for tedious lawsuits and technical legal decisions, not always in accord with substantial justice. This could best be done, not by recourse to law courts, or by pressing them through a labyrinth of legal forms, but by submitting them to a well-chosen Commission, which could deal with every case fairly and promptly. I can tell you, although grumblers might construe into tyranny and injustice the course Her Majesty's Government has determined to pursue with reference to the lands, that the course to be adopted is, nevertheless, not so.

9. Note here that Gordon's situation was neither one of general or natural indeterminacy, as if all situations are the same, nor one of indeterminacies created especially by Gordon's own strategies, as if all order exists only subjectively (compare Miyazaki, Chapter 9, this volume). The issues here include efficacy as well as self-knowledge, interactions and enactments that fashion actual institutions as well as the genesis of particular texts, specific hopes pursued rather than generalized hope attained, and the consequences of actions for others as well as the aesthetics of selves.

10. Even in his anxieties about sofas for his draughty house? Yes. In the focus of these letters, one has to remember that he is preparing his own very local parts of Fiji, also, for the arrival of Lady Gordon, a crucial force for the rituals of hierarchy in imperial terms. Where his own lordship is compromised by the robust terms of his travel and the heterogeneity of his interactions, she will stand for something more purely. As he told the settlers, "Circumstanced as this colony is, I have no belief whatever in sitting at a table behind a big inkstand, with a bundle of quills on one side of me, and a bundle of red tape on the other." However, he emphasized to the chiefs, "When we compare Fiji with many other countries, it is but a small place after all; nevertheless, a Chief of rank in Great Britain has been appointed to govern Fiji," and proper respect for those higher was vital. Gordon was not going to drag Lady Gordon through any mud if he could help it, and he wanted her acutely sensitive to matters of rank in an imperial register. After his visit to the Joskes of Suva at home, he was more impressed with them all and wrote to his wife of their "nice flower-garden inside a bamboo fence, where good roses and bright flowering plants flourish. Mrs. Joske is rather nice, and almost a lady" (letter of July 23) (Gordon 1897:147–148). To Lady Gordon herself, a week later he wrote, "You have perfect taste and are a perfect lady." In the same letter, he wrote that governing Fiji just then was "certainly the right work for me" (1897:154).

11. This point is well established in the Fiji literature. For example, see

France (1969:109): "The Council of Chiefs was directly subject to Gordon's authority, the regulation which provided for its establishment stating: 'The Governor is the originator of the Council and he alone can open its proceedings.'" Before Gordon instituted the Great Council, high chiefs rarely gathered. When they did, France argues, it was usually an occasion restricted to gift exchanges with rigid protocol, not "councils" discussing political affairs. He cites Wilkinson, who "although a pillar of the orthodoxy, would not accept that the Council of Chiefs was a body based in Fijian tradition: 'The Fijian custom being that high Chiefs seldom, if ever, meet each other in Council'" (1969:192). See also Chapman (1964:193): "This 'Great Council' or 'Bose vaka Turaga' was an innovation." Gordon (1879:14) wrote in his 1879 paper on taxation that district councils *(Bose ni Tikina)* were part of an organization "purely native, and of spontaneous growth. To it has now been added a meeting annually of the Roko Tuis with myself, thus completing the chain from the village to the Governor. This Bose vaka Turaga, or Great Council, is also attended by the Native Stipendiary Magistrates, and by two Bulis from each Province, chosen by the Bose vaka Yasana."

12. Here I can only touch on the theme of the entailments of lawgiving in the British Empire. Martha and I are writing a book, Kaplan and Kelly forthcoming, in which lawgiving and its consequences are central themes.

13. In fact, I reserve most of my observations on this theme—including the history of the Polynesia Company, stock market scams, the chiefs and settlers' debts and hopes for cession, and the significance of finance in colonial history more generally—for another essay, "The Other Leviathans," Kelly 1999.

14. Gordon (1897:137) fit the doom of the settlers into a travelogue he wrote to his wife on July 10, showing more anxiety over his own house: "Both at Tavia and Mbureta there were schools, and that at the former place seemed an efficient one, though as unlike a European school as could well be fancied. The Wesleyans, wise in their generation, have adapted their lessons to the old national songs and dances, and we were informed by a great swarm of brown boys and girls, chiefly dressed in green leaves and flowers, that 'four times five shillings makes a pound,' with all the movement, gesticulation, and swaying about which mark one of their regular *mekes*. We stopped at a few white settlers' houses, and found them all complaining of their want of money, and of the hard times they had had. It will require a new set of men to come in before there is any real prosperity in the colony. Most of the present holders of the land will sell, and, as is usual in all new settlements, the first-comers will be ruined and go to the wall. We are getting on with the house. Of course you must not expect it to be really

comfortable, but we may, I think, make it shift passably till we build a better one elsewhere. The great fault of the existing house is its draughtiness...."

15. On the other hand, I strongly suspect that he acquired it in 1879 for use as he prepared his own paper, "The System of Taxation in Force in Fiji," years after the period on which we focus. Lending it to Fison would follow his own actual use of it. In Gordon's 1879 talk (1879:13), one finds the only other reference I am aware of in his papers to Maine, a reference that is indirect and, nota bene, at least partly dismissive:

> The political unit [in Fiji] is the village. In every one of these is found a local chief, practically hereditary, but nominally appointed by the District Council, of which I shall hereafter speak. He is assisted by a council of elders and certain executive officers, a magistrate, frequently the chief's brother, one or more constables to carry out his decisions, a town crier, (an hereditary and important officer,) and a garden overseer. The resemblance of this organization to that of an Indian village will at once strike everyone; but as there is certainly no Aryan strain in the Fijian race, I am inclined to conceive that this form of organization is not essentially Aryan, but simply the shape into which the first elements of society when emerging from barbarism naturally crystallize.

Gordon has no disquiet replacing Maine's conceptions with his own; if it is anthropology, he shows no amateur trepidation.

16. In this sense, Maine was no Orientalist (in Said's usage). Gordon's reconception of his theory in the taxation talk changed it far more by asserting stages that "naturally crystallize" than by universalizing the stages. For a fuller scholarly review of the issues raised by Maine's critique of Austin, see Rumble 1988.

17. Intriguingly, something kindred to this was the theme of the speech by J. B. Thurston at Hercules Robinson's ceremony on October 10, 1874. Thurston (speaking, to recall note 4, as King Cakobau's "Chief Secretary") presented to Robinson a gift from Cakobau to Queen Victoria: "The King gives Her Majesty his old and favourite war-club, the former, and, until lately the only known, law of Fiji. In abandoning club law, and adopting the forms and principles of civilized societies, he laid by his old weapon and covered it with the emblems of peace.... [His people] having survived the barbaric law and age, are now submitting themselves, under Her Majesty's rule, to civilization" (quoted in Derrick 1950:249). Whether Thurston was a reader of Maine et al. is an even cloudier question. According to Scarr (1973:102,141–142), Thurston also was "a serious student of ethnology" and a reader of intellectual works who by 1874 had studied

works by Morgan, Humboldt, Macaulay, Matthew Arnold, and Washington Irving—but no trace of Maine, to my knowledge.

18. From the trial of Hastings, accused of corruption and failure to institute decent government in his overestimation of the value of local administrative structures, through controversies over how to determine the proper landowning units and systems of rent or tax collection, and through many failed projects to find useful law in the translation of classic texts thought to be law codes, the British East India Company had recurrently failed to establish a smoothly functioning legal foundation for its state in articulation with any previous system of governance. On Hastings' trial, see Suleri 1992; see Guha 1981 on Bengal's "permanent settlement"; see Stein 1989 on Munro and the *ryotwari* system.

19. To finish the story for India, in place of the search for law in the courtly worlds of Sanskrit shastras and the Islamic legal schools, the principle of "personal law" was invoked, that Indians carried with them into court a personal, customary law particular to their community, which had to be far more aggressively specified by way of census, survey, and legal precedent. As Cohn (1989) has discussed, over time, this documentation found its way entirely into English-language court decisions, the published texts of which provided courts of law the precious precedent that could make the Anglo-Saxon jurist armed and ready. "What had started with Warren Hastings and Sir William Jones as a search for the 'Ancient Indian Constitution' ended up with what they had so much wanted to avoid—with English law as the law of India" (Cohn 1989:151).

20. In Indian agriculture, following the Mutiny, "the promotion of the free market (regardless of social consequences) gave way to the protection of Indian institutions (regardless of their economic drawbacks). It is impossible to explain this metamorphosis without reference to Henry Maine" (Dewey 1991:353). In official reportage and policy, village institutions and even caste went from abominations against civilization and reason to indispensable sources of social cohesion (1991:367). This shift was particularly important in the management of Punjab, where officials literally schooled on *Ancient Law* and *Village Communities East and West* sought to support Indian institutions thought necessary and threatened by British rule. In Punjab and elsewhere in western India, from the 1860s onward, "government measures constrained the sale of agricultural lands to moneylenders, protected the Indian aristocracy and princes, and sought to determine and codify the custom of local clan and caste rather than to purvey the general principles of either English or brahmanical Hindu law" (Bayly 1991:391). Bayly further ties the legacy of Maine to the explicit founders of systems of "indirect rule," Lugard in

West Africa and Swettenham in the Federated Malay States. "The colonial admin-istrator, it appears, was making a slow transition from the status of social engineer to that of social conservator and anthropologist-as-legislator" (1991:391).

21. This language cuts to the heart of Fiji's legal and political confronta-tions in 2000 and 2001, as courts attempted to reinstate and enforce the 1997 constitution while a "Caretaker Government," the army, and the Great Council tried to subordinate the legal questions to their politics (see Kaplan, Chapter 6, this volume).

22. Four long passages from his 1879 taxation paper (forty-three paragraphs total, in original order) reappear in the 1897 introduction. Views kindred to Maine's abound, such as this: "Indeed it is probable that as much real wrong has been inflicted by the conscientious but narrow-minded desire to act in accor-dance with maxims in themselves generally sound, but not of universal applica-tion, as by violence and consequent tyranny" (Gordon 1897:197, 1879:9). "I came therefore to the conclusion that the wisest course to pursue would be to preserve as far as possible the existing native organization of village communities, to uphold the authority of the Chiefs and local councils, and generally to maintain existing native laws and customs, modifying them where necessary, but working them mainly through native agency" (1897:199). Both the 1897 introduction and the 1879 taxation paper cited Earl Grey as an authority on the virtue of tithe-type produce taxes for those "in a rude state of society" (1897:204, 1879:24).

23. A sign that Chapman, for example, did not pursue the connection is that his text reproduces Gordon's erroneous citation of the title, which was actually *Java; or, How to Manage A Colony*, and misreports his name as E. B. instead of J. W. B. Money.

24. These are some examples from the taxation paper, repeated (with a spelling error corrected) in the 1897 introduction:

> Something—perhaps much, perhaps little—is done for the native; nothing is left to be done by him, or in his own way. (Gordon 1879:10, 1897:197).

> But it is not enough to abstain from seeking hastily to replace native institutions by unreal imitations of European models....A native may suffer very patiently...but if rights really cherished by him be touched, if his moral sense be shocked, or his honour seriously wounded, it may be doubted whether he will ever again entertain any belief in the justice of those who have, he conceives, wronged him...whenever white and native races meet, such offenses are sure to be committed, partly in

careless indifference, and as frequently through well-meant blunder-
ing. It is therefore of the utmost importance to seize, if possible, the
spirit in which native institutions have been framed, and endeavour so
to work them as to develop to the utmost possible extent the latent
capacities of the people for the management of their own affairs, without exciting their suspicion or destroying their self-respect. (Gordon
1879:10–11, 1897:198)

25. Money relies entirely on a vocabulary of race but does not adduce a unitary conception of what makes European and Native races different. At times, he
uses specific allochronic measures, European laws of the nineteenth century
meeting Oriental systems equivalent to Europe's of three to six centuries before
(for example, see Money 1861a:99, 1861b:56). However, he also quite generally
contrasts European energy with native laziness, sometimes with enervating climate
mentioned, a straightforward "myth of the lazy native" (as Alatas [1977] named it).

26. I will not seek any critical evaluation of Money's account as a description
of Dutch Java's culture system. It would be interesting to track more about
Money's account in the histories of Java, India, and Dutch and British colonial
policies. Here I trace only one thread: Via Gordon's agency, what Money claimed
about Java was translated into what the government did in Fiji.

27. Gordon received and accepted the yaqona (kava), with perhaps his first
speech in Fijian language, which he had studied on the ship. The sequence of
events: Cakobau took the yaqona from a *matanivanua*

and laid it at my feet, breaking off at the same time, rather nervously
and hastily, one of the smaller portions of it and placing it in my hand.
This was the decisive act of vassalage. I said, *Au sa tara oqo: ena vinaka
sara ko Viti* (I accept this: may it be well with Fiji). Then they raised the
shout of *Mana!* and clapped hands....He was a good deal agitated, as
was not unnatural, for, though he has signed treaties of cession and
hauled down flags, this is probably the first time in his life that he ever
performed a personal act of homage to another, and that too in the
presence of his people. The effect has been electric. Wherever I go now
the natives shout *Woh!* and crouch down, as before their own great
chiefs, and they admit and understand that I am their master. (Gordon
1897:128)

On July 6, "Cakobau came to see me this afternoon. He is very anxious that
all should tama to me now that he has done so" (1897:135).

4

Talking Back to Law and Empire

Hula in Hawaiian-Language Literature in 1861

Noenoe K. Silva

This chapter is about the first publication of the *moʻolelo* of the goddesses of hula. A moʻolelo is a story, history, literature, or any kind of narrative. Because I am about to share details of a moʻolelo that few people in the world have the ability to read, I must begin by stating my relationship to this moʻolelo and to the knowledge of the native people of Hawaiʻi. Before proceeding, I will explain why so few people in the world have access to this literature and what that has to do with law and empire in the Pacific.

I am the granddaughter of Kathleen Kauhiliʻiliʻi Jay Decker, who was born in Kalāpana, Puna, Moku o Keawe (Island of Hawaiʻi). She was the daughter of Mary Kauila, who was the daughter of Lāhapa Lehuloa, who was the daughter of Kauhi. All of them (and their *kūpuna*) were born in the Kalāpana area, near Pele's home, Halemaʻumaʻu, Kīlauea. Hula in literature is mainly connected with the moʻolelo of Pele. My grandmother was of the first generation purposely raised to be ignorant of the language and literature of their mothers and grandmothers. She was raised to speak Chinese and English, but despite her parents' efforts, she understood spoken Hawaiian and knew hundreds of songs in the Hawaiian language. Her daughter, my mother, also knew many songs, but much less Hawaiian. I grew up knowing even less. As an adult, I returned home to Hawai'i nei and began to learn my great-grandmothers' language at the university. As I became fluent, my teachers impressed upon me that this language I had fallen in love with was nearly extinct.[1] Those of us who have managed by our various means to learn it are privileged in our community because most Kānaka 'Ōiwi still face serious barriers to learning the language and to higher education. We therefore bear a "merciless weight of responsibility" when we decide to reveal, interpret, and analyze the writing of our kūpuna (Benton 1987). To do so puts "scholars and authors into the role of brokering knowledge," as Amy Ku'uleialoha Stillman (2002:131) has put it.

Furthermore, the texts of hula have come down to us in two ways. One is through the oral tradition, passed down from kumu hula (hula master) to kumu hula over the generations. As we will see, hula was often disparaged and at times virtually banned, so the knowledge had to be passed along in secret. Because of mass death from epidemics, land dispossession, and other reasons, some of the knowledge did not survive. I am not a dancer and have not earned the right to the body of knowledge that did survive in hālau hula (hula schools). In an unevenly parallel stream, some of this knowledge was recorded in writing, in manuscripts, and, starting with the mo'olelo I will share, in literature published in Hawaiian-language newspapers. That written knowledge has been difficult to access for many kumu hula, especially for those not fluent in written Hawaiian. To complicate matters further, institutions whose archives contain such manuscripts have sometimes blocked access to the written mele (songs and chants) associated with hula (Stillman 2002:141, 2001:193–194). In the twentieth century, when most kumu were unable to access the Hawaiian-language literature, some used the two books written by Orientalist Nathaniel B. Emerson as primary sources. However, Dr. Emerson (1965), despite the title of his work, Unwritten Literature of Hawaii, obtained much of that knowledge from the written literature in Hawaiian newspapers. It is obvious, for example, that Emerson (1978) took much of his book Pele and Hiiaka from the text we will examine. He did not credit the author, even though the mo'olelo was published under the author's name, M. J. Kapihenui (see Charlot 1998).[2]

My relationship to the mo'olelo is therefore multilayered. In a culture that greatly values genealogy, I am a descendant of the people who live(d) close to the *akua wahine* (deities) that the moʻolelo is about. I am also the recipient of the gifts of prescient ancestors who wrote the moʻolelo, foreseeing that today's generations would want and need it. I honor the depth of knowledge that kumu hula have earned and acknowledge that I do not speak as an authority on hula but as a student of language and literature. Finally, I respect the responsibility to make known what I discover while I do research in Hawaiian-language texts, because I am one of the few able to do so. The moʻolelo concerning hula may be some of the most important to Kānaka ʻŌiwi today because interest in traditional hula practice has blossomed in recent years, along with the movement to revitalize the language, cultural practices such as long-distance voyaging in traditional *waʻa*, traditional medicine, and certain religious practices. Moʻolelo of every kind are important to the revitalization of our traditional culture, which is, in turn, important to the collective recovery of our community from the harms caused by the colonial past and neocolonial present.

It is important to understand, as well, that the text of the moʻolelo and the text of the mele within the moʻolelo are of primary importance to hula. Stillman (2002:133) has noted that "the poetic text is absolutely central to performance as recited song and enacted dance. The dance combines hand and arm gestures that depict selected aspects of the poetic text...." In fact, there is no such thing as hula without accompanying text.

In this chapter, I seek and develop (incomplete) answers to the following questions: Why was the very first written version of the *Moolelo o Hiiakaikapoliopele,* the moʻolelo of the hula goddesses, published in 1861? What circumstances motivated and allowed for its publication? Why did anyone feel that there was a need to translate the oral tradition into literature? What was the relationship between the attempt to ban hula legally in 1859 and the publication of this moʻolelo in 1861? Finally, was the hula the Calvinist missionaries sought to ban the same as the hula as Kānaka ʻŌiwi thought of it? That is, I suggest that the missionaries had a particular idea of what hula was, based on what they saw and what they assumed went on in dance halls and theaters in Honolulu and Lāhainā, and this idea differed radically from hula in the minds and practices of the *Kanaka Maoli.*

LANGUAGE LOSS, THE LAW, AND IMPERIALISM

First, why do Kānaka 'Ōiwi no longer speak their heritage language? Also, what does that have to do with law and imperialism in Hawai'i? Paul Nahoa Lucas (2000:3) notes that "beginning in 1846, the Hawaiian legislature declared that all laws enacted were to be published in both Hawaiian and English." He quotes Chief Justice Albert F. Judd as remarking, "Of necessity the English language must be largely employed to record transactions of the government...because the very ideas and principles adopted by the government come from countries where the English language is in use" (Lucas 2000:3). Although legal documents were written and court conducted in both languages, there was a struggle for linguistic and cultural hegemony throughout this time. By 1859, the legislature had enacted a law dictating that where Hawaiian and English versions of laws differed, the English version would be binding (Lucas 2000:4).

Government officials, especially former missionary Richard Armstrong, were at the forefront of the movement to shift the language of the land to English. "During Armstrong's administration, the first government-sponsored school in English was established in 1851, and by 1854, government-run English schools were effectively competing with the Hawaiian-medium schools" (Lucas 2000:5). In 1896, following the military intervention and coup d'état that established a colonial oligarchy in Hawai'i, that government legally ended both public and private Hawaiian-medium schools (Hawai'i 1896:189). (Although Hawai'i was not a political colony until 1898, the processes of colonialism began much earlier. See Merry 2000 and Silva 1999.) When the United States took over the government in 1900, it reinforced the sole use of English in schools. The shift to English was part of a gradual process of colonialism that used law, in addition to churches and schools, to change the culture of the Kanaka Maoli and establish American hegemony in Hawai'i (see Merry 2000). The English-only law was cruelly enforced in schools. Lucas (2000:9) reports that "Hawaiian was strictly forbidden anywhere within schoolyards or buildings; physical punishment could be harsh. Teachers...were threatened with dismissal for singing Hawaiian...and, at times, teachers were even sent to Hawaiian-speaking homes to reprimand parents for speaking Hawaiian to their children." No wonder that several generations grew up deprived of the mo'olelo their kūpuna had so carefully and conscientiously written down.

Here is the other part of this story. By the mid-nineteenth century, most of the population was literate in Hawaiian. The mission had established several newspapers, starting in 1834. Missionaries had controlled all the Hawaiian-language newspapers, including the one sponsored by the government, *Ka Hae Hawaii*. Kānaka worked at all these papers in every capacity, from typesetter to assistant editor. They quickly realized that their knowledge, which was disappearing with the many people dying in the severe population collapse of the time, could be preserved for future generations—in print. They began to write it all down. J. H. Kānepuʻu, for example, urged editors not to shorten moʻolelo or mele:

> *Ua ike au, ua hakina ka moolelo o Hiiakaikapoliopele, ua hakina kona mau mele e pili ana i na "huli," a pehea la anei e loaa ai na koena i na hanauna hope o kakou, ke makemake lakou e nana, aole no e loaa, e hele ana kakou i ka nalowale, e hele ana o Kau ka makuahine o M. G.* [sic] *Kapihenui i ka nalowale. E makemake ana ka hanauna Hawaii o na la* A.D. *1870, a me* A.D. *1880, a me* A.D. *1890, a me* A.D. *1990.* (Kānepuʻu 1861)

> I see that the moʻolelo of Hiʻiakaikapoliopele has been broken off [that is, shortened]. Its "Hulihia" mele have been broken off, so how will the remainder get to the generations coming after us? They are going to want to look [at them], and they will not have [them]. We will be gone; Kau, the mother of [author] Kapihenui will be gone. Generations of Hawaiians will want [this literature] in 1870, 1880, 1890, and 1990.[3]

In addition, in the mid-1850s, the American Board of Commissioners for Foreign Missions (ABCFM) ended financial support for missionaries to Hawaiʻi. Those desiring to remain in Hawaiʻi had to devise their own livelihood. Some were supported as ministers by the members of their churches, many took government jobs as judges, land surveyors, schoolteachers, and the like, and many others established themselves in businesses, particularly as owners of sugar plantations. The ministers of the Calvinist Congregational Church also established the Hawaiian Evangelical Association (HEA), which took over some of the activities previously administered by the ABCFM.

For forty years, these Calvinist missionaries had been converting and "civilizing" the Kanaka Maoli. They quickly expanded from preaching at church to establishing schools, taking active part in creating constitutional government, and influencing how the *Mōʻī* and other *aliʻi* (rulers, chiefs) thought about business, politics, and law (Merry 2000; Osorio 2002). As important, they waged a discursive battle in the name of "civilization." That battle represented traditional moʻolelo as part of what was *naʻaupō,* or uncivilized and ignorant, and needed to be stopped.

In 1857, the HEA began a campaign to use the law to eradicate hula. The ministers conducted the campaign in newspaper editorial pages and also drafted a bill, succeeding in getting it heard in the Kingdom's legislature in 1859 (Silva 2000). Note that this same legislature made the English versions of laws the binding ones. I have demonstrated elsewhere (Silva 2000) that the motivation for the attempted legal ban was linked to the desire of the missionaries cum planters for laborers. By this time, most of the *aliʻi nui* had converted to Christianity (see Collier, Chapter 2, this volume), with varying levels of sincerity and conformity to the rules of morality dictated by the new religion. They both assisted and resisted the attempted legal banning of hula. The result of the attempt was a law prohibiting the public performance of hula unless the performers purchased a license at a cost of $10 per performance. Licenses were given only for Honolulu. This resulted in a virtual ban everywhere else in the islands and for everyone except successful businesses.

Just two years later, a group of Kanaka men formed an association named the *Ahahui Hoopuka Nupepa Kuikawa* (The Special Newspaper Publishing Association) to publish their own newspaper, *Ka Hoku o ka Pakipika (The Star of the Pacific)*. They were frustrated that all the newspapers in their language were controlled by the Calvinist missionaries. In a discursive insurrection, they demanded a place in print where they could tell their own stories, preserve the oral traditions, and talk back to the increasingly oppressive actions of the HEA. Not surprisingly, the HEA attempted to shut down their newspaper (Silva 1999).

During this period, long moʻolelo, which included mele and *pule* (prayer), first flourished as published literature. (According to John

Charlot [in a personal communication in 2001], professor of Polynesian religion, the form existed in unpublished manuscripts before this time.) It is difficult to say with absolute certainty when the first moʻolelo of this type were published. The same processes that worked to eradicate the Hawaiian language and culture at that time have had long-lasting consequences for contemporary scholars: The newspapers in which our literature appeared have not been comprehensively indexed, and American scholars such as Martha Beckwith include only translated works in their bibliographies (see Beckwith 1940). With that caveat, I will venture to say that the translation of moʻolelo from the oral traditions into literature, including mele and/or pule, first occurred at this time.[4] The first example was published in *Ka Hae Hawaii* (the government newspaper) after the death of Richard Armstrong in 1860. *He Wahi Moolelo (A Story)* by S. K. Kuapuʻu, a narrative of the story of Pākaʻa, is the first that I know of, running as a serial from April to June 1861 (Charlot 2001). This was followed by *He Moolelo No Kamapuaa (A Story of Kamapuaʻa)* by G. W. Kahiolo, which ran from June to September 1861, also in *Ka Hae Hawaii* (Charlot 1987:4), and which Charlot (1987:93) says was bowdlerized, no doubt as a result of missionary pressures. When *Ka Hoku o ka Pakipika* began, it ran *Moolelo no Kawelo (Story of Kawelo)* by S. K. Kawailiula on its front page, beginning with the first issue on September 26, 1861. *Ka Hoku o ka Pakipika* thereafter ran several types of moʻolelo.

The missionary camp was incensed that these Kānaka Maoli were celebrating their traditional ways of life, thinking, and poetics in the moʻolelo and in mele. The missionary John S. Emerson especially attacked the publication of moʻolelo, fearing that it reinforced the traditional beliefs. He wrote an editorial in the HEA newspaper protesting the publication of moʻolelo:

> *He mea pono anei e paiia maloko o na Nupepa, a me na palapala e heluheluia e na keiki, o na kaao a me na mooolelo lapuwale no Pele, a me Kamapuaa ... O ka mea nana i papa mai, "Aole ou akua e ae imua o koʻu alo," ua papa mai oia i na hana a pau e hoala ai i ka makau i na akua kahiko o Hawaii nei.* (J. S. E. 1861)

> Is it right that there should be published in the Newspaper or any documents read by children, the legends and the

worthless stories about Pele and Kamapuaa?...The one who commanded, "You shall have no other god before me," has forbidden every action that might awaken fear of the old gods of Hawai'i nei.

In contrast, readers expressed their appreciation for the *mo'olelo,* as in this opinion piece:

> *O ka mooolelo, oia ka mea i hoakaka mai i na mea i hanaia e kanaka e like me kakou, o ka poe i ola i na manawa okoa, a me na wahi okoa.... O ka mooolelo ua like ia me he aniani la e hoike mai ana i ka hana a ke kanaka i hana'i mamuli o kekahi kumu.... Ua hoike mai ka mooolelo i ka hope oia mau hana, ina he maikai, a ino paha, i loaa mai i ke kanaka...e hana ana ia mau mea.* (Kaukaliu 1861)

> Mo'olelo is what explains the actions taken by people like ourselves, people who lived in other times and/or other places....Mo'olelo is like a mirror showing the action a person takes for a certain reason....The mo'olelo shows the results of these actions, if they were good or bad, [and their effects] upon the person doing those things.

Kaukaliu argues that people can learn *pono* (righteous) behavior through reading the mo'olelo. This is in opposition to the missionary discourse that pono can be learned only in the education provided by the mission. Because of this love for the mo'olelo and mele and the assertion that they had value, the missionaries tried to shut down *Ka Hoku o ka Pakipika* (Silva 1999).

In the face of this direct missionary opposition, *Ka Hoku o ka Pakipika* published the first written version of *He Moolelo no Hiiakaikapoliopele (A Narrative of Hi'iakaikapoliopele)* in serial form from December 1861 until July 1862. Hi'iakaikapoliopele is the youngest sister of Pele, the volcano. Both are major deities of the hula. To the missionaries, Pele is also the most dangerous akua (deity) of the Hawaiian pantheon because she is female and she lives: She is an akua the people can see—the volcano is alive and continues to erupt. The mo'olelo represents hula as an aspect of the Pele religion.

A BRIEF EXPLANATION OF HULA

Before I present the descriptions of hula in the story, a general explanation of a more contemporary, indigenous view of hula might be helpful here. Mary Kawena Pukui (1895–1986) was a kumu hula, a native speaker of Hawaiian, and an extraordinarily talented and educated person in Hawaiian culture. She authored or co-authored most of the standard reference works on the Hawaiian language. For many years, she worked at the Bishop Museum, collaborating on projects with anthropologists and translating from the Hawaiian-language manuscript archives and newspapers. Pukui (1980:74) also wrote a series of articles about hula, from which the following descriptions are taken:

> Every country in the world has its folk dances, and we have ours in Hawaii. These are not of one type only but a large number generally called the hula. Some were peculiar to one island; some originated in one locality and spread to others; and some belong to the whole group, but had many versions. I should say there were not less than 36 different kinds of hula in Hawaii.

> In the days when every island had its own ruling chief or chiefs, hula dancing was much practiced by chiefs and commoners, by the aged as well as by children.

Pukui (1980:76) describes hula training as imbued with prayer and ceremony, as religious ritual:

> Keahi [Pukui's hula teacher] remembers seeing her sisters come out of the halau [hula school] early every morning to the pool called Poolimu where they had their hiuwai or ceremonial bathing before returning into the halau....These pupils returned from Poolimu pool to the halau with prayer chants every step of the way....A kuahu or altar to Laka was built in their halau or school, and there Keahi learned not only the meles and dances but the rites, ceremonies and prayers of the hula.

Pukui (1980:93) adds,

> All these old hula...were decent dances in ancient times.
> The mixture of indecency in modern times is not the fault of
> the dancers but of the disreputable persons who have
> money to spare and bring in this element for their own
> enjoyment. It is the dollar that has brought low the hula of
> Hawaii nei.

In this statement, Pukui points out the differences in perception of the
hula—that foreigners perceive it as a dance by women for men and
contrive to make it more so and to profit from it. She mourns that the
solemn, religious, yet entertaining traditional hula is so misunderstood. This perception of the hula was undoubtedly widely shared
among the Kanaka Maoli of the 1860s. Missionaries in the mid-
nineteenth century shared the foreigners' perception that hula was
danced by women for money as entertainment for men.

HULA IN THE MOʻOLELO

The story of Pele's migration to Hawaiʻi was also well known to the
Kanaka Maoli of the nineteenth century, that is, the readers of the
Hawaiian-language newspapers. Several versions of the story seem to
coexist peacefully in the shared consciousness of the people. In all versions, some kind of dispute over a man occurs between Pele and one of
her sisters. As a result, Pele leaves Kahiki (perhaps Tahiti, perhaps
another foreign land) and sails with many of her brothers and sisters to
the Hawaiian archipelago. She arrives in the northwest islands of Nihoa
and Niʻihau and travels eastward to each of the islands, looking for a
home. Along the way, certain family members decide to stay at various
places. Pele, some of her brothers, and her younger sisters settle at
Kīlauea, the live volcano, in the crater named Halemaʻumaʻu. Pele lives
in the volcano but also is the volcano, whose "primary function [is] creating new land" (Kanahele and Wise n.d.:37). The Hawaiian word for
both *volcano* and *lava* is *pele.*

Kapihenui's version of the moʻolelo begins when the family is
already well settled in Hawaiʻi. Pele has eight sisters, all of whose names
begin with *Hiʻiaka* and who live together in Halemaʻumaʻu. The
youngest and favorite is Hiʻiakaikapoliopele (Hiʻiaka in the embrace of
Pele). The brothers seem to live supernaturally in the cliffs, in the

ocean, or in the heavens; they have godly powers. Pele is simultaneously a woman who engages in romances with handsome young men and a fearsome, unreasonable volcano that regularly erupts and consumes the landscape in fire. Her sisters appear more human, with no discernable supernatural powers—except for Hiʻiakaikapoliopele. According to kumu hula and Kanaka Maoli scholar Pualani Kanakaʻole Kanahele, Hiʻiakaikapoliopele is the most popular of all the Hiʻiaka forms and is recognized as a deity of great importance whose functions are equal to those of Pele. Her functions are those of a *kāula* (prophet or seer) and a medical practitioner who heals land as well as people. She has the ability to function as an *ʻanāʻanā* (one who is able to take life and restore or save life). Hiʻiakaikapoliopele also allows the growth of new vegetation on new lava flows and is the female counterpart of Kāne, the akua of the rising sun (Kanahele and Wise n.d.:15–16).

Therefore, Hiʻiakaikapoliopele is also a powerful female force, and in a way that is complementary to Pele: After Pele erupts, destroying the landscape to create new land, Hiʻiakaikapoliopele creates plant life there. Other relatives also exist simultaneously as people and as features of the landscape, such as Pele's father, who is said to be the mountain peak Kānehoalani on the island of Oʻahu. An unmistakable feeling emerges through the text that people, the gods, and the landscape are all members of the same family.

Innumerable hula songs and dances are dedicated to Pele and to Hiʻiakaikapoliopele. Pele manifests not only in fires and molten lava but also in thunder, storms, and the flashing of lightning. *Lapa* is the word for "lightning flashing," and its variant, *ʻōlapa*, is the word for "hula dancer." In many dances, the sounds of the instruments and the movements of the dancers evoke the sounds and movements of the eruptions and their attendant storms.

The frame of Kapihenui's story of Hiʻiakaikapoliopele is this: Pele meets a handsome young aliʻi, Lohiʻau, on the island of Kauaʻi while she is in a spirit state. Desiring to consummate their relationship in the flesh, she sends Hiʻiakaikapoliopele on a journey to fetch him, promising that after Pele has enjoyed his company for five nights, her sisters would be free to enjoy him also. Hula is featured prominently several times in the story, beginning with the very first scene (Kapihenui, 26 December 1861).

Pele says to her sisters that they should take a trip from their upland home down to the seashore to fish. (This is the eastern shore of the easternmost island in the archipelago.) When they arrive at Pu'upāhoehoe (Hill of pāhoehoe lava), a young woman, Hōpoe, and her male friend, Hā'ena, dance for Pele and the sisters at the shoreline. Pele likes this hula very much and asks her sisters to perform a hula in return, but they refuse, except for Hi'iakaikapoliopele. Hi'iakaikapoliopele composes a chant and dance of praise for Hōpoe on the spot. She is clearly enchanted with Hōpoe, even appearing to fall in love with her:

Ke haa la Puna i ka makani,	Puna is dancing in the wind,
Haa ka uluhala i Keaau,	The pandanus grove at Kea'au is dancing,
Haa Haena me Hopoe,	Hā'ena dances with Hōpoe,
Haa ka wahine ami i kai o	The woman dances an 'ami [a step] at
Nanahuki la,	the sea of Nānāhuki
Hula lea wa—le,	Such an entertaining hula,
I kai o Nanahuki—e,	At the sea of Nānāhuki
O Puna kai 'kua i ka hala,	Puna the godly sea with pandanus trees,
Pae ka leo o ke ka—i,	The voice of the sea strikes the ear,
Ke lu—la i na pua lehua,	Scattering the lehua flowers,
Nana i kai o Hopo—e,	Look at the sea of Hōpoe,
Aloha wale no hoi o Hopo—e,	So beloved is Hōpoe,
Ka wahine ami i kai,	The woman who does an 'ami in the sea,
O Nanahuki—la,	Of Nānāhuki,
Hula lea wale,	Such an entertaining hula,
I kai o Nanahuki—e,	At the sea of Nānāhuki.

In this song, Hi'iakaikapoliopele is so entranced by Hōpoe's dancing that the landscape itself seems to be dancing with her: The district of Puna is dancing, and the pandanus trees of Kea'au are dancing. *Hā'ena* is the name of both the dancer and the place where they were dancing. The repeated place name *Nānāhuki* is composed of two words, *nānā* (to watch) and *huki* (to pull), giving the hearer or reader the feeling that as

Hiʻiakaikapoliopele watched the hula of Hōpoe, she was pulled toward her in a romantic attraction. Kanahele (Kanahele and Wise n.d.:67) notes another meaning: "The haʻa or dance which she exhibits is a creative exposition in praise of the environment around her and a celebration of the regenerative power of the coupling of land and flora." This is Hiʻiakaikapoliopele's godly power to regenerate the land. As always, Hiʻiakaikapoliopele and Hōpoe appear at once as women and as the landscape. As the scene ends, Hiʻiakaikapoliopele leaves Pele and her sisters and goes off with Hōpoe to dance and surf.[5]

The hula that Hōpoe and Hāʻena do is not described in words or movement but is nevertheless understood to be a welcoming for Pele and her sisters. This fits in with Polynesian protocol. Hōpoe, the *kamaʻāina* (resident), performs her hula as a welcome; then the godly guests respond. The protocol establishes friendly relations between Pele and company and the permanent residents of the area. They have received permission and are now welcome to fish and camp there. Note that the hula is performed by a woman and a man for a company of women. Hiʻiakaikapoliopele's song completes the protocol but also serves to begin the romantic friendship with Hōpoe.

Hula plays a big role in the next section of the story as well. As the other Hiʻiaka sisters go off to fish, Pele remains behind with one sister, Hiʻiakaikapuaʻenaʻena. Pele tells her sister that she is going off to sleep and that no matter how long she is asleep, she is not to be awakened. If she must be awakened, only her brother, Keowahimakaakaua, or Hiʻiakaikapoliopele are allowed to awaken her. In her sleep, her spirit (*ʻuhane*) hears the sound of hula drums. Her spirit follows the sound of the drums across the island, then across the channel to Maui, continuing westward to Molokaʻi and Oʻahu, and finally to the westernmost of the large islands, Kauaʻi. There she sees the young handsome aliʻi Lohiʻau playing the hula drum, with his hula teacher, Mapu, his *aikāne* (friend and/or homosexual lover), Kahuakaiapaoa, on either side of him and others, playing another kind of drum or bamboo pipe (*kaeke*), surrounding them. It is a kind of hula festival. An audience is present, listening and watching the hula for entertainment. Pele transforms herself into a beautiful young woman adorned with the forest greenery of Puna. After chanting back and forth, she and Lohiʻau retreat to his house, where they stay for several days without emerging for food.

The *pahu* (hula drum) in the first part of this sequence is an enticement to Pele; she is excited by the sound and cannot help but follow it
to its source. After Lohiʻau is in the house for a couple days, the hula
festival is still going on, and his friends begin to wonder about him
because hula is his favorite activity.

> *Ia manawa, haohao na makaainana, a me ke aikane a ia nei, a me ke*
> *kumu hula a laua nei. A me na mea a pau, i ka hemo o kana mea nui*
> *o ka hula, akahi wale no a hemo, nolaila, manao wale iho no na mea*
> *a pau ua make o Lohiau.* (Kapihenui, 26 December 1861)

> At that time, the common people wondered, and so did his
> friend and their kumu hula. And so did everyone, because
> of his staying away from his most important activity, the
> hula[;] this was the first time he ever stayed away, so every-
> one thought that Lohiʻau had died.

Lohiʻau was performing hula because it was important to him, and
he was also sharing it to entertain the common people of his area.
Although the text does not tell us what particular hula were being
performed, it is significant that Lohiʻau, his aikāne, and his kumu were
playing the pahu, the shark-skin drum. According to Adrienne Kaeppler
(1993:6), "in pre-Christian Hawaiʻi, there were two main contexts or
activities...performed in conjunction with shark-skin-covered drums:
(1) worship of the gods in sacred situations, and (2) honor of the gods
as an element of formal entertainments." The described scene is consistent with the second type of performance. Perhaps Pele's spirit was
called to the scene because hula was being performed in her honor.

When Pele arrives, however, the performance takes on another
dimension: It inflames Pele's passion for the handsome aliʻi. The scene
becomes one in which a woman's sexual desires are aroused by the
sights and sounds of a man performing hula. This is not a singular
occurrence in Hawaiian literature; other examples may be found in the
story of Kawelo (Hoʻoulumāhiehie 1909) and the story of Limaloa, of
whom it was written, "He was always an unlucky fellow with women....If
he had learned to do the hula he might have been successful" (Pukui
n.d.:18). It is important to note, however, that Lohiʻau is not performing hula for that express purpose. Pele is represented here as a woman

exercising unfettered agency in her sexual life: She is attracted to Lohiʻau and freely pursues him.

After a few days, Pele must return to her body on the island of Hawaiʻi. She tells Lohiʻau that she will send a woman to bring him to her and that he must not sleep with anyone else in the meantime. Again, she is exercising not only agency but also power: She sets the terms of their relationship. When she awakens in Hawaiʻi, she asks each of her sisters, in turn, to go fetch Lohiʻau, but none will go. She summons Hiʻiakaikapoliopele, who is still with Hōpoe at the shore. Hiʻiakaikapoliopele agrees to go, providing that Pele does not destroy Hōpoe while she is gone. She takes along a human young woman, Wahineʻōmaʻo. They walk across the island of Hawaiʻi, battling *moʻo* (spirits that take various forms, usually described as large lizards or dragonlike), as well as dangerous sharks and the like. Early in the journey, Hiʻiakaikapoliopele realizes that Pele has broken her promise not to destroy Hōpoe; Hōpoe and her grove of lehua flowers are consumed in Pele's fires. Hiʻiakaikapoliopele, however, continues on her errand for Pele, with grief and a growing desire for revenge. The two young women sail to Maui, which is where the next incidence of hula occurs.[6]

Hiʻiakaikapoliopele and Wahineʻōmaʻo are standing on a cliff at Honolua, looking down at the water and at Manamanaiakaluea, a young girl described as *mumuku* (maimed or having amputated limbs). She is being tossed in the waves. When the waves carry her out to sea, she gathers seaweed and shellfish; when they carry her back in, she lands on the flat rocks and performs hula. She sees Hiʻiaka and Wahineʻōmaʻo and performs in an entertaining way for them. In chant and hula, she tries to guess where they are from and finally succeeds. She then returns to her home and prepares a meal for them. When the meal is ready, Hiʻiakaikapoliopele reveals to Wahineʻōmaʻo that Manamanaiakaluea is actually dead and that her spirit (*ʻuhane*) has been entertaining them. Wahineʻōmaʻo wants Hiʻiakaikapoliopele to restore the girl to life, and although Hiʻiakaikapoliopele seems reluctant to intervene, *"no ka nui o na hana maikai ana i na malihini no laila hu ke aloha o na malihini a lapaau ia ai oia a ola ia la, o ke ola aela no ia o Manamanaiakaluea"* ("because of the all the good deeds that [Manamanaiakaluea] did for the visitors, the affection of the visitors

for her grew, and she was treated with medicine [by Hiʻiakaikapo-
liopele], and Manamanaiakaluea was restored to life") (Kapihenui, 6
February 1862). The following day, however, the girl died again.

As a girl, Manamanaiakaluea performs hula to make friends with
Hiʻiakaikapoliopele and Wahineʻōmaʻo. At the same time, she is a spirit
communicating with her deity. The hula is so entertaining and the girl
shows her love and respect in such a way that Hiʻiakaikapoliopele is
induced, against her first instinct, to bring the girl back to life. For the
first time in the story, we see Hiʻiakaikapoliopele's ability to use medicine. That power to heal and to bring the dead back to life is a recurring theme in the moʻolelo.

Hiʻiakaikapoliopele and Wahineʻōmaʻo travel from Maui to Molokaʻi,
through Oʻahu, and finally to Kauaʻi. They have several important
encounters and adventures but no instances of hula until their arrival
at Lohiʻau's land. Lohiʻau has died; he committed suicide when Pele
did not return. His spirit is hovering in the cliffs above his home.
Hiʻiakaikapoliopele does not go directly to him, however. She first
observes a man named Malaehaakoa. He is described as ʻoʻopa (lame);
each morning his wife, Wailuanuiahoano, carries him to the shore to
fish and returns midday to carry him back to their house. Malaehaakoa
is chanting while he fishes, and Hiʻiakaikapoliopele answers one of his
chants:

> *Alaila lohe ae la o Malaehaakoa i keia leo, nana ae la o*
> *Malaehaakoa i luna, aohe ike o ia nei i ka mea nona keia leo, o*
> *ka malu nae kai uhi iho maluna oia nei, alaila, i ae keia, nou*
> *ka hoi keia la malu nui la e ka wahine ai laau o Puna....*
> (Kapihenui, 20 February 1862)

> Then, Malaehaakoa heard this voice; Malaehaakoa looked
> up but did not see the person to whom the voice belonged.
> A feeling of peace (blessing) covered over him, and then he
> said, "This great peace belongs to you, the forest-consuming
> woman of Puna [Pele]....

It is unusual for ordinary people to recognize Hiʻiakaikapoliopele;
when they do, she bestows blessings on them. Malaehaakoa sings one
more chant in return as he throws out his fishhook once more. Then

he stands up and walks briskly back to his home—Hiʻiakaikapoliopele has healed his lameness. Again, because she is recognized and respected, she exercises her healing powers. At his home, Malaehaakoa tells his wife that they must prepare a meal for the goddess, and they do so. When the meal is ready, Hiʻiakaikapoliopele and Wahineʻōmaʻo appear. Wahineʻōmaʻo eats the meal, and while she is eating, the couple dances a very long hula, which the author says is a "hula Pele," a Pele type of hula, or hula in honor of Pele. After the first three verses, Kapihenui tells us that Hiʻiakaikapoliopele likes the hula very much and whispers to Wahineʻōmaʻo to eat very slowly so that the couple will continue to perform. The author does not describe the movements of the dance nor the instruments. What is important are the words. The hula is 234 lines long. It tells of Pele's migration from Kahiki, her travels on all the major islands, and her settling on Hawaiʻi. It speaks of the akua Kāne and the akua wahine Haumea and Hiʻiakaikapoliopele, among others. Verses are punctuated with the line *"Elieli kau mai"* ("May a profound reverence alight") (Pukui and Elbert 1986:41). *"O ka pau ana ia o ka ai ana a Wahineomao, hoonuu o Wahineomao i kana wahi mea ai, pau, o ka hoonoa ana no hoi ia o ka pule a Malaehaakoa ma, oia hoi keia mele maluna."* (Kapihenui, 6 March 1862) ("Then Wahineʻōmaʻo was finished eating; Wahineʻōmaʻo had eaten heartily of her food, and when it was finished, the prayer of Malaehaakoa and his wife was freed [sent up to the deity], the prayer being the above song.")

Here hula is performed as a prayer to Pele and Hiʻiakaikapoliopele. The reader feels the affectionate relationship between the couple, particularly the man, Malaehaakoa, and the goddess. Furthermore, it is not merely friendly protocol, as we have seen previously, but also a religious ritual in which Pele is worshipped as an *akua nui* (a major deity). In this, we can see the Pele and Hiʻiaka moʻolelo functioning as counternarrative to the discourses claiming that the major gods of Hawaiʻi are male (for example, Valeri 1985:8). The counternarrative is one that celebrates female power. It is understood that in Hawaiian mele, two ways of enumerating the islands are common: The first is from Hawaiʻi Island to Niʻihau, and the other from Niʻihau to Hawaiʻi Island. The first way is associated with the story of Papa and Wākea and reinforces the hierarchy that includes female subordination to the male. Briefly and incompletely, the story is this: The couple Papa and

Wākea give birth to Hawai'i Island and then to Maui and Kaho'olawe. Papa returns to Kahiki, and while she is gone, Wākea takes up with another woman, Hina, who gives birth to Moloka'i. In retaliation, Papa sleeps with another man, Lua, and bears O'ahu. The couple then reunites, and finally Papa has the islands of Kaua'i and Ni'ihau. The islands are born in order, from east to west.

In that same origin story, Wākea, the sky father, conspires with the male *kahuna* to institute the *'ai kapu,* in which men are separated from women while eating and also during certain nights of the month. Wākea does this because he wants to sleep with their daughter, Ho'ohōkūkalani, and does not want Papa to know about it. Ho'ohōkūkalani gives birth to the taro, Hāloa, and then to the first man, also named Hāloa. Jeanette Marie Mageo (2001:26) has analyzed these kinds of stories: "When you hear origin stories, you know there is an attempt to establish a hierarchy....Origins establish a social order and are well-springs of authority." This tale—beloved as it is because it conveys the metaphorical familial relationship of Kānaka 'Ōiwi to the older sibling, the taro, and to the earth and sky—nevertheless can be read as the one that legitimates female subordination to male authority in the Hawaiian religious system. The Pele stories and mele, on the other hand—by literally coming from the other direction, enumerating the islands by reiterating her migration from west to east, from Ni'ihau to Hawai'i—disrupt this narrative and assert an unruly female power.[7]

After receiving this tribute from Malaehaakoa and Wailuanuia-hoano, Hi'iakaikapoliopele goes to find Lohi'au and brings him back to life. The three begin their journey back to Pele on Hawai'i Island. When they arrive at Honolulu, they hear that a night's entertainment, the *kilu* game, is planned for that evening by the ali'i wahine, Pele'ula. In kilu, players chant and hula and then slide a stone or coconut cup to try to hit a post. To win, a player must accurately hit the post ten times. Two teams alternate turns, each side first performing a chant and/or hula and then sliding the kilu. Lohi'au is well known as a talented player of this game. For this and other reasons, Hi'iakaikapoliopele decides that the company should stop and take part in this entertainment.

Hi'iakaikapoliopele uses her magical powers to cause Lohi'au to lose. When he loses, *"o ka hula ka uku o ka eo ana"* (Kapihenui 17 April

1862) ("hula was the penalty for losing"). After he performs a little, *"ke mahalo nei na mea a pau o loko o ua hale kilu nei, no ka lea o Lohiau i ka hula. O Hiiakaikapoliopele kekahi e mahalo nei i ka lea o ua kane nei a laua i ka hula"* (Kapihenui, 17 April 1862) ("everyone in the *kilu* house appreciated how entertaining Lohiʻau was at hula. Hiʻiaka also appreciated how pleasing their man was at hula.").

While Peleʻula is aroused with desire for Lohiʻau, Lohiʻau is thinking of Hiʻiakaikapoliopele. True to his name (*Lohiʻau* meaning "to be slow"), he still has not fully recognized that Hiʻiakaikapoliopele is a goddess, nor does he realize the danger he is in, that he is about to die at Pele's hands. He naively wants to give up the journey to Pele and return to Kauaʻi with Hiʻiakaikapoliopele. Hiʻiakaikapoliopele desires him also but wants to wait until they arrive at Kīlauea so that she can avenge the killing of Hōpoe by defiantly making love to Lohiʻau in front of Pele. This sequence of hula kilu is the only one in the moʻolelo with overt sexual content. The emphasis in the game is on *leʻaleʻa,* which, in addition to "entertainment" and "amusement," also means "sexual pleasure" (Pukui and Elbert 1986:198). Unlike the foreigners' idea of hula, the *women,* Peleʻula and Hiʻiakaikapoliopele, are filled with desire when witnessing the handsome man performing the dance. The text suggests that the players of the game would usually end such an evening with sexual activity. It was up to the winner to decide whether he or she wanted to sleep with the opponent. This evening was different because Hiʻiakaikapoliopele wanted to keep Lohiʻau away from all other women because of Pele's kapu (taboo) on him and her own plan for revenge. This is the last instance of hula in the moʻolelo.

CONCLUSION

In entering the world of the moʻolelo, we find that hula is a part of daily life as protocol and as entertainment that creates bonds of affection between visitors and hosts, among community members, and between individuals and their gods. Hula can be performed as prayer or as part of a night's games of seduction. Study of this moʻolelo makes it clear that the indigenous tradition of hula was an important part of life in traditional times. To the nineteenth-century Kanaka reader and to the generations before, hula was profoundly spiritual but also entertaining and, at times, sexy.

What hula never appears to be is a trade; never is it performed in exchange for goods. Never in the moʻolelo do women perform this dance for the titillation of men. It is a very different world from the European/American dance hall in which sailors paid to see women dancing. This other world is possibly even more dangerous to the "civilizing" project. In the world of Pele and Hiʻiakaikapoliopele, women have power: They act on their desires, they travel, they kill, and they heal. Viewing hula in this context enables us to see that missionaries such as Emerson felt compelled to ban hula not only because it celebrates a rival religion and created obstacles for the colonial capitalist economy but also because a major missionary goal was to discipline female sexuality and restrict female power in order to establish patriarchy. It was equally important to him to attempt to ban the moʻolelo as well, which possibly had as much power as hula and much more lasting power after it appeared in print.

The emergence of the moʻolelo in print was clearly in response to both legal and cultural imperialism being put into place by puritanical, and capitalist, missionaries. It was a refusal on the part of Kānaka ʻŌiwi to despise their ancient culture and was, instead, a way to celebrate the artistry of the oral traditions and of the hula itself. It was a way to keep the traditions alive during times when the public performance of hula and chant was not permitted. The moʻolelo talked back to the oppressive colonial powers in indirect yet powerful ways. As important, the moʻolelo was being read by thousands of people across the entire archipelago, binding them together as a *lāhui*. It also, however indirectly, reminded women that their female ancestors were powerful and that there were alternatives to being subordinated to men.

From this time until its demise in 1948, moʻolelo of various genres were published continually in the Hawaiian-language press. Both hula and moʻolelo play important roles in the shared consciousness of Kanaka Maoli today as we attempt to recover from the devastation of colonialism. The emergence of the moʻolelo now is part of the new movement to revitalize the language and the culture. Continuing research into the moʻolelo and mele informs contemporary hula practice (Stillman 2002).

This and other moʻolelo are also important politically because they celebrate (and explain) our ancestors' close and affectionate relationship to the *'āina* (land). More of our 'āina is being occupied by the US military than ever before, and even more is being taken over and destroyed by "development." The mo'olelo inspire us to seek indigenous ways of governing ourselves as we work to protect ourselves and the 'āina from the contemporary neocolonial processes. The greater understanding of the thought of *ka po'e kahiko* (the ancient ones) from hula traditions and mo'olelo can be a powerful force in our decolonization.

Acknowledgments

I am grateful to Houston Wood, Jorge Fernandes, and Lia Keawe for reading several versions of this chapter, to Sally Engle Merry and the other advanced seminar participants for sharing their insights and assistance, and to Anne Keala Kelly, *ku'ualoha ho'omanawanui,* and Gabrielle Welford for helpful conversations about it. *Mahalo nui* also to John Charlot and to Joan Hori, curator of the Hawaiian collection of Hamilton Library at the University of Hawai'i at Mānoa.

Notes

1. These influential teachers were 'Ekela Kanī'aupi'o-Crozier, Sam L. No'eau Warner, and Tuti Kanahele.

2. I have added diacriticals to names where such spelling is now standard, e.g., Hi'iakaikapoliopele, or where the meaning is readily apparent, e.g., Kānepu'u. Otherwise I have left the spelling of all names as they appear in the original text.

3. All translations are my own.

4. I have checked the available indexes, including the Bishop Museum's Hawaiian Language Newspaper Index, the Hawaiian Language Newspaper Index Project of the Native Hawaiian Culture and Arts Program (NHCAP), and John Charlot's extensive bibliography, and I have spot-checked the early papers.

5. See Kanahele and Wise (n.d.) for a complete explanation of the importance of the land in this and other songs for Pele and Hi'iakaikapoliopele.

6. Some of this account is taken from another version, Bush and Paaluhi (1893), because an installment of the 1862 version (January 30) is missing from the microfilm. Except for the very beginning, the two versions are nearly identical.

7. I am indebted to No'eau Warner for his insight into the significance of the different ways the islands are enumerated.

5

Law and Identity in an American Colony

Sally Engle Merry

Law is a crucial element in the constitution of ethnic identities, creating affinities and oppositions, inclusion and exclusion. Comparing Hawai'i to Fiji demonstrates dramatically how legal arrangements constitute ethnic relationships and conflicts. The designation of citizenship and of rights to land differed significantly in the two places, leaving legacies of ethnic tension and crisis of quite different configuration. Fiji and Hawai'i developed under the regime of chiefdoms and shifted to sugar plantation capitalism and nationalism in the nineteenth century. Differences in colonial legal regulations, however, produced dramatically different ethnic relationships and tensions. Hawai'i has not polarized on the basis of ethnicity to the same extent as Fiji, nor is there a history of violent ethnic conflict, with the exception of the white settler coup of 1893. There are enduring inequalities among ethnic groups in Hawai'i but not sharply bounded, politicized ethnic communities. On the other hand, the Native Hawaiians' desire for political autonomy and land remains unsatisfied, in contrast to the success of ethnic Fijians in retaining political power and control over land. Unlike Fiji, where Riles (Chapter 7, this volume) shows that the difficulty of inserting Part-Europeans into the nationality structure of colonial Fiji provoked crises in governmental knowledge and relegated them to marginal statuses, people in Hawai'i of mixed Hawaiian, Chinese, and white ancestry were gradually absorbed into the category of local and then indigenous. In conjunction with the chapters that discuss Fiji, this chapter demonstrates how changing legal arrangements governing landownership and political participation produced ethnic affiliations and conflicts.

This chapter traces the evolution of ethnic identity in Hawai'i through the social and legal history of the past two centuries. It looks at the legal constitution of identity as a historical phenomenon. It examines the construction of ethnicity in the light of shifting legal definitions of personhood to show the significance of law in forming these identities. This illuminates how other forms of identity emerged as oppositional. Whereas some ethnic affiliations were based on legal categories such as citizenship and rights to political participation, others emerged in reaction to the dominant structuring of identity and power. They were formed as oppositional structures of inclusion and exclusion: ways that subordinated groups distanced themselves from powerful groups and denigrated those groups' claims to belonging in the islands. This chapter discusses the nineteenth-century transition from chiefdom to nation, the impact of the exclusion of Asians from citizenship and equal status on the plantations, the emergence of Japanese-dominated electoral politics in the 1950s, and the growth of the separatist Hawaiian sovereignty movement in the 1980s and 1990s.

Four principles underlie the designation of ethnic identity in Hawai'i: genealogy, nationality, residence, and indigeneity. Nationality and indigeneity have clear legal grounding, but genealogy predates nation-state law, and residence emerged in opposition to it. *Genealogy* emphasizes descent and connections to the land. It developed during the two thousand years Polynesians lived in the islands before Europeans arrived. As is common within chiefdoms, rank and spiritual power depend on ancestry, kinship relationships, and actions (see Collier, Chapter 2, this volume). During the nineteenth century, this system gave way to liberalism and the conception of the nation-state, while the second principle of identity, nationality, assumed increasing importance. *Nationality* has several meanings, of which the two major ones are citizenship in a polity and national origin in the sense of a primordial, racialized identity. *Residence,* the concept of "local," refers to birth and rearing in the islands. It appeared in the early twentieth century in opposition to the growing economic and political dominance of the white elite. The language of "local" emphasized long-term residence and working-class status and asserted that local people had greater legitimacy on the land than elites and newcomers. *Indigeneity* refers to a group's priority, based on first arrival in the islands. It is a product of the late-twentieth-century, transnational indigenous rights movement that introduced the conception of an indigenous identity for people of Polynesian descent. Indigeneity separated Native Hawaiians from other locals, who were redefined as "settlers," and emphasized the division between settlers and indigenous people. It re-emphasized descent and land, two themes basic to belonging in Hawaiian chiefdoms. As Martha Kaplan points out in Chapter 6, these themes are also basic to contemporary ethnic-Fijian notions of belonging. All four of these principles appeared in Fiji as well, although the concept of local was far less important there.

LAW AND ETHNIC IDENTITY

Ethnic identities are produced under legally constituted historical conditions. As a cultural system of meanings and identities, law sorts groups by national origin and race to determine who can be a citizen, who can own land, who can run for office, and who can consume alcohol. Law defines identities such as "alien" or "contract laborer" and in various ways allocates access to schools, jobs, and citizenship. Particular regulations such as permission for immigrant males to bring women with them have profound effects on the formation of families and ethnic communities. Regulations about naturalization and citizenship similarly affect the way an immigrant group can move to a mainstream social position. The use of the legal form brings legitimacy and state power to dominant groups who deploy it in acquiring and extending their control over the wider society.

Law plays a critical role in defining personhood because of its capacity to draw on concepts of rationality. As Collier, Maurer, and Suarez-Navaz (1995) have argued, social contract theory defines some people, usually those with property, as subjects of law and capable of rational action, but others are understood to be governed by custom or nature. As Collier (Chapter 2, this volume) notes, the logic of liberal capitalism links personhood with property, so only through controlling property (even if this property is no more than one's own labor) can one claim autonomy and therefore equality with others. In nineteenth-century Hawai'i, whites arrogated to themselves the mantle of rationality and adulthood and welcomed Hawaiians into this sphere if they were willing to convert to Christianity, become literate, and remain sexually constrained in marriage—that is, to conform to "civilized" Christian behavior. By the end of the nineteenth century, to be entrusted with governance of the state, it was also necessary to be male and to hold property. The political and legal systems the whites established allowed Hawaiians to be admitted as equals under these conditions. If they failed to acquire and hold property, the whites redefined them as children, incapable of rational behavior, although not alien. This new conception of adulthood justified protracted efforts at social reform of those Hawaiians apparently (to the whites) unable to govern themselves.

In contrast, the whites viewed the peoples from China, Japan, Korea, and the Philippines as unalterably alien. When whites gained effective political control of the Kingdom in 1887, they insisted that Asians be denied the right to become naturalized citizens and, implicitly, to be seen as responsible, self-governing persons. Chinese, Japanese, Koreans, Filipinos, and Portuguese were the major groups brought to the Kingdom of Hawai'i to work on the sugar plantations during the nineteenth century. Arriving as contract laborers under three-year contracts, they were subject to penal sanctions for failure to work. Although this was a quasi-slave status, when the contract was completed, they were free to take other employment. Many did, either on the plantation or in farming, fishing, or urban occupations. Viewed as labor units instead of potential citizens, the Asian workers were understood as separate and "other" rather than as childlike. Thus, the division between Hawaiians and Asians paralleled that between Fijians and Indians in labor status and in the whites' conceptions of their rationality and responsibility.

After annexation to the United States in 1900, elite whites realized that even though the immigrants were excluded from citizenship by laws against the naturalization of non-whites, under US law their children would be citizens capable of voting. As the number of Japanese Americans increased, some whites feared that they would lose political power to what they labeled a new "racial voting bloc." New concerns were voiced about the resistance of the Japanese community to assimilation, their failure to marry non-Japanese, and their commitment to Japanese-language schools for their children. With the increasing dominance of the military in the 1920s and 1930s, first- and even second-generation Japanese were defined as a security threat, based on fears that they would be loyal to Japan rather than to the United States in the event of a war (Okihiro 1991). This way of thinking emphasized the alien status of Asians, underscoring their inability to participate politically in the nation. In response, Asian Americans claimed for themselves the mantle of law and rationality, talking in terms of rights and democracy in early union movements and in electoral politics after World War II.[1] Facing discriminatory social practices, Japanese Americans responded by claiming citizenship and rights. The participation of Japanese Americans in World War II greatly facilitated their acceptance as citizens and their entrance into electoral politics. Kelly and Kaplan (2001:64–81) contrast their experience with that of the Indo-Fijians who refused to join the war, claiming discriminatory treatment. Although ethnic Fijians fought energetically for the British Empire in World War II to "prove" themselves to the whites, as did the Japanese in Hawai'i, the Indo-Fijians resisted (Lal 1002:117–121). Of course, second-generation Japanese Americans were already citizens and able to vote on a common roll at the same time that the Indo-Fijians were marginalized by their exclusion from landownership and the communal, racialized system of voting.

Thus, the relationship between the colonizing whites in Hawai'i and the Native Hawaiians was sharply different from the relationship between whites and Asian Americans. The Hawaiians could be incorporated into the realm of the civilized as long as they were willing to reform their social practices. Frequent intermarriage between Hawaiians and whites underscored this incorporation. Adult civilized status, however, was always contingent on conduct and was frequently withheld, and even political participation became circumscribed by property and gender. Asians, in contrast, were always treated as alien by the dominant whites. When they failed to assimilate as rapidly as the whites desired, they were deemed a threat to national security (see Okihiro 1991). The discourse of nationality underscored the whites' conception that these groups were fundamentally different. Ethnicity was called "nationality" in Hawai'i, a term that referred to an essentialized, racialized conception of national origin.

The struggle over incorporation and identity was about claims to rationality and self-governance and their intersection with race. Those who promoted the rule of law and claimed to be governed by law—the whites, in this case—simultaneously asserted their own capacity for self-governance on the basis of race and property ownership. Native Hawaiians, in contrast, had to prove their rationality and social adulthood through personal conduct and property ownership and achieve adult status in a more contingent way. Perhaps this is why legal strategies are now so central to the Hawaiian sovereignty movement (see Osorio, Chapter 8, this volume). Those who were denied admission as citizens on the basis of race (nationality) were deemed unfit to participate at all in the governance of the community. By the late nineteenth century, the ideas of personhood and responsibility promoted by the economically and politically dominant whites crystallized the notion of ethnic identity as nationality. This identity designated some individuals as full members of Hawaiian society on the basis of birth and race while underscoring the permanent alien status of those newly arrived from other countries.

As Linnekin and Poyer (1990:7–9) note, the nationality model is based on a western conception of ethnicity as natural, unambiguous, and rooted in the blood, whereas Oceanic conceptions foreground social relationships, shared social activities, and shared place. Howard (1990:263–268) contrasts a European (colonial) perspective emphasizing genetic inheritance with an Oceanic view recognizing the importance of genealogical transmission but also common substance on the basis of being fed or nurtured by the same source. The Oceanic model stresses a person's specific relational history and place, along with the history of that place. There is a strong emphasis on the land—the place of rearing. Yet, under pressures of colonialism and cohabitation with peoples who hold more European ideas of ethnicity and deploy these conceptions to allocate rights and privileges, there is a tendency to adopt more biologically based conceptions (Howard 1990:267). Thus, conceptions of ethnicity for Native Hawaiians are quite different from race and nationality but are under pressure to become more similar.

FROM CHIEFDOM TO NATIONALITY
IN THE NINETEENTH CENTURY

In the eighteenth century, membership in the chiefdoms of the Hawaiian Islands depended on descent and connections to the land. In the mid-nineteenth century, non-genealogically connected individuals could become members of the Hawaiian Kingdom by swearing an oath of loyalty and renouncing loyalty to any other political entity (see Osorio, Chapter 8, this volume). Nationality here referred to membership in a political entity on the basis of loyalty. However, by the late 1880s, under pressure from Americans, the Kingdom's laws became more exclusionary on the basis of race. With the increasing economic ascendancy of Americans and Europeans at the end of the nineteenth century, access to voting, political power, and adult status was restricted to wealthy male whites and Hawaiians, and after the 1893 overthrow, to Hawaiians willing to swear loyalty to the new government.[2] By the end of the nineteenth century, a new language of nationality became more important as the Kingdom was overthrown and replaced by a republic based on the political structures and legal arrangements of the United States. Following the US model, *nationality* became a code word for *race*, referring to a discrete racial identity with presumed attached cultural characteristics marked by country of origin. In the Republic (1893–1898) and Territory (1898–1959) periods in Hawai'i, the exclusion of non-whites from citizenship via naturalization was very important in maintaining the status of Chinese and Japanese as outsiders. The shifting relations of power during the twentieth century, including the incorporation of Hawai'i into the United States as a colony and then as a state, further altered forms of membership and exclusion, giving rise to new configurations of ethnic identity. Although non-whites were excluded from naturalized citizenship during the early part of the twentieth century, their Hawai'i-born children were citizens with equal rights to participate in politics and with the ability to vote on a common roll regardless of their ethnic identity.

Earlier, for the Polynesian migrants to the Hawaiian Islands, membership had depended on genealogy and kin ties. At the time of the Europeans' arrival in 1778, they had developed, over a period of 1,500 years, highly stratified chiefdoms, with privileges and responsibilities allocated to various ranks and authority concentrated in the highest-ranking chiefs, or *ali'i* (Kirch 1985; Sahlins 1992; Ellis 1969; Kamakau 1961; see also Merry 2000). This system joined political and religious authority. Most people worked the land as commoners, or *maka'āinana,* and a small chiefly class of ali'i controlled the land on which maka'āinana had use rights. Patterns of conquest and succession led to redistribution of lands within the chiefly class, although the maka'āinana were not generally evicted in these land transfers (Wise 1933). Chiefly rank and distinction were articulated through a system of *kapu* that demarcated various statuses, including those of men and women, regulating their relations to one another. Local communities of commoners were governed by rules focusing on respect and reciprocal obligations (Kame'eleihiwa 1992; Kamakau 1961; Sahlins 1992). Thus, membership in society depended on genealogy (which determined rank) and location on the land. Those who had established several generations' residence on the land had stronger claims on it and became known as *kama'aina,* "people of the land" (Sahlins 1992).

After Captain Cook's arrival in Hawai'i in 1778, the islands became convenient watering and restocking sites for the European and American merchants engaged in the China trade and the fur trade in the Northwest Coast (Sahlins 1992). By 1820, the ali'i were deeply in debt to merchants who supplied them with generous quantities of silks, porcelains, and clothing in exchange for promises of sandalwood harvested from the mountains, available in ever-dwindling amounts. As Collier notes in Chapter 2, under the logic of chiefdoms, the chiefs sought to gain power through incorporating the goods of the Westerners. The introduction of guns spawned devastating wars that unified the islands under a single paramount chief, Kamehameha, by 1810. In 1819, the ruling chief, Liholiho, declared that the kapu on men and women eating together was broken, in effect dismantling much of the political-religious system undergirding chiefly authority (see Valeri 1990). The ravages of introduced diseases and rum decreased the population by three-quarters in the first forty years after contact, according to the reports of a missionary touring the islands in 1823 (Ellis 1969; see Stannard 1989). This population decline produced a crisis in the logic of chiefdoms and probably hurried the transition to nationhood.

The first contingent of New England missionaries, arriving in 1820, interpreted the abolition of the kapu system as an act of God, reinforcing their belief that they were carrying out God's mission to the heathen. These missionaries, predominantly Congregational, brought with them a stern moral code that condemned all sexual activity outside marriage, as well as strong drink, gambling, and forms of recreation and spiritual practice involving bodily display, such as dancing, surfing, and swimming. They demanded rigid adherence to the Sabbath as a day of rest and set high standards of social and sexual conduct as the threshold for membership in their churches. In the giddy years of the 1820s, they overcame initial resistance and in 1823 succeeded in converting Keopualani, the most sacred chieftess, on her deathbed and in 1825 several other powerful chiefs (Sinclair 1969:8). The American missionaries quickly became influential advisors to the ruling chiefs. To the ali'i, the missionaries spoke for a new and powerful god, Jehovah. It was common practice for a chief or king to select a god from the vast pantheon of deities as his personal god, to build temples to him and make offerings in the hope of support for his endeavors. Conversion to Christianity meant adopting the new god Jehovah, consonant with existing political-religious practices (Sahlins 1992). The new religion offered a way to return the troubled Kingdom to a state of *pono* (righteousness) and counter the massive and frightening depopulation (Kame'eleihiwa 1992).

American advisors brought liberal ideas of the nation and the rule of law to Hawai'i between 1825 and 1852. Appropriating the Anglo-American legal system seemed a route to sovereignty in an imperialist world. It enabled the *mo'i* (king) to deal with the squabbling merchants in Honolulu and to present the Kingdom to the world as a civilized nation under the rule of law. The whites proposed their own legal system as the legitimate basis for the emerging colonial social order. Using concepts of civilization and rationality, *haole* (white) lawyers from New England and missionaries employed by the Kingdom encouraged the sovereign Kingdom of Hawai'i to adopt their legal institutions and codes. Laws modeled on American prototypes created the conditions of land ownership and labor power that made possible the transition to capitalist agriculture. Anglo-American whites, in conjunction with Hawaiian elites, also used the law to reform Hawaiian patterns of sexuality and marriage, alcohol consumption, and gambling, a process I have discussed in more detail elsewhere (Merry 2000).

The Kingdom of Hawai'i established a unitary instead of a dual legal system in the mid-nineteenth century, incorporating both whites and Native Hawaiians as equals. This unitary system was unusual because, at the time, colonial policies in other parts of the world favored dual systems that subjected each group to a separate legal system (for example, see Roberts and Mann 1991; Mamdani 1996). The United States intervened in Hawai'i under the rubric of a republican and liberal regime, not the paternalistic, restrictive one characteristic of much British colonialism, including that in the Pacific. The Hawaiian incorporation into empire was led by a group of white missionaries who endeavored to include Hawaiians in Anglo-American legal and political institutions as relatively equal participants, as long as they were willing to convert to Christianity and transform their way of life. Inspired by abolitionist sentiments, these influential whites resisted creating separate legal and political institutions for whites and Native Hawaiians. There was to be only one system, but it was an Anglo-American one. Marriage and sexuality were governed by Christian laws that criminalized adultery and fornication and prohibited divorce under most circumstances. To settle for a separate legal system was to surrender the hope of transforming conduct. This approach drove Hawaiian customary law and practices underground, where they survived in rural areas or in close-knit urban communities.

The unitary legal system severely undermined Hawaiian land ownership and kinship arrangements and dismantled the chiefly system and its rituals of respect, or kapu. Moreover, it dramatically changed land use and labor patterns. In 1848, the king was persuaded to convert chiefly titles to land historically allocated through use-rights to followers into fee-simple ownership, leading to a massive and permanent division of the lands among the chiefs, called the *Mahele* (Wise 1933; Chinen 1958; Kelly 1980; Lam 1985; Kame'eleihiwa 1992; Sahlins 1992). The common people were allowed to petition for ownership of the lands they worked, but for a variety of reasons, few did. At the same time, the government allowed foreigners to purchase land. The land quickly passed out of the hands of both aliʻi and makaʻāinana, reducing many to the status of landless laborers (Osorio 2002). In 1850, the government also adopted legal regulations for importing foreign labor under contracts enforced by the penal system. Access to land and labor fueled the growth of the sugar plantation economy, increasingly controlled by whites. The result was a dramatic shift in landownership from chiefly Hawaiians to whites, only some of whom were citizens. By 1896, 57 percent of the land area paying taxes belonged to whites, and Native Hawaiians owned only 14 percent of the taxable land (Morgan 1948:139, n. 59). At midcentury, many white missionaries, missionary children, merchants, and bankers present in the islands began to buy up large tracts of land that became the basis of personal fortunes. For example, in 1882 William Shipman, son of a missionary, and two partners bought 64,275 acres for $20,000 near Hilo from the estate of the deceased King Lunalilo, an area of land Shipman expanded in the 1880s and 1890s, forming the basis for the family's vast future wealth (Cahill 1996:165–166, 189).

By 1876, the booming sugar-plantation economy demanded a larger labor supply than the dwindling Hawaiian population could provide. Decades of labor importation from Asia and Europe produced an extraordinarily heterogeneous community by the turn of the century: Plantation regions consisted of a largely Chinese, Japanese, and Portuguese labor force under the management of predominantly American and British supervisors and plantation managers. By 1887, the economic power of whites was sufficient to impose a new constitution on the monarchy with a far more restrictive suffrage, limiting the vote to men with property at a level that excluded many Hawaiians and denying Japanese and Chinese the vote that had been promised to Japanese under the Hawaiian-Japanese Treaty of 1871 (Fuchs 1961:29; Okihiro 1991:57; Takaki 1983:73). The 1893 overthrow, a white settler coup supported by US forces, and the 1900 annexation to the United States encountered considerable Hawaiian resistance through petitions (Silva 1997) and military endeavors. Nevertheless, this ended Hawaiian sovereignty, although not the desire for sovereignty.

At annexation in 1900, white leaders resisted universal male suffrage and tried to retain the restricted suffrage of the Republic (1893–1898), arguing that the Hawaiians were like children and could not be trusted with the vote (Fuchs 1961:39). Because American laws denied naturalization to Asian immigrants, nearly 60 percent of Hawai'i's population at the time of annexation was disenfranchised (Okihiro 1991:13). Antagonism to Chinese and Japanese had taken on the essentialized understandings of race characteristic of the United States at this time. This was an era of increasing nativism and exclusionism, marked by the passage of laws in California in 1913 that prohibited aliens from owning land, thus denying land ownership to all non-white groups excluded from naturalization (Takaki 1989:203).[3]

In the Territory period, the notion of citizenship based on loyalty to the king pledged by oath gave way to a new conception based on race. Under this system, so-called alien races were permanently excluded from citizenship. The language of nationality was applied predominantly to the imported workers on the plantations, although the dominant whites also described Europeans and Hawaiians in terms of nationality. As you will see in the next section, these national origin identities served as the basis for the social order of the plantations. In contrast to the earlier Polynesian notion that identity depended on genealogy, loyalty, and attachment to the land, this new discourse emphasized birth, race, and nation. Nation was a primordial category and, like race, was unchanged by alterations in citizenship. A second-generation citizen of Japanese or Portuguese ancestry was still referred to as "Japanese" or "Portuguese." The terms are widely used without hyphens (for example, "Japanese-American") because they really mean race, not membership in a national polity. Because everyone had a racialized national identity, there was a sense of equality to the system: Everyone had a nationality. However, sharp economic and political differences existed among these racial/nationality groups. The discourse of nationality remained powerful during the first four decades of the twentieth century. By the late twentieth century, it had morphed into a new discourse of multiculturalism, a system in which everyone has a culture and therefore can still be conceived as equal but different.

THE PLANTATION ERA OF THE EARLY TWENTIETH CENTURY: THE HEGEMONY OF NATIONALITY

The plantation era of the early twentieth century solidified the notion of racialized nationality as the basis for ethnic identity, encoding nationality in a wide array of legal and customary regulations. Asian Americans were typically descendants of people who arrived as plantation laborers and faced the exclusionary practices denying Asians citizenship and subjecting them to unequal pay and working conditions on the plantations.[4] After formal annexation in 1900, the contract labor law was eliminated, but planters continued to deploy legal strategies in their increasingly intense struggles with workers. During the 1920s, the Hawaii Sugar Planters Association (HSPA) helped the planters to act in concert to break strikes. Plantations employed local law enforcement officials or hired their own deputies to put down strikes and evict strikers from their plantation houses.[5]

From annexation until 1946, a small, interrelated group of haole businessmen exerted enormous political and economic power over a numerous and heterogeneous non-propertied class (Fuchs 1961; Okihiro 1991:13). Island politics revolved around the delegate to Congress, the governor appointed by the US president, and the territorial legislature. During the 1930s, the so-called Big Five companies controlled thirty-six of the Territory's thirty-eight sugar plantations, as well as banking, insurance, transportation, utilities, and wholesale and retail merchandising. Interlocking directorates, intermarriages, and social associations bound this financial oligarchy closely together. By 1940, a dozen or so men managed the economy. During the Territory period, fewer than eighty individuals owned almost half the land, and the government owned most of the rest, producing a concentration of wealth and power more extreme than elsewhere in the United States (Fuchs 1961; Okihiro 1991:14–15; Kent 1983). These white elites conceptualized work on the plantations in terms of gender and nationality, assigning specific jobs to members of particular nationalities typically conceived as racially suited to a specific kind of work (see Merry 2000). Nationality and race were interchangeable in this form of ethnic categorization. By 1923, one white commentator noted that "there are practically no Anglo-Saxon laborers in Hawaii, or at least no field-laborers. The Anglo-Saxon element is of exceptional quality. The men who control the industries are largely of 'Old American,' British, German, and Scandinavian stock" (Sullivan 1923:533).

The white planter elite also linked nationality to particular patterns of labor unrest and criminality. A 1903 report on the conditions of contract labor in Hawai'i published by the American Economic Association soon after annexation clearly reflects planter perceptions (Coman 1903). In the author's preface, she thanks prominent white leaders for assistance, implying that the report reflects their views. In 1901, 27,531 of the 39,587 plantation laborers were Japanese. The author noted that an "epidemic of strikes" occurred immediately after the end of the contract labor system and that of twenty-two strikes recorded in 1900, twenty were by plantation laborers, all of whom were Japanese (Coman 1903:47). The demands of the strikers, she says, throw "a good deal of light on the aspirations of the inscrutable Jap" (1903:47). These demands were, not surprisingly, for higher wages and better working and living conditions. Yet, she reports that the Japanese were never entirely satisfactory laborers: "From the outset they were difficult to deal with, proving to be restless and self-assertive to a degree hitherto unknown in the cane fields of Hawaii" (1903:45). Moreover, the Japanese workers left the plantations for the skilled trades even more rapidly than the Chinese (1903:46). "As a race, these men are restless, ambitious, and eager for change. In marked contrast to the patient, industrious Chinaman, the Japanese is quick to take offense, ready with his fists and altogether a difficult and unreliable employee" (1903:59). In a discourse redolent of future accusations of resistance to assimilation, Coman complains that the Japanese were "remarkably clannish, clubbing together for the championship of their common interests in a way that was distinctly embarrassing. They showed no disposition to marry with the Hawaiians, and, while readily adopting American dress and ways, cherished allegiance to their native land with peculiar tenacity.... The danger that Hawaii might be orientalized was greater than in the days of unstinted Chinese immigration" (1903:46–47). Coman's depiction is intriguingly similar to British colonial views of Indians in Fiji during the same period (Kelly 1991, 1997).

Okihiro (1991:79–86) documents the widespread portrayal of Japanese as anxious to take control of the islands, nationalistic, resistant to assimilation, and threatening to "Japanize this American territory," spearheaded by military leaders and some civilian white leaders in Hawai'i, particularly after the 1920 strike. As white leaders recognized that in time there would be large numbers of voters of Japanese ancestry and that there was a threat of military conflict with Japan, rhetoric about the "Japanese menace" escalated. The Japanese became a national security problem (Okihiro 1991:101).

In the context of this intense racism and discrimination, some Japanese began to speak the language of rights and equality, of citizenship and nation (Fuchs 1961:129). They referred not to a racially defined grouping but to a political entity. Fuchs (1961:219) notes that at the time of the earliest union movements of the 1910s, some Japanese organizers were talking about their rights and equality, even as their opponents were complaining about the inability of Japanese to assimilate to the American way. They sought membership in the nation through claims to legal rights and citizenship and rejected the racialized designation of membership in the nation. Pablo Manlapit, a prominent Filipino labor leader in the 1924 strike, also articulated his goals as American: "The keynote of Americanism, for the laborer, is the opportunity to advance—to better his condition. It is one of the cherished American ideals that each generation shall stand in advance of the preceding one, better physically, mentally, spiritually. And America demands for her workers this opportunity for development" (quoted in Kerkvliet 1996:8). The sugar planters, however, brought a series of questionable legal charges against Manlapit and finally had him imprisoned (Kerkvliet 1996:9).

Schoolteachers also brought ideas of rights and equality to the plantation workers. Fuchs (1961:263–298) emphasizes the impact of public school education on children in Hawai'i in the 1920s and 1930s as they learned the principles of equality before the law, liberty, and democracy—ideas starkly at odds with the tightly controlled and closed racial hierarchy in which they lived. In his novel about plantation life, Murayama (1988:33) describes a plantation schoolteacher, a haole newcomer from the mainland, trying to persuade his Japanese American students to support the Filipino strikers in the 1937 strike. The teacher is astounded by the feudal nature of society and by the way the plantations effectively use divide-and-rule techniques to separate ethnic groups.

The union movement mobilized rights language and used legal forms such as petitions in the earliest strikes in the twentieth century (Fuchs 1961:219, 223; Okihiro 1991:48–51). In the 1909 strike, workers' demands for higher wages were framed in terms of equal rights: "Is it not a matter of simple justice, and moral duty to give [the] same wages and same treatment to laborers of equal efficiency, irrespective of race, color, creed, nationality, or previous condition of servitude?" (Okihiro 1991:50). The planters responded by evicting the striking workers from plantation housing. By 1910, union leaders argued that the plantation was "undemocratic and un-American" and charged plantations with discrimination (Fuchs 1961:117–118). In 1920, the strikers were even more explicitly American in their claims. Although some Japanese used respect and humility to achieve acceptance, others advocated using strikes and the courts (Fuchs 1961:126–127, 131, 219). As Okihiro (1991:55) notes, the irony for Japanese workers was that their desire to become Americans through demands for equality indicated their Americanization, but they were labeled foreigners, undesirables, and seditionists. There were also substantial efforts to regulate the Japanese-language schools created by Japanese families to teach their children, yet successful lawsuits by Japanese plaintiffs thwarted white efforts to eliminate these schools.[6]

One of the early labor struggles was between the dockworkers in Hilo and the local police, who opened fire on a group of strikers in 1938, precipitating the Hilo "massacre." Although no one was killed, several were severely wounded. One of these, Bert Nakano, went on to a long career as a union organizer. In 1991, he told me in an interview how difficult it was to get on to the plantations to speak to the workers in the 1940s, and he described the enthusiasm of the workers for the union message. Laws passed by the territorial legislature in 1923 and 1925 prohibited trespassing on plantations and interference with the "right to work," imposing criminal penalties on those who entered plantations without permission. These laws were frequently used to exclude labor organizers (Okihiro 1991:99–100). Martin Pence, a midwestern white lawyer, described in an interview in 1992 how plantations on windward Hawai'i fought to keep him away from their workers in 1937, as he was campaigning for himself and for Tom Okino, one of the first Japanese American candidates for political office.

During this period, the first forty years of the twentieth century, the old haole/Hawaiian alliance persisted, although uneasily. This alliance was premised on a religious, social, and cultural linkage between haoles and Hawaiians dating back to the missionary days, an alliance frequently cemented by marriages between white men and Hawaiian women. It was reinforced by the unitary legal system, with its commitment to the incorporation of Hawaiians into white society if they converted to Christianity and adopted practices the whites defined as civilized. In the early twentieth century, Hawaiians held a majority of positions as judges, lawyers, and teachers and were particularly numerous in the police force (Fuchs 1961:69). In 1927, Hawaiians held 46 percent of the appointive executive positions, 55 percent of the government jobs, more than half the judgeships and elective offices, and virtually all the law enforcement positions (Fuchs 1961:162). The whites needed Hawaiian votes, essential for electoral success for the small white population at a time when the Asians were excluded from voting. However, Hawaiian aspirations for greater control over their country and for real political power were disappointed. Washington never appointed a Hawaiian as governor. Although Prince Kuhio Kalanianaole served as non-voting delegate to the US Congress for many years, he was only able to achieve the Hawaiian Homelands legislation designed to rehabilitate Hawaiians by returning them to the land (Fuchs 1961:71). Underfunded and lacking much good land, the program never adequately responded to the alienation of Hawaiian people from their lands. This uneasy Hawaiian/haole alliance excluded the alien immigrants imported to work the white-owned plantations

The 1930s to 1950s was a period of disillusion for Native Hawaiians, as their fraction of the electorate fell and their political power eroded. They were the majority of registered voters until the late 1920s and remained the largest voting bloc until 1940 (Fuchs 1961:80), but as the alliance with the haoles weakened, it no longer guaranteed political power. Meanwhile, economic conditions worsened, and Hawaiians began to fall to the bottom of the social class hierarchy. By midcentury, Hawaiians were largely abandoning the Hawaiian language and were pressured not to use it in school, in part by the predominantly Asian American schoolteachers, who were also experiencing pressures to assimilate to dominant white culture.

THE EMERGENCE OF THE "LOCAL"

During this period, Native Hawaiians, working-class whites, and working-class Asians, many of whom had plantation backgrounds, began to develop a shared identity as "local." The concept of *local* emphasized class and residence in the islands. *Local* described working-class people of color who were born in Hawai'i and spoke pidgin—the English Creole language of Hawai'i (Rosa 2000:94; Okamura 1998). Neither newcomers nor elite whites raised in the islands could speak pidgin, by and large. Local people shared a common history of oppression by the tight-knit haole elite. The identity of local blended immigrant and indigenous groups through their common experience of subordination to white elites. They used this term to mark themselves as different from the dominant haoles. Local identity was based on a cultural mosaic of island food, music, arts, and values, as well as birth and rearing in the islands. It was fostered by the creation of multiethnic labor unions in the struggle against the plantations during the 1920s to 1950s and by interethnic sociability within certain plantation camps (for example, Damaso 1996:31; Revilla 1996:57; Andaya 1996:109). The flood of mainland white tourists, military personnel, and settlers in the years after statehood further emphasized the difference between outsiders and those born and raised in the islands.

The term *local* was used throughout the twentieth century by Native Hawaiians, Asian-, Portuguese-, and Puerto Rican–descended groups to distinguish themselves from more recent immigrants, tourists, and the military (Rosa 2000:94). Developed during the Depression, it achieved sharper focus and widespread use after World War II, spurred by the emergence of an urban, multiethnic population. Incidents of white racism, such as the Massie case in 1931–1932, promoted the conception of the local. In this case, a group of local men were falsely accused of raping a white military wife. After being acquitted, they were attacked by the aggrieved husband, who killed one of them. However, the murderer received only a token sentence. As this story was told and retold over the years, it reinforced the sense of local as a subordinated but resistant identity (Rosa 2000). With the poststatehood surge of mainlanders, *local* stood for a blending of Asian and Hawaiian cultural practices that set apart these groups from the haole newcomers. This is, however, an ambiguous concept that is constantly being produced and reproduced, showing, as Ferguson and Turnbull (1999:94) argue, "anxiety about and resistance to hegemonic structures of meaning."

THE POSTWAR PERIOD: JAPANESE AMERICAN
POLITICAL ASCENDANCY

The tight grip on the economy and governance held by the small group of white elites loosened after World War II, although whites continued to dominate the economy and legal system. With the rise in numbers and political participation of the second generation of Japanese Americans, along with the 1952 Walter-McCarran Act allowing non-whites to be naturalized as citizens, the white population of Hawai'i lost political predominance in electoral politics. World War II offered nisei (second-generation) Japanese a way to prove their loyalty as citizens. The much celebrated 442nd Regiment, which fought in Europe, formed the basis of a postwar shift to Democratic Party dominance under Japanese American leadership. When questions about the patriotism of Japanese American young men obstructed their entry into the military and, as Ferguson and Turnbull (1999:159) point out, the order of mature masculinity that military service offers, they responded by appealing to rights, asserting their right to defend their nation.

Citizenship rules and demographic changes were shifting the power at the polls also. As early as the 1910s, some whites noticed that the number of Japanese voters was likely to increase, causing great anxiety (for example, Harvey-Elder 1910). The tight-knit alliance of white sugar-plantation managers and owners, financial and business leaders, and Hawaiians would no longer control political life in the future. Indeed, in the 1950s, returning war veterans and Democratic Party leaders from the mainland united to revive the Democratic Party and managed to achieve a dramatic shift in political leadership from the Republican Party to the Democratic, based largely on Japanese American voters and others disaffected with the haole elite. By 1949, 27 percent of the legislators in Hawai'i were of Japanese ancestry, and by 1955, 47 percent. This proportion continued to be nearly half until 1981, when it dropped to one-third. Japanese registered voters were 40 percent of all voters in 1961 and 46 percent in 1970 (Haas 1992:42, 43). In 1954, Democratic Party victories based on a strong Japanese vote, along with that of other ethnic groups, ended the long domination of the haole-controlled Republican Party as the Democrats gained control of both houses of the territorial legislature (Fuchs 1961; Okamura 1998:276). The 1954 election swept the Republican Party from power and replaced it with a labor-friendly Democratic Party dominated by Japanese Americans. Yet, as Cooper and Daws (1990) point out, the new Democratic leaders quickly joined forces with the whites in promoting massive land development on the islands, a project that enriched the Chinese and Japanese, as well as the whites.

Thus, despite a history of exclusion of Japanese Americans and other Asian Americans, their energetic pursuit of unionization, education, political participation, and military service enabled them to move into political prominence and higher social class positions. These victories were accomplished despite considerable resistance. For example, one of the prominent Japanese American judges in Hilo said that he was discouraged from pursuing a legal career by a teacher in the plantation school in the 1930s who felt that it was above him. One of the most successful Japanese American politicians, George Ariyoshi, who served as governor of Hawai'i from 1974 until 1986, said in a 1977 interview that because he lived in town, he had experienced far less discrimination as a child than his friends who grew up on plantations (Brown 1977:6). He felt that discrimination did not exist when he was growing up in the 1930s, but after he returned from law school on the mainland in 1952, he became aware of the barriers. As he started his law practice and tried to make a living, he relates, "I began to see the discrimination, the barriers that existed, how difficult it was for some people to rise above a certain level. No matter how competent, how able they were, they couldn't crack those barriers. Better jobs were always reserved for somebody else who was brought in from the outside, somebody who was married to the right family, running around in a certain social structure" (1977:6). He noted that his friends who grew up on plantations felt much more prejudice and recognized more fully that haoles ran things and that they were at the bottom (1977:6).

One sign of change is the increasing numbers of lawyers, judges, and police officers of Japanese ancestry. Largely dominated by Hawaiians in the early twentieth century, police departments are now hiring more Japanese Americans. Although there were virtually no Japanese lawyers in 1920, by 1992 they were 27 percent of all lawyers in the state (Haas 1992:103). In Hilo, one of the major towns, Japanese

Americans constitute a significant proportion of judges, attorneys, social workers, and police officers. The Japanese ancestry population has moved substantially into middle-class occupations, holding many professional and government jobs. As early as 1979, the median income of Japanese males was the highest of any ethnic group. In 1990, 55 percent of all civil service administrators were of Japanese ancestry; from the 1950s to the 1990s, so were nearly 40 percent of all state civil service employees (Haas 1992:39, 45, 46).

THE HAWAIIAN SOVEREIGNTY MOVEMENT AND INDIGENOUS IDENTITY

World War II and statehood in 1959 brought enormous changes to Native Hawaiians as well. During this period, the whites shifted their primary alliance from Native Hawaiians to Asian Americans, particularly to the most numerous group, the Japanese Americans. This arrangement has left Native Hawaiian interests largely ignored by dominant Japanese groups such as the Japanese American Citizens League and powerful Senator Daniel Inouye, according to some critics (Yoshinaga and Kosasa 2000). Newly excluded from political power, Native Hawaiians began a movement of cultural rejuvenation in the late 1960s (Burgess 1992:15; Hasager and Friedman 1994). Inspired by decolonization in the Pacific (beginning with Fiji in 1970), black struggles in the United States, and the Native American movement, Native Hawaiians turned to cultural revival and alignments with new political movements based on their status as indigenous peoples. Hula *halaus* (schools) gained wider prestige and membership, canoe clubs became more popular, the interest in Hawaiian language increased, the practice in natural medicines developed, and many people became more familiar with Hawaiian history. Hawaiian names were used prominently. Land soon became another focus of contention, with major struggles in the Kalama Valley on Oahu and the movement to protect Kahoʻolawe from bombing by the Navy, an important challenge to the military establishment (Burgess 1992).

By the second half of the 1970s, new Hawaiian organizations began to raise the issue of Hawaiian sovereignty and self-determination. The Blount report from the 1890s, challenging the legality of the overthrow, received new attention. In evictions from land occupations in Sand

Island, Makua Beach, and Waimanalo, activists challenged the jurisdiction of the courts over Hawaiian citizens (Burgess 1992). Some of this movement has involved legal strategies, such as cases demanding gathering rights for medicinal plants on private lands and access to shorelines. Ka Lāhui Hawai'i, an organization seeking to establish a separate Hawaiian state, developed its own constitution and system of citizenship and sought to establish a separate legal system (Trask 1993; Osorio, Chapter 8, this volume). The vision of Hawai'i as an independent nation with citizenship settled not by racial extraction but by relationship to the land has also expanded, along with new forms of protest, such as refusing to join the pledge of allegiance in schools, stand for the national anthem, file tax returns or pay income taxes, and accept the jurisdiction of American courts when charged with criminal offenses (Burgess 1992). In the 1990s, some Hawaiians refused to use license plates, claiming that the state of Hawai'i did not have jurisdiction over them. As Jon Osorio notes in Chapter 8, Ka Lāhui emphasizes descent and race as indices of membership, but an alternative movement focuses instead on citizenship in the nation of the Hawaiian Kingdom of the nineteenth century. He describes the significant differences in the ideas of membership and identity within each of these movements.

During the 1980s and 1990s, the sovereignty movement began to ally itself with other indigenous peoples seeking to overcome colonization. Native Hawaiian representatives appeared at the United Nations (UN) Working Group on Indigenous Peoples in Geneva. One of the most prominent spokespersons for the movement, Haunani-Kay Trask (1993), included the UN draft declaration on indigenous peoples in her book on the movement (see also M. B. Trask 2000a and b). Many activist leaders are now adopting legal strategies for reclaiming land and seeking reparations, seeing law as an important terrain to contest the past history of colonialism and displacement. A peoples' trial in 1993 found the United States guilty of breaking its treaties with the Kingdom of Hawai'i in the nineteenth century (Hasager and Friedman 1994; Merry 1997). Some leaders in the sovereignty movement seek independence from the United States, or at least some degree of autonomy, relying on the international human rights system to accord them the rights of self-determination for indigenous peoples. Thus, the sovereignty movement has been substantially influenced by international law and its conception of indigenous peoples' rights.

A distinction is now emerging between settlers and indigenous peoples, with all the immigrant groups, rich and poor, old and new, lumped into the settler category. Native Hawaiians have conceptualized themselves as indigenous peoples in human rights terms and have formed links with other indigenous groups around the world through the global indigenous rights movement based in the UN and its Human Rights Commission. This movement demands self-governance and reparations or return of lands and waters based on indigenous peoples' human rights to self-determination. In contrast to the earlier movements of the immigrant groups, this movement seeks some form of nationhood, not freedom from discrimination (H. Trask 2000; M. B. Trask 2000a and b; Hasager and Friedman 1994). Many seek a separate nation with a constitution and citizenship, an autonomous state governed by law—the goal of Ka Lāhui Hawai'i, the best established and most widely recognized sovereignty group (H. Trask 1993, 2000; M. B. Trask 2000a and b). As Osorio (Chapter 8, this volume) notes, this model bases membership on descent rather than on nationality, the criterion of an alternative organization that stresses nationality defined as loyalty to a state. Even though many members of the sovereignty movement agree that some form of self-determination is desirable, there is considerable contestation about the shape of that autonomy.

In conjunction with the growing assertion of an indigenous nationhood by Native Hawaiians, some Native Hawaiians have increasingly emphasized the distinction between the situation of Asian settlers and that of Native Hawaiians, a move that fractures the category of local . One of the most outspoken proponents of Hawaiian sovereignty, Haunani-Kay Trask, castigates Asian Americans for focusing on the hardships of their plantation pasts and distancing themselves from whites yet cooperating with the whites, ignoring Native Hawaiian concerns, and denying their complicity with whites in taking Hawaiian lands and resources (H. Trask 2000:6). They are, she points out, settlers just as the whites are and are also using the lands and resources of the Native Hawaiians. She argues that Asian Americans identify as local to avoid being categorized with haole in the context of Native Hawaiian insurgency (H. Trask 2000:7). They continue to talk about freedom from discrimination and equal rights under the law and justify their economic and political success in terms of the hard work that enabled them to overcome their marginal position as immigrants. Yet, they are also settlers. This idea tears the concept of local and replaces it with a settler/indigenous dichotomy. Some Japanese Americans are shocked by this idea, which deviates from their image of themselves as immigrants who succeeded in a democratic and egalitarian society (Kasoso 2000:89). As Fujikane (2000:xx) writes, Asian Americans have framed the Hawaiian sovereignty movement as a domestic civil rights issue rather than as an international human rights one: "Asian settler scholars confuse indigenous struggles for nationhood with settler struggles for equality, and in so doing, such academic projects exploit indigenous sovereignty issues in order to further settler self-interests and our own political dominance. Our ideological indoctrination as settlers and our inability to understand the full complexity of Native struggles lead us to make damaging academic assertions that actually support a system of U.S. colonialism." However, she points out, the Native Hawaiian movement is not about equality but nationhood (Fujikane 2000:xx).

In sum, both the assertion of rights to organize and to vote by Asian Americans and the assertion of rights to land and self-determination by the Native Hawaiians reflect legal definitions of identity and are part of movements that mobilize law to improve their situation. The legal conception of indigeneity grows out of Hawaiian ideas of connections to the ancestors and to the land. Nationality is similarly defined by law. Local, in contrast, is an identity that grows out of resistance to the privileges that law created for the white elites.

THEORIZING ETHNIC IDENTITY IN HAWAI'I

How are these conceptions of ethnicity and their legal grounding related to contemporary ethnic relationships and tensions? The dominant model of Hawaiian society has long been based on the idea of nationality. Histories of the making of Hawaiian society typically fall into several distinct narratives, each tracing the history of one of the ethnic groups making up the present social fabric of the islands. Each major ethnic group in Hawai'i—whites, Chinese, Portuguese, Japanese, Filipinos, Koreans, and Puerto Ricans—tells the story of its particular journey to the islands and experiences of adaptation and struggle. The consciousness of separate identities based on nationality is facilitated by the distinctive historical circumstances surrounding each group's entry into the island scene and the conditions of its inclusion in or exclusion from the dominant society. Workers of different national origins were housed in racially segregated areas, assigned different tasks, and paid different wage rates (Takaki 1983:34–51). Before World War II, nationality identities determined most aspects of a person's life, from his or her baseball team, to school, to housing. These categories were included in police reports as late as 1938. The Waipahu Plantation Village Museum on Oahu replicated this ethnic model in the early 1990s, when I visited there. The museum contained perhaps ten workers' houses, each furnished according to the cultural artifacts of a particular ethnic group and juxtaposed to other workers' houses along a path, regardless of the variations in the period each group worked on the plantations. Ethnic associations furnished the houses, described as "the Portuguese house," "the Japanese house," "the Korean house," and so on. Even though the Hawaiian story is fundamentally different, immigrants often understand Hawaiians in nationality terms as well.[7] This Michenerization of Hawaiian history as a tale of parallel but separate stories is widely followed by academic and popular writings, literary accounts, and museum and tourist displays. Tamura (2000) notes that it has been a dominant approach to studying ethnicity in Hawai'i throughout the twentieth century, although it is now being supplemented by new, more multiethnic frameworks.

In recent years, Hawai'i has been portrayed as a model of multiethnic harmony. Pointing to extensive intermarriage, the absence of intergroup violence, and the shared culture of the local, social theorists have celebrated the emergence of a multicultural and peaceful society. They note that boundaries among groups are relatively fluid and overt conflict is minimal. The indigenous community did not contest the immigrants' rise to political power with coups, as it did in Fiji. Social science scholarship, generally produced by whites, stresses the interethnic harmony of the islands and the high levels of interpersonal sharing and tolerance. Andrew Lind (1938, 1980), the predominant scholar of race relations in Hawai'i from the 1940s to the 1980s, developed this image of multicultural harmony and peace (Okamura 2000:125).

The extensive intermarriage among the ethnic groups on the islands over the past two centuries supports his argument, although not all groups have intermarried equally.[8] The US Census 2000 allowed multiple racial identifications, revealing that 78.6 percent identified themselves as having a single race, but 21.4 percent described themselves as having two or more races. The model of multicultural harmony is based on the nationality concept because it posits a collection of distinct but equal nationalities that treat one another with tolerance.

Yet, some argue that the image of ethnic harmony has been overdrawn (Okamura 1998:284). Significant inequalities in power and wealth exist among the groups in contemporary Hawai'i, and a virulent racism maintains these inequalities (Okamura 2000:125; see Chang 1996). Although proponents of multicultural harmony argue that all immigrant groups will achieve social mobility eventually, in practice, the whites (including Portuguese), Chinese, and Japanese have become relatively affluent, and other groups, especially the Samoans, Filipinos, and Native Hawaiians, have remained relatively impoverished (Okamura 2000, 1996:41; Haas 1992; Revilla 1996:60). In the 1950s, the newly politically powerful Japanese Americans were co-opted by the white economic elites into a power-sharing arrangement that increasingly excluded Native Hawaiians and immigrant groups such as Filipinos, Samoans, and Puerto Ricans (see Cooper and Daws 1990; Chang 1996; Okamura 1998). Ethnic identity, although fluid and not marked by sharp boundaries, continues to mark inequalities in resources and power. The multicultural harmony model argues that all nationalities will follow the same pattern of social mobility as the Chinese and Japanese have if only they will be patient, because it envisages all nationalities as the same. This ignores the differential patterns of racism and exclusion that these groups have encountered.

Alongside billiard ball models of multiple nationalities and romanticized images of multicultural harmony, the class-based notion of the local persists. This identity still crosses national and ethnic lines, uniting the Hawai'i-born in opposition to newcomers and the dominant white elite. Yet, it is now being reframed with the rise of the indigenous rights movement. At the same time, identity based on genealogy and descent persists, among both Native Hawaiians and white families long resident in the islands. Hawaiians define themselves through genealogies and spiritual connections to the land, much as the Fijians do. In a sense, the whites do also. For example, the descendants of the white missionaries of the early nineteenth century gather to celebrate their ancestors and compete to see which group of missionaries, or "company," has the largest contingent of descendants present. In the recent Supreme Court case *Rice* v. *Cayetano,* which Osorio discusses in Chapter 8, a long-established white resident contested the priority of Native Hawaiian claims, based on his own four generations' residence in the islands.

CONCLUSION

These examples show how law contributes to shaping ethnic distinctions and fostering ethnic conflict. The law defines political participation and access to land through social categories such as citizenship, race, nationality, and locality and sets groups against each other, as it did Native Hawaiians and Japanese Americans. Law allocates rationality and adulthood when it designates who can vote for whom, who can run for political office, and who can be a citizen. Those given identity within the law as citizens and deemed capable of contractual relationships were defined as rational and civilized; others were labeled irrational, animalistic, and dangerous. Clearly, whites and Hawaiians occupied the former status in the nineteenth and early twentieth centuries, and Japanese struggled to attain this position in the mid-twentieth century. In recent years, the international human rights system has conferred the status of indigenous identity on Native Hawaiians, a population increasingly beleaguered by its political and economic marginalization.

The use of law as a political strategy reinforces claims to the status of rationality and adulthood. In its own unique way, each group has relied on law to better its situation. Asian Americans searched for civil rights and freedom from discrimination. Native Hawaiians worked toward self-determination and national control over their lands and resources, also pursuing paths more culturally focused than legal. As marginalized non-citizens, Japanese Americans sought freedom from discrimination while acquiescing to assimilation. The white strategy of excluding Asians from citizenship and placing burdens of discrimination on them, as well as suspecting them of disloyalty on the basis of nationality, encouraged Asians to assert rights as citizens and to assimilate into the dominant society through military service and their own bloodshed if necessary. After being abandoned by the whites, Hawaiians increasingly emphasized their separate identities, developing regimes of citizenship in separatist organizations and recuperating a distinctive language, law, and culture. Whites sought to retain their political and economic control through legal strategies such as exclusion of aliens from citizenship and, more recently, lawsuits such as *Rice* v. *Cayetano*. As managers of the dominant political and legal structure, whites used the regulation of citizenship, access to voting, and access to jobs to maintain economic and political control. Legal mechanisms such as land ownership patterns, voting requirements, and contractual labor arrangements surrounded their acquisition of power with an aura of legitimacy. The enduring identity of local testifies to the resentment this strategy produced.

The differences between the Hawaiian recourse to law and ethnic-Fijian reliance on coups that trump law are intriguing to note. Ethnic Fijians, Kaplan argues in Chapter 6, ground themselves in negotiations and relationships instead of legal claims. She shows how ethnic Fijians who lack legal ownership of land nevertheless assert that it belongs to them. Their linkage to land and God supersedes law, justifying claims and coups. The Hawaiians, in contrast, who made Anglo-American law their own in the nineteenth century, continue to use the law to contest their exclusion from control over land and water. Perhaps the Hawaiian Kingdom's incorporation of the colonized and colonizers in a single legal system that confers legal adulthood and rationality on all encouraged the Hawaiian enthusiasm for law in a way that the Fijian protectionist and plural legal system did not.

However, although the Hawaiian system created fewer boundaries than the colonial regime in Fiji, it did not prevent the alienation of the colonized population from its land, resources, language, and culture. Defining Hawaiians as equal members of the Anglo-American system of law rather than as a second tier in a dual legal system incorporated them into the Anglo-American world at the price of suppressing many indigenous customs and practices and allowing the massive dispossession of Native Hawaiians from the land. Like the Indo-Fijians, those excluded from control over land have relied extensively on legal strategies to gain it. In the end, ironically, the weapon of the weak is law.

Acknowledgments

This research was generously supported by grants from the National Science Foundation, both the Cultural Anthropology Program and the Law and Social Sciences Program, and from the National Endowment for the Humanities. I am grateful to Jane Collier and to Noenoe Silva for valuable discussions and comments and to the other participants in the SAR advanced seminar for their comments.

Notes

1. Although ethnicity is commonly talked about in terms of national identity, the term *Asian American* is increasingly common, adopted from the mainland.

2. The Republic, established after the overthrow in 1893, increased property qualifications for voting, making Hawaiians fewer than 20 percent of all registered voters (Haas 1992:11).

3. The early twentieth century saw the growth of racial exclusion, racially based nativist movements such as the Ku Klux Klan, and the passage of a racially based immigration law in 1924 excluding the Japanese and many European groups, a law that applied to Hawai'i as well (see Takaki 1989:209; Higham 1955).

4. Immigrant sugar workers came from China, Korea, the Philippines, and Japan. The Chinese were 22.6 percent of the population in 1884, but since the 1930s, their numbers have dropped to between 4 and 7 percent of the population. The Japanese were the largest ethnic group in Hawai'i from 1900 to 1940, forming 37 percent and 43 percent of the population during that period, but were only 20 percent of the population by the end of the 1990s (Tamura 2000:63). The Koreans, who began to arrive in 1903, constitute only 1 to 2 percent of the population. The Filipinos, who came between 1906 and 1935 and after 1965, were the third largest and the fastest-growing ethnic group by the 1990s (Tamura 2000:65). Unlike the earlier Asian immigrants, the Japanese immigrants brought wives, but usually only after they had arrived and sent for them, often as strangers selected from photos—called "picture brides" (Takaki 1983, 1989). This increased the ability of the Japanese immigrants to create families and communities in the early twentieth century and to bear American-born children eligible for citizenship.

5. A series of letters from the executive director of the HSPA to the Onomea plantation reveals something of the way this organization mobilized the law during one of the early strikes in 1924. On June 16, 1924, plantation manager Moir sent a wireless message to Kohala plantation managers, requesting Sheriff Pua to authorize deputies in Kohala specifically to commission additional police

officers (up to twenty) as required by Kohala plantation mangers to protect their property in the event of a strike. Men were to be equipped with regulation badges, uniforms, and arms, and the HSPA would pay.

6. The haoles attempted to regulate the language schools of the Japanese, Chinese, and Korean parents by screening textbooks and imposing per-student state taxes. Two military intelligence reports, the Merriam Report of 1918 and the Summerall Report of 1922, concentrated on the threats of Japanese-language schools, the proportion of Japanese voters in the future, and the high birth rate in Japanese families (Okihiro 1991:118–120). As a result, laws were passed in 1920 and 1922 regulating Japanese-language schools and putting their curriculum under the authority of the Department of Public Instruction (Okihiro 1991:137). The Supreme Court overturned this regulatory effort in 1927 in *Farrington* v. *Tokushige* (273 US 284) (Haas 1992:59; Okihiro 1991:154).

7. Museums in Hawai'i portray these groups quite differently. As Kelly notes in Chapter 3, there are multiple representations of Hawaiian culture in Hawai'i, including the exhibits in the most prominent museum, the Bishop Museum in Honolulu, but relatively little portrayal of the experiences of immigrant groups (Kelly 2000a). When museums do include a space for these immigrant communities, as they do in the Bishop Museum in Honolulu and the Lyman Memorial Museum in Hilo, these communities are typically represented as family units in national costumes. In contrast, the Waipahu museum offers not only a series of plantation camp houses, each furnished (by members of that community) to represent a single ethnic community, but also a substantial exhibit about the union movement of the early twentieth century led by Japanese and Filipino workers.

8. Rates of interethnic marriage have increased from 12 percent in 1912 to 34 percent in the 1980s, with a low of 13 percent of white women and a high of 87 percent of Hawaiian men (Haas 1992:60). My interviews with residents of plantation camps in the 1940s and 1950s, as well as reminiscences, suggest that marriage into other ethnic groups was rare and looked down on (see Andaya 1996:109). If one examines police records and other self-report data, though, people frequently do list multiple identities or describe themselves as mixed.

6

Promised Lands

From Colonial Lawgiving to Postcolonial Takeovers in Fiji

Martha Kaplan

A major question for contemporary postcolonial societies is understanding how legally defined identities have shaped contemporary social groups. In Latourian fashion, I would like to generalize this question to ask as well about entities and events: How have legally defined entities in Fiji's colonial history shaped contemporary events? We will consider how Sir Arthur Gordon's structuring of the relationship of courts, markets, and other systems more powerful than law at the inception of colonial Fiji has shaped contemporary events in a dialogical colonial history. We will also think about ethnic Fijians as agents and consider how they have remade Gordon's structures, indeed, how they have taken them over.[1]

Takeovers in Fiji have challenged or ignored constitutional rule, electoral democracy, and legal titles. Coups have twice ousted democratically elected national governments in Fiji. Some Fiji citizens, notably Indo-Fijians and Labour Party supporters, have been dispossessed of political rights. Other Fiji citizens have reclaimed property, or newly claimed it, especially land. This introduction first describes the coups, the legal challenges to them, and some of the resulting landholding and dispossession. Then it describes the events of a more local takeover. At both the national and very local levels, we will observe a dialogical transformation of "ownership" as a ritual and political category. The juxtaposition of events of recent national history with the story of one rural takeover enables us to pose this question: What is the connection between colonial legally defined entities that established rule to current assertions of ownership and current ethnic-Fijian certainties about God's promises to them?

In 1987, Fiji had been independent for seventeen years. At Independence, there were 715,375 Fiji citizens. *Indo-Fijians,* people descended from Indian indentured laborers (and from other immigrants from South Asia), were 48.7 percent of the population, and *ethnic Fijians,* people of Fijian Pacific islander descent, were 46 percent (Fiji Bureau of Statistics 1989). In 1987, a multiethnic Labour Party coalition, headed by an ethnic-Fijian commoner, was democratically elected, replacing the colonially groomed, ethnic Fijian-dominated, chiefly-led Alliance Party government that had governed Fiji since Independence.[2] Colonel Sitiveni Rabuka led a military coup against the Labour government, claiming to do so on behalf of ethnic Fijians.

Following this coup, under the government led by Rabuka, a pro–ethnic Fijian and racially discriminatory constitution was promulgated in 1990. In 1997, it was replaced by a well-crafted, far more democratic constitution. In free, well-conducted elections in May 1999, a multiethnic coalition led by the Fiji Labour Party defeated and replaced Rabuka's government and made Labour leader Mahendra Chaudhry Fiji's first Indo-Fijian prime minister.

In 2000, a failed businessman named George Speight, past head of the Fiji Hardwood and Fiji Pine Commissions in the Rabuka government, saw his carefully laid plans to sell Fiji's mahogany reserves (planted by colonial planners in the 1950s) to a US buyer overruled by the newly elected Labour coalition government. Speight had incited and championed the ethnic-Fijian landowners (on whose rented land the mahogany was growing) to back his plans for its sale (Kahn 2000). On May 19, Speight got the jump on other potential coup leaders and led a group of armed soldiers into Parliament to begin a coup against Chaudhry's Labour coalition government.

Speight's haphazard coup was overtaken and solidified, from the top down, by ethnic-Fijian stalwarts, including high chiefs and the military. An interim government installed ethnic-Fijian bureaucrat Laisenia Qarase as prime minister, with Fiji's military forces under Commander Frank Bainimarama as guarantor. Qarase then began to announce and implement a range of programs to solidify ethnic-Fijian paramountcy in the nation.

However, a suit by an Indo-Fijian farmer, arguing that Speight's coup and the ensuing abrogation of the constitution violated his civil rights, led Justice Gates of the Lautoka High Court to rule that the 1997 constitution should not have been set aside. On March 1, 2001, the ruling was upheld by the five-member Appeals Court, and it was not appealed to the Supreme Court. This ruling would seem to declare the coup and the interim government illegal. On the one hand, it required new elections under the 1997 constitution. On the other hand, though, rather than return the elected Labour coalition government to power, the ruling allowed the army-backed interim government to remain in power until the elections held in late August 2001. Interim government Prime Minister Laisenia Qarase and his Soqosoqo Duavata ni Lewenivanua (SDL) party won that election, joining its thirty-one seats in coalition with the six seats of the Matanitu Vanua-Conservative party. Twenty-seven Fiji Labour Party representatives were elected (Ali 2001:10).

Taking advantage of the takeover of the nation in May 2000 and the following months, ethnic Fijians carried out or attempted many local takeovers of roads, power stations, tourist resorts, and factories, asserting (as in the national takeovers) the rights of ethnic Fijians as landowners.

Something that had not happened by 2003: a final disposition of the expired ALTA leases, that is, of lands leased by Indo-Fijian cane farmers. Eighty-three percent of Fiji's land is owned by ethnic-Fijian patrilineal kin groups *(mataqalis)*. These lands were reserved for ethnic Fijians at the behest of the first British governor, Sir Arthur Gordon, who established the Native Lands Commission in 1880 to identify owning kin groups and their territories. Ownership of "Native land" is by kin group membership (on the Native Lands Commission, see also Miyazaki, Chapter 9, this volume). In 1940, the colonial government created the Native Lands Trust Board (NLTB), which continues to oversee rental of "Native lands," especially to Fiji's Indo-Fijian sugar cane farmers. As Independence approached, in 1970 the Agricultural

Landlords and Tenants Ordinance (ALTO), later named the Agricultural Landlords and Tenants Act (ALTA), set uniform and secure twenty-year leases with ten-year extensions. Agricultural land in Fiji, owned by ethnic Fijians, was leasable for only thirty years. Crown land leases, notably in urban locations, have in some circumstances been ninety-nine-year leases.

Many of the thirty-year agricultural leases expired in and around the year 2000 (see France 1969; Lal 1992:224–227). By 2002, more than 4,000 agricultural leases had expired. Only 30 percent were renewed to the Indo-Fijian tenants. Much of the non-renewed lease land is not being farmed by the ethnic-Fijian owners but has "reverted to bush" (Dakuvula and Naidu 2002:10). Since 2000, sugar cane production has declined from 4.2 million tons to 2.8 million (Dakuvula and Naidu 2002:13). A few Indo-Fijians have taken residential leases on land they used to farm. Others have moved in with relatives whose farm leases have not yet expired, and many have moved to urban or peri-urban squatter settlements, or to other parts of Fiji as agricultural laborers. Some displaced farmers are staying in "refugee camps" (Dakuvula and Naidu 2002:14). (Interestingly, one would expect the Indo-Fijians facing expulsion from lands farmed for decades and generations to create major disruptions. Instead, the dispossessed Indo-Fijians—and Indo-Fijians in general—have mounted absolutely no armed or illegal seizures of any kind.)

Let us discuss these national events, coups, ethnonationalism, and disposession and their connection to colonial lawgiving—by way of an apparent detour—through a takeover event with an apparently happy ending. On Thursday, November 18, 2000, the *Fiji Daily Post* ran an editorial titled "Vinaka Fiji Waters "[Thank You, Fiji Waters]:

> Today Fiji will be blessed with a $40 million much needed boost to the economy.
>
> This is when Natural Waters of Viti Limited opens the extension to its Yaqara facility today.
>
> While other investors are adopting a wait and see attitude on whether Fiji will be able to secure a political and social foothold in these treacherous times, the owners of Fiji

Waters David Gilmore [sic, should be *Gilmour*], with this gesture has instilled a lot of confidence into the 790,000 inhabitants of these 300 or so islands.

This paper wishes to commend Mr. Gilmore for having that trust and loyalty in a land which in many aspects cannot be compared to his beloved America and for having confidence in the people of Fiji.

The risks Fiji Waters has taken today will be offset by the dynamic team comprising its owner, workers and high quality product it ceasingly [sic] produces.

Our economy has taken a battering and been stretched to its limit, and the road to recovery has been rough and turbulent.

But this country is blessed in the fact that there are courageous people like Mr. Gilmore, who through its [sic] actions are reminding us that the good inherent in our people coupled with our God given resources are the springboard to economic recovery and future prosperity.

The new water bottling plant will employ close to 100 people and its spin-off to the immediate local population will be enormous

By turning out 80 million bottles of top of the range quality mineral water per year, Fiji Waters will dramatically increase Fiji's Gross Domestic Product, increase rural income and further diversify Fiji's export base.

All this to be emanating from a remote location such as Yaqara is a good sign of things to come for the rural population which makes up more than 60 percent of the country's population.

Fiji Water's decision to establish its Yaqara facility will help Government in its efforts to keep urban populations down which already have limited employment opportunities in the formal sector and overly strained social services.

Apart from that, a percentage of national income is distributed to the Rakiraki rural area.

Only time will tell, but if development flourishes at Yaqara, then it would not be surprising if it evolved into a township of its own.

Remote Yaqara will today be full of people with beaming faces.

The people of Ra will stand proud knowing they have given something back to this wounded nation and thanks to Fiji Waters for reminding us that this country has what it takes to speed up our journey along the road to recovery.

The *Post*'s editorial reflects post-coup normalization rhetoric in Fiji: Coups are to be forgotten; the nation must pick itself up and get on with rebuilding. Yet, there are some oddities to this rare bit of good news for Fiji's post-coup economy. First, Gilmour and Natural Waters of Fiji's investment is all the more interesting because, following a three-year struggle, a group of local ethnic Fijians, of *yavusa* Vatukaloko, took over the plant and demanded various forms of compensation for the use of "their" land and the spring water flowing from it. And, happily for them, legal prosecution has been withdrawn. Second, there is much to be said of this "their" and of the "our" ("our God given resources" in the *Post* editorial), and of who the "nation" is who will be blessed and rewarded by their use.

In general, in the history of Fiji, Vatukaloko people have been atypical ethnic Fijians in their relationship to land and resources. Natural Waters of Fiji, Ltd., bottles from pipes sunk down into the aquifer in land near the springs from which the prophet leader Mosese Dukumoi, also known as Navosavakadua, dispensed *wai ni tuka* (water of immortality) in the 1870s and 1880s. Navosavakadua preached an articulation of powerful gods, simultaneously Fijian and Christian, attempting to form his own polity to combat encroaching eastern, Christian, chiefly kingdoms and colonials. In an atypical Fijian colonial experience, Navosavakadua's kin did not receive legal title to the land they occupied in the 1870s. Equally atypical was their very particular Fijian-Christian narrative of exile and return to their promised land, in which

Navosavakadua as Moses played a prominent part (see Kaplan 1995). The Vatukaloko might seem exceptional, unusual. The intersection of their land and water rights, historically claimed in ritual-political terms, and the thanks of coup backers for foreign investment, also couched as God's design, may seem coincidental. However, other ethnic Fijians, too, had articulated powerful themes in ethnic-Fijian culture with Christian and colonial projects. As I will show, the Vatukaloko narrative and a more orthodox Christian-Fijian understanding of Jehovah, land, and colonial authority have moved close together in Fiji's dialogical colonial history.

For there is a curious feature that links coup leader Rabuka, coup leader Speight, bureaucrat Qarase, and the rural Vatukaloko people. It is their theory of an ownership that need not derive from market contracts, nor from colonial and postcolonial courts, nor from a social contract of "we the people." This is why what is so interesting about the Vatukaloko, among all the takeovers, is that—unlike many ethnic Fijians—they do not have legal title to the land on which the plant is located. The land is "theirs" as Fijians, by custom, history, God's promise. The god who has promised is a synthesis of Jehovah and gods of the land. Their conviction that it is their water mirrors the conviction of Speight, Rabuka's government, and many landowners that the colonially planted mahogany was theirs, not the nation-state's. In this sense, the Vatukaloko feeling of entitlement, their theory of ownership, may shed some light on that of Rabuka, Speight, Qarase, and others. After all, Rabuka and Speight did not win the election but still felt compelled to proclaim their rights to the nation-state. The takeover of Natural Waters, Speight's disposition of mahogany, and the takeover of the nation are events that eschew claims about legal titles, electoral processes, or constitutional rule and argue for ethnic-Fijian entitlement based on Fijian special rights, on the rights of Christian indigenes. But what can be the relationship between God's promises and Gordon's colonial law? In this chapter, I will seek to connect God's promise to the Vatukaloko (and all ethnic Fijians) to colonial events of the past in order to show how legally defined entities of Native Administration and Native Lands Commissions—which do not sound like God's promise—have shaped colonial and postcolonial events. Gordon's initial plan and these colonial structures began with a subordination of law to other entities. The fashioning and refashioning of these entities, especially their transformation as Fijian-Christian, is our story in this dialogical colonial history.

PROMISED LANDS/COLONIAL ENTITIES

To seek the connections between what Gordon set up and the recent ritual politics of owning Fiji, between colonial structures and contemporary events, I will begin with a history of the polity within the colonial polity, focusing on the Native Administration, the Native Lands Commission, and the Native Lands Trust Board and their Christianization. Then I will return to a fuller story of the Vatukaloko and the events of their takeover amid the takeover of the nation. In each case, both the ongoing impacts of Gordon's colonial entities and their articulation and transformations in the encounter with ethnic-Fijian entities and projects are the main points.

We need not see a dynamic colonial history encountering a structured Fijian culture. Quite clearly, Gordon's colonial project gained its strength from its articulation with ongoing and differing chiefly Fijian projects of rule (Kaplan 1988, 1989a and b, 1995). Fijians in general, and the Vatukaloko in particular, have always innovated, borrowed, rejected, or adopted new concepts and practices. Over the past two centuries, it is clear that such history-making has used a framework of *itaukei/turaga* (land/sea, people/chiefs, or foreign/indigenous relationships) in a variety of ways (for nineteenth-century versions, see Sahlins 1985; Kaplan 1995; for postcolonial political deployments, Rutz 1995). The latest takeovers of "god-given resources" create another moment in colonial dialogue.

Around 1800, the term *itaukei* (people of the land, or owners of the land) had primary meaning as "commoner installers of the chiefs." *Itaukei* were ruled by powerful chiefs (chiefs constructed as foreign in their *mana*) but retained the ritual privileges of superseded autochthones. This was understood in coastal Fijian kingdoms via the myth and ritual narrative of a dangerous, powerful stranger who comes, marries a woman of the land, and founds a line of chiefs who incorporate the power of their foreign father with the powers of their mother's gods of the land, superseding the mother's brother's line. In the great coastal kingdoms such as Bau, the chief thus held the *lewa* (rule) but not ownership of land (Sahlins 1985). In some nineteenth-century

Fijian polities, for example, among the Vatukaloko, different narratives emphasized continuing ruling powers and sovereign autonomy of the original people vis-à-vis claims to sovereignty by powerful chiefs. The Vatukaloko live, after all, close to the heart of the Kauvadra Range, home of the gods of the land. In such polities, chiefly leadership was contested by "land" leaders, who embodied land gods more directly, such as the warrior priests and installing people of the interior. From the mid-1800s on, "ownership" changed variously in the encounter with settlers (for example, see France 1969). Beginning in the 1860s, white settlers began to "buy" land in the areas where the Vatukaloko held sway. More systematically, from 1874 on, it changed under the codifications of the colonial Native Administration (later renamed the Fijian Administration) and the Native Lands Commission, a part of the system of indirect rule.

Gordon's plan established a polity within the colonial polity (for example, see Clammer 1975; Kaplan 1988; Kelly 1988, Chapter 3 in this volume; Lal 1992; Macnaught 1982). At colonial inception, Fijians were already typically Methodist in colonial expectation. (London Missionary Society missionaries had begun arriving in the 1840s. By 1854, with the conversion of Cakobau, the most powerful eastern-coastal chief, the majority of Fijians were nominally Methodist; one colonial observer called it the "Established Church" [Joske 1922].) The Native Administration created standardized districts and an official hierarchy, staffed largely by ethnic Fijians, especially Fijians of chiefly rank: officials called *Rokos* headed provinces, *Bulis* headed districts, and *Turaga ni koros* headed villages.

The British authorized chiefs from the top down and systematically de-emphasized the installing powers and rights of itaukei. Simultaneously, however, the British emphasized and elaborated on land ownership, instituting a Native Lands policy eventually establishing the ownership of 83 percent of Fiji's land by Fijians. In this system, still in place, Fijian land became private property, but the Fijian owners of this land were colonially researched, patrilineal kin groups who could not sell the land that was legally judged to be theirs "traditionally." The commissioners of the Native Lands Commission were British officials and Fijian high chiefs; Ratu Sir Lala Sukuna, who also served as the Native Lands Commissioner, headed the Native Lands Trust Board. (See below for a detailed account of the *Vatukaloko* encounter with the 1917 Native Lands Commission and with Ratu Sukuna's Native Lands Trust Board inquiries of 1940.) The Fijian Administration and the Native Lands Commission's authority linked Methodist Christianity, custom as law, fixity, chiefly leadership, communal non-market economics, and Fijianness. Via deployment of ordinances such as the Disaffected and Dangerous Natives Ordinance of 1887, they criminalized Fijian gods, oracle priests, Fijian commercial enterprise, and claims to ownership and sovereignty by non-chiefly Fijians. Always in colonial peripheral vision, Indo-Fijian rights and claims formed a fearful reservoir of disorder, a counterpoint to use to unite Fijians to colonial projects (Kaplan 1989a and b; Kaplan and Kelly 1994).

The Fijian Administration set up district leaders, laws, and separate courts and magistrates for Fijians. The Native Lands Commission inquiries established Fijian landholdings and registered yavusa and mataqali (kin group) membership, crucial for rights in landownership and more recently in voting and citizenship issues. As already mentioned, in the 1940s the colonial government established the Native Lands Trust Board to regulate leasing of Fijian land by sugar cane growers, by then largely Indo-Fijian.

Here, with a vignette of Ratu Sukuna and the workings of the Native Lands Trust Board, let me illustrate the linkage of chiefs, land, god, and rights these colonial institutions put into place.[3]

The Native Lands Trust Board was established after several years of planning. Both the Colonial Sugar Refinery and the cane growers had complained for decades about difficulties and irregular expenses faced by the growers, mostly Indo-Fijians, when arranging land leases with ethnic-Fijian landowners. Previous reforms had required approval of leases by district commissioners (British district officials added to the colonial hierarchy in the early 1900s) and the Native Lands Commissioner in Suva. This had added delays and risks but had not changed local situations in which lands were allotted irrespective of commercially efficient use and in which cash gift contests determined which grower a Fijian chief would endorse for lease (Lal 1992:134; see also Moynagh 1981:141). The Native Lands Trust Board became a major vehicle for further developing and ensconcing ethnic-Fijian bureaucrats under the direct supervision of the highest government authorities. Its first, crucial commissioner was Ratu Sir Lala Sukuna, the Fijian chief who preeminently embodied the consolidation of official and chiefly power in the mid-twentieth century. As Native Lands Reserves Commissioner, he demarcated lands to be rented from lands to be reserved for the owners' present and future uses. His hagiographic biographer, Deryck Scarr (1980:136–137), describes vividly how Sukuna did this:

> At the steady, earth-devouring pace he had perfected during his twenty years in the Native Lands Commission, he walked the rich river flats and the barren hills; you had to be able to outwalk anybody, he held, if you were going to be taken seriously when you made decisions about the land you trod. By night, he sat at the head of the yaqona circle quietening apprehension in these Western [Western side of Viti Levu island] people who he saw as particularly parochial; "Their main characteristic of importance here is their disregard of all authority outside their own tribal chiefs, who are regarded as the repositories of initiative and judgment and the first court of appeal in all matters." They knew full well they were handing over to the government leasing rights they had hitherto used profitably themselves, as the ransacked, rack-rented Indian could often bear witness. And the sacrifice was not easily made. At Vuda...Ratu Sukuna ran into opposition from the Tui Vuda..."Eventually, out of deference to his wishes," said Ratu Sukuna, "a tabua [whale's tooth] was presented ending in the prayer that we might be pleased to pack up and be gone." Ratu Sukuna obliged by moving to Vitogo so that by starting elsewhere, and "by quietly demonstrating the entire absence of sinister motive," he could "expose the Vuda faction to what natives universally dread, the ridicule of their fellows."
>
> He was very much the great Eastern chief in all this, insisting on the use of Bauan rather than local dialects when he sat formally, and made all the more powerful by his government offices. As Talai [Secretary for Native Affairs] he was just below God and the King, with only the Governor intervening.

As one who dealt authoritatively with land, he was practically a god himself. And while he impressed the Governor with the care and labour he put into the reserves work, Ratu Sukuna's power of decision astonished even the decisive Mitchell. It looked as though the Reserves Commissioner paid little attention to hereditary right and that, in fact, he took the position of an administrator charged solely with administering the land to the best advantage of the people but was entitled in doing so to disregard private interests and rights. If that was the position, and it could be maintained, it was a happy one from the point of view of land use, said the Governor.

Thus, an ethnic-Fijian bureaucracy came to build its own necessity into ever-deeper grooves in land, society, and government. Via the efflorescing institutions initially set in place by Gordon and high chiefs, Sukuna and other bureaucrats claimed to represent the truest interests of all ethnic Fijians. They relied on top-down alliances to replace "parochial" local autonomy with a wider "Fijian" bureaucratic order and insisted that the language, formality, and hierarchy of the eastern-coastal, Christian high chiefs become basic vehicles of government action.

In the 1980s, in his inaugural speech as leader of the new Fiji Labour Party, Dr. Timoci Bavadra argued that "the Native Lands Trust Board must be democratized so that it comes to serve the interests of all Fijians and not just the privileged few and their business associates" (quoted in Lal 1992:300). The matter was simultaneously urgent and limited. More democratic representation had to come, but a Fiji without a Native Lands Trust Board and the racial "ethnic-Fijian" interest it administers so autonomously has become almost unimaginable.

PROMISED LANDS/CHRISTIANIZATION OF OWNERSHIP/FIJIAN BIBLES

Gordon's land system had come to link gods, traditional rights, chiefly leadership, and (what would become) Fijian paramountcy.[4] Ironically, the Native Lands Commission inquiries might be read as having desacralized many ancestor gods, turning them into ancestors and legitimators of property rights. But simultaneously, property rights themselves—or at least ethnic-Fijian land ownership—became sacralized in ethnic Fijians' eyes through the workings of the commissions. The link between gods, land, and ethnic-Fijian paramountcy has been sustained in three ways: first, precisely through its association with Fijian chiefly leaders, which has slowly "democratized" into a broader set of rights of ethnic Fijians as a racial/political category; second, through the separation of ethnic Fijians from the market; and third, through the role of the Fijian Administration and the Native Lands Commission as repository of "Fiji's Bibles," sacred, customary, traditional knowledge.

First, the role of chiefly leadership in routinizing the link between gods, land, and ethnic-Fijian paramountcy has a long history in Fiji. As Sahlins (1985) has shown, the great Fijian chiefs of the 1800s were living gods, incarnate syntheses of foreign mana and the gods of the land. Like Tongan kings, they made an alliance with Jehovah in the mid-1800s. In the colonial era, their godliness came less from gods of the land and more and more from the top down, from the foreign Christian god and British Christian queen.

In the chiefly coastal kingdoms, chiefs in articulation with foreign gods and the foreign colonial government created well-known moments of conversion, dividing time into before and after Christianity, just as time had also been divided into before and after Cession. Certainly, Fijian chiefs, especially high chiefs, have remained divine, but their divine source of authority is more complex. On the one hand, in the installation ceremonies of Christian Fiji, a Christian preacher *(Talatala)* lectures the newly installed chief. On the other hand, of course, founding ancestor deities *(kalou vu)* are still remembered, as are the constituting relationships with women of the land, which found the lines of "child chiefs," reborn as gods of the land. However, now chiefly ancestors may be reckoned more as heroes of myths, founders of lines, and political talismans than as divine figures. In colonial reifications, the active participation of the people of the land in choosing the chief has been de-emphasized in favor of the top-down designation of the true inheritor by agencies such as the Native Lands Commission on the basis of ultimate knowledge of genealogy. Through this colonial process, chiefs became less dependent on priests and more dependent on the authority of the colonial state and Christian god. Christianity became the necessary divine sanction for chiefs but unnecessary to the definition of any particular chief, not distinguishing in any way. Present chiefs, who have come to have definition as a class, are different from their grandparents, who were more specifically the synthetic representatives of particular polities, the embodiment of specific gods of the land.

Crucial narratives of ethnic-Fijian political rights locate God's promise of sovereignty to them in a special covenant made by ethnic Fijians with Jehovah. In some versions of this narrative, the covenant was sealed when the high chiefs ceded Fiji to Queen Victoria, and this relationship with both God and Queen, possibly with God in a Queen, lodges in chiefs a special leadership right. In other narratives, ethnic Fijians' right to rule is lodged in the Christian itaukei as a whole (see Rutz 1995).

Second, the sense of Fijian ownership as an entire people, or "race" (bypassing explicit discussion of chiefly leadership), has roots in the articulation of Gordon's separation of Fijians from the market with objectifications of nineteenth-century Fijian exchange practices. As I have described in more detail elsewhere (Kaplan 1990), missionaries translated "salvation" or "Christ's grace," his gift of salvation to mankind, as *loloma*. Loloma also means gift exchange among kin. The phrase *vuravura vakaloloma* (world and way of life in the way of loloma) is routinely contrasted with the *vuravura vakailavo* (world in the way of money), said to be practiced by non–ethnic Fijians, especially Indo-Fijians and whites. In Gordon's plan, Fijian life in the way of loloma was explicitly contrasted to life in the way of money. Ethnic Fijians were separated (for example, see the colonial Masters and Servants laws) from it, but Indo-Fijians were organized via contracts and life in the way of money (Kaplan 1990). The ethnic-Fijian *soli* economy (from small-scale contributions for kin group projects to major fundraising festivals), with its unusual elaborations into the present, is a consequence. In particular, some have considered stocks and shareholding as suitable means for ethnic-Fijian entrance into the world of business. But the ethnic-Fijian practice of shareholding (discussed in later sections of this chapter) denies the individual property rights and individual agency in transacting that are a hallmark of the joint stock corporation. Instead, ethnic-Fijian shareholding practices have tended to conceptualize shareholding as participation in a community activity with political and social import. Fijians have understood themselves as set apart from the market, and they now remake the world of the market. In this sense, they continue to refuse to become alienated.

This history gives us an insight into the logic of takeovers, as opposed to other means of intervention, such as lawsuits. It is striking that ethnic Fijians such as the Vatukaloko historically eschewed courts and suits, but Indo-Fijians were historically known as extraordinarily litigious. Throughout both the colonial era and independence years, ethnic Fijians sent or took their questions directly to the Native Lands Commissioner or other chiefs and bureaucrats.[5] For example, in the 1990s, Vatukaloko people held discussions about their need for land with parliamentarian William Toganivalu. I have several accounts from very different observers, all of whom begin by noting that the meeting "began with traditional Fijian chiefly ceremonies." Similarly, Fijian takeovers through occupation impel negotiation and face-to-face meetings instead of removal to court sites where ethnic-Fijian relationships may not be mobilized.

Third, institutions of the Native Lands Commission and the Native Lands Trust Board themselves have been sites of the routinization of the link between gods, land, and ethnic-Fijian paramountcy. In the 1880s, the colonial government held inquiries to rule on claims made by Europeans to land purchased before 1874. Sir Arthur Gordon, setting up his system of indirect rule, had decided to halt alienation of Fijian lands after 1874 and to systematize Fijian ownership of land. From the 1880s on, the Native Lands Commission elicited testimony on local kinship groups—mataqalis were settled on as the ostensibly traditional owning groups—and the lands they "traditionally" owned. Throughout Fiji, people came up with appropriate kin groups, with names, clear apical ancestors, genealogies, and lists of living members and traditional boundaries; this information was keyed to maps of the area.

To be sure, ethnic Fijians have had a conflicted relationship with the Native Lands Commission and Native Lands Trust Board records because these simultaneously allot land but also maintain ethnic-Fijian political separation and paramountcy. The Vatukaloko are, of course, not the only people in Fiji whose polity, autonomy, and lands were altered or diminished by the Native Lands Commission's colonial codifications. Certainly some polities were augmented and effloresced as the new forms of commissions and districting were successfully used by claiming groups or were mobilized by Fijian officials of the Native Administration. In the 1980s, the original records of Native Lands Commission testimony (especially the Evidence Books) were not publicly available. Published listings of yavusa and mataqali groups with constituent subdivisions and the boundaries of the lands they own were available, as were maps keyed to these books. The actual records recorded by G. V. Maxwell (including "tribal histories" and Evidence Books) are part of the entire set of Native Lands Commission records, held in the Native Lands Commission building in Suva. A bust of Ratu Sukuna is set in the front wall. However, access to the actual records has been by permission, and often only via selections, of the Native Lands Commissioner. Fijians who were dissatisfied with or had questions about land apportionment frequently came into the building. They were seated, records were fetched and read to them, and they were told that there could be no reopening of land matters. "These records are like the Bible," several staff members said to me.

In the mid-1980s, the Native Lands Commissioner himself took on the duty of settling succession and land disputes and told me that he had to take the volumes and read them to the people, who, he said, "often are ignorant of their true history." Yet, from Sukuna's time on, certain land questions have been reopened. In 1986, the Vatukaloko were given permission to use Yaqara land for planting after having appealed personally to the governor general and to the prime minister in an election year. Yet, simultaneously, dissatisfaction with individual judgments of the Native Lands Commission, past or present, is hard to raise because it seems to call into question the rights of ethnic Fijians as "owners of the land," a status authorized through the truth of the recording of custom in the Native Lands Commission's bibles (see Kaplan 1988, 1990, 1995).[6] Post-1997 coups' constitutional revisions invested Native Lands Trust Board officials with the authority to use the kin group membership records *(Ivola ni kawa bula)* to determine "racial" membership crucial to the rights to vote on ethnic-Fijian rolls and run as ethnic Fijians for national office (Riles 1997a). Thus, the institutions themselves sustained the nexus of connection between ethnic-Fijian political and social rights, land ownership, and God's grace.

This entire history is set against the backdrop of contrast with Indo-Fijian experience. As Kelly and others have noted, there was no parallel colonial reification of Indo-Fijian culture, no administration via ostensibly customary political leadership, no system of customary law for Indo-Fijians in colonial Fiji. Instead, contracts, courts, the Colonial Sugar Refinery, and the market more generally were major colonial entities in Indo-Fijian history.

PROMISED LANDS/STOLEN WATERS: VATUKALOKO LAND AND WATER IN PARTICULAR

Now I want to focus on a particular local history to consider the ways in which Gordon's colonial intervention articulated with a hinterland Fijian group. If eastern coastal chiefs developed a Christianized entitlement of all Fijians within the colonial and then national polity, what can we learn from the history of contentious and contesting hinterland Fijians?

The Vatukaloko are atypical ethnic Fijians in two ways. They are preeminently itaukei ritually and have very little land. They claim close relationship to autochthonous gods of the land located in the Kauvadra mountain range, and they tend to contest the rights of chiefs and powers deemed foreign. Generally, the Vatukaloko have done this by finding that if anything colonial is truly powerful—such as Jesus—it must be Fijian in origin, that is, of the land. Second, unlike most Fijians, they did not fare well in the colonial Lands Commission processes, and, therefore, they are itaukei with very little actual land. (At the end of this chapter, I return to the ways in which some of the Vatukaloko today are not atypical, the ways in which their takeovers and national takeovers are parallel.)

The land in question here is approximately 17,000 acres in the north of Viti Levu Island, not far from the coast. When I first went there, beginning research with the Vatukaloko people of Drauniivi and nearby villages in the 1980s, it was part of the Yaqara Pastoral Company and also was described to me as "the yavutu" ancestral lands—lands of significance in the history of Navosavakadua, the famous ancestor of the Vatukaloko who led a ritual-political movement in opposition to other Fijians, the colonizing British, and the Christian missions in the 1870s (see Worsley 1968; Burridge 1969; Kaplan 1991, 1995).

European settlers in the area, Tom Burness and W. T. Thomas, made land purchases in the late nineteenth century. These were established, registered, and acknowledged by colonial Land Inquiries that considered European claims to land (ELC) in 1884 and 1908. The land was sold in part and leased in part to the Colonial Sugar Refinery, the colonial-era sugar-refining monopsony in 1926. At Independence in 1970, the new Fiji government bought the land and in 1973 established a private company owned by the Fiji government (Yaqara Pastoral Company 1981). In the 1990s, the Rabuka government leased part of this land to Natural Waters of Fiji, a corporation owned by David Gilmour.

By the 1870s, Wesleyan missionaries had been in the coastal areas of Fiji for thirty years. White planters had flooded the islands in the cotton boom of the 1860s. The Cakobau government, an uneasy coalition of chiefs and settlers, was about to be replaced by British colonial government in 1874. The Vatukaloko in the 1870s gave their name to a small hinterland polity, stretching in territory from their yavutu (origin village) in the Kauvadra Range, home of Fijian ancestor gods, down to the coast where present-day Drauniivi stands. They were headed by a chief from the line of the Tui Vatu, mataqali Nasi. Other subdivisions are mataqali Wakalou, the line of the chief's warriors, and mataqali Nakubuti, the line of the installing people and priests. Nakubuti people were distinctive in the power of their warrior priests. Originally from the interior, the Vatukaloko had conquered and married some of the coastal people, so their polity included people that some in the area today call the *Tini ka Rua na Yavusa,* "the Twelve Tribes (of Israel)." The Vatukaloko were on the borders of larger, far more hierarchical, chiefly-led polities and had a history—from the 1840s, at least—of asserting autonomy in relation to encroachments by bigger kingdoms, most notably in 1873, when they killed a labor recruiter from the kingdom of Bau and fought against white settlers and coastal troops sent up by the Cakobau government. I have always understood the Vatukaloko of this period to have been operating with a sense of themselves as autochthonous and ritually prior, linked to the powers of the Kauvadra range. In the 1870s, most of the Vatukaloko people followed

Navosavakadua, a Nakubuti man, an oracle priest, and a member of the installing kin group, who sought to establish a new kind of polity. Instead of being authorized by the "foreign" mana of a chief's lewa, Navosavakadua's polity was made powerful by its connection to the center of autochthony, or indigenousness, the Kauvadra range. It was what I call a "land-centered polity."

Navosavakadua's vision of a polity skillfully gave meaning to foreign and indigenous powers and then realigned them. Whereas Cakobau and other eastern chiefs took Christian gods and British forms of rule as powerful foreign forms, Navosavakadua preached that what was powerful was powerful because it was Fijian. Thus, Jesus and Jehovah were Fijian gods. Water was quite important in Navosa's polity. He and later followers sent out wai ni tuka (water of immortality) to those who wanted to join his polity and to mobilize against the encroaching coastal chiefs and colonizers.

The colonial administration suppressed Navosa's land-centered polity. He was sent to the island of Rotuma in 1886, and his followers were deported to Kadavu, where they stayed from 1891 to 1903. They were allowed back to Ra and stayed from 1903 to 1909 in Nanukuloa, where the Roko (Fijian colonial provincial governor) kept an eye on them. In 1909, they were allowed to rebuild Drauniivi village. In the intervening years, the Thomas brothers and Tom Burness had consolidated their land purchases. The Vatukaloko had two opportunities to get their land back, at two sittings of the Native Lands Commission in Ra in 1917 and 1924.

Lands Commissions are an integral part of this Vatukaloko history: In the 1880s, when the colonial government held inquiries to rule on claims made by Europeans to land purchased before 1874, white settlers living near the Vatukaloko had already made claims to land ownership in the area. From the 1880s on, as noted earlier, the Native Lands Commission elicited testimony on Fijian landholding. It inquired into local kinship groups (mataqalis) and the lands they "traditionally" owned. During the process, Fijians developed standard lists of named kin groups, each with a founding ancestor, and group membership from inception to present. The Lands Commission keyed the kin group names to maps, showing boundaries. In 1917 and 1918, G. V. Maxwell held Native Lands Commission hearings in Ra. The Vatukaloko sent three spokesmen, one for each of the three mataqali. They produced the required tribal statement and answered questions about how they were connected to larger local kingdoms, but said that they had always been autonomous. The commissioners listed them under the kingdom of Rakiraki. The older history of the Vatukaloko polity did not make it into the Native Lands Commissioners' conclusions. At this hearing in 1918, the Vatukaloko tried to claim the land stretching from the shore where Drauniivi was located back through Vugala on the hilltop near the coast, to the flatland sites of Nakorowaiwai and Vale Lebo close to the Kauvadra range, all the way back to Vatukaloko, their yavutu. They did not get it. Only the people of Wakalou mataqali got some land via genealogical connection to the Togavere and Nasaro people.

The Native Lands Commissioners' decisions and records were not the only description of the disposition of Vatukaloko lands. As the official records were returned to the capitol and housed at the Native Lands Commission, in 1918 Jovesa Bavou, a Vatukaloko intellectual, created his own record of the commission's visit. An entry dated 24 January 1917, written in Bavou's precise handwriting in a large bound book kept by a descendant in Drauniivi, is headed "History of the beginning of the yavusa (ritual kin group) Vatukaloko and the yavusa who share its descent from the beginning of the world in the olden Days."

> The Lord Jehovah (Na Kalou ko Jiova) made two people. A man and a woman. He named the man Rasari and named the woman Naikanivatu. He gave them land of which they were owners *(me rau taukena)*, and it was called VATUKALOKO. Then they had three children. First, LEWANAVANUA was born. Then later the twins BULIBULIVANUA and SAUMAIMURI were born. When they were grown, their father decreed that they should have different lands. He gave LEWANAVANUA the land called BUKELELEVU. He was the eldest. He gave BULIBULIVANUA the land called NARAWARAWA. He gave SAUMAIMURI the land called NASARO. They then went their separate ways and married, and their descendants multiplied over time and became people [instead of ancestor gods] of the three mataqali of our yavusa of VATUKALOKO and of all the different yavusa

of all the parts of FIJI and the WORLD. [My translation, his capitals]

The narrative then traced the histories of the three mataqali of Vatukaloko and their subdivisions. After those histories, he turned to other peoples of Fiji, through accounts of the many wives of founding ancestor Degei and the lands founded by their children. His genealogical scheme is unusual in two interrelated ways. It begins with creation by Jehovah (who does not appear in his tribal history as recorded by the Native Lands Commission). Further, it presents a Kauvadra-centric vision of the world, claiming that from the ancestors of the Vatukaloko spring all the kingdoms of Fiji and, indeed, all the peoples of the world. (A longer account of Bavou's book and its place in Vatukaloko history is in Kaplan 1995:149–159.)

The records of colonial Land Inquiries both made and displayed colonial order, seeking to fix and record set boundaries to contain Fijian land and Fijians in set hierarchies of province, district, village, and kin group, and, of course, to fix legal ownership of land as property. The record kept by Jovesa Bavou set a parallel but different order. He chronicled the relationship of the Christian god, Vatukaloko ancestors, and lands. In this vision, even as the Native Lands Commission denied its land claims, the Vatukaloko have temporal, genealogical, and ritual precedence over far-flung peoples and polities, whether eastern coastal chiefs in Fiji or colonial powers, no matter how powerful they may be. Where the colonial inquiries altered the divinity of ancestor gods in the service of the specification of ownerships, the Vatukaloko pressed Jehovah into service to create a framework for their universal claims.

In 1924, land ownership throughout Fiji was again up for review. Ratu Sukuna held hearings to establish Native Lands Reserves, Fijian mataqali-owned land that would be leased to Indians and Indo-Fijians to grow cane or would be used for government development projects. Koresi Nataranuku, the Vatukaloko chief, tried to claim the lands at Nakorowaiwai. Sukuna noted in the records of the inquiry that, although the Vatukaloko were in Kadavu, certain lands were sold "and the money paid out to the wrong people" (Sukuna in Native Reserves, Vol. 44). However, by then the Colonial Sugar Refinery had leased and bought the land and wanted it for a cattle run at Yaqara, so he denied the claim. At Independence in 1970, the Colonial Sugar Refinery became the nationally owned Fiji Sugar Corporation, and lands it owned became nationally owned Crown land. Since those days, the Vatukaloko have lived near the Yaqara cattle ranch and fields and have sometimes worked there, frequently calling the area the "yavutu" (origin place). They have never gone to court to sue for it and probably would have lost if they had. Since 1998, when David Gilmour built the Natural Waters of Fiji bottling plant, having obtained a ninety-nine-year lease on this nationally owned land, the Vatukaloko have had three main responses.

First, there has been acquiescence, enthusiasm, and cooperation. When Gilmour first set up the plant, a number of Vatukaloko people got jobs there. In 1998, the Vatukaloko chiefs set up a corporation, the Vatukaloko Investment Company, Ltd., to provide security, maintenance, groundskeeping, and catering for the plant and its workers. In a typical organizing form, the chairman is the *Tui Vatu*, and the chiefs from the various villages make up the board of directors of the firm.

Second, there was some disillusionment with Natural Waters. Some Vatukaloko people felt undercompensated and sought to make deals with other investors. As my main informant described it, they wanted to manage the investment and not see Gilmour profit on Vatukaloko resources. Other local mataqalis, including villagers from Naseyani, sought to open their own bottling project, using springs at Nananu. This critical position intertwines a vein of protest that has appeared in the newspaper columns, from a writer who criticizes both colonial and recent governments for depriving the Vatukaloko of their land and then dips back into a more prophetic tone to evoke Navosavakadua, mysteries surrounding his death, and (as I read it) hints of his return if the land is not returned. "What will the Chaudhry government do? Therein lies its destiny. Time is the essence. Na Gauna" (Sokonibogi 1999). In this somewhat apocalyptic version, the fate of the national government rests on the fate of the Vatukaloko lands.

The third response to Natural Waters of Fiji was the takeover. On July 12, 2000, almost a month into the national crisis during which Speight held Prime Minister Chaudhry and his cabinet hostage, the *Daily Post* (Sharma 2000) reported:

Over 80 villagers armed with spear guns, knives and sticks seized the Natural Waters of Viti Ltd factory....The men of mataqali Nakubuti, Yavusa Vatukaloko from Drauniivi in Rakiraki surrounded the Yaqara plant...they asked the workers to leave, seized all communication lines and told the chief engineer to step aside.

The spokesman said...the villagers would release the plant after the Prime Minister, President, or Minister for Lands visits them to discuss their grievances.

The villagers want access to the lease of the land on which the factory is constructed and a written agreement with the company for one cent per sale of a bottle of water to go to the landowners.

Mr. Tuifagalele said the company should employ people from the village and give them opportunities to rise to the levels of supervisors and managers. He said the factory should not operate on Sunday no matter how tight the demand was.

The villagers had set up a roadblock in front of the plant....

"The new administration should understand that the land is sacred and central to our continued existence and identity," a spokesman said.

"We want them to open up all the files regarding Vatukaloko people and no Fijian should live off the breadcrumbs of past colonial injustices.

"The villagers have tolerated more than enough and despite many appeals to former governments we have never been able to achieve what we are entitled to.

"This time we want answers and until then the factory will remain closed."

The takeover ended with the arrest of the occupiers. Eventually, charges against them were dropped. It does not seem surprising that the agents of the takeover were people of Nakubuti mataqali, acting perhaps in the tradition of Navosavakadua. The company continues to contract for services with Vatukaloko people and has sponsored a number of initiatives for local development, including building kindergartens in local villages and settlements.

What always seems to me remarkable about the Vatukaloko has been their refusal of alienation. Their very tenacious sense of ownership, of being vested, and of entitlement to the returns on that ownership has endured through more than a century. Since the days of Navosavakadua, Vatukaloko people have had a distinctive self-understanding as people of the land, ritually powerful and opposed to external incursions. Water from the springs near the Kauvadra range figured in this history as a ritual and political gift from Navosavakadua to his followers. The Vatukaloko experience was always shaped by colonial structures yet also shaped them in new ways, as Jovesa Bavou's record of the Native Lands Commission in 1917 reveals. This unusual narrative challenged colonial assumptions about Vatukaloko polity affiliation and eastern-coastal chiefly claims of sovereignty in the area. Yet, it also participated in the same process we have seen in the Native Lands Commission bibles. Bavou's book and the Vatukaloko sense of the gods' gifts of land and water, never alienable from them, are in parallel with the more general, ethnic-Fijian result of colonial legal forms set in the 1870s. In each case, a sense of the nature of Fijians as a group, their attributes and their ownership, their place and their rights, is generated. Followed into the present, what is most striking to me is the conviction felt by my Vatukaloko friends that if land records and files are opened, the obvious ownership of the Vatukaloko cannot help but be revealed.

CONTEMPORARY CRISES

The takeover of the Natural Waters of Fiji plant is at once a sign of Fijian refusal of alienation and of the Christianization of entitlement pervading Fiji's colonial history. It mirrors the ethnic-Fijian takeover of the nation. (On the 2000 coups, see Kelly and Kaplan 2001; Lal 2000b.)

Following the coups, Fiji's military-backed interim government began routinizing takeovers on a grand scale. Following Speight's coup, the military and Fiji's chiefs had installed Laisenia Qarase as prime minister. At first, Qarase anticipated an indefinite period of rule to administer, write a new constitution, and eventually hold new elections. Then, following the court ruling that an election must be held under the rules of the 1997 constitution, Qarase's government also worked to position itself for the election (which he won), while continuing its agenda of normalizing the coups in multiple ways. In outlining his blueprint for Fiji's political and economic future, Qarase said, "We are absolutely mindful of the special needs of the different communities of the country. The vast contributions of our brothers and sisters in the Indian and other communities has been crucial in our development as a nation. But the most important contribution has been from the indigenous Fijian and Rotuman community. They are the majority landowners in this country and it is through their good will and generosity that today we are a multiethnic and multicultural society" ("New PM addresses nation," Fijilive Website, July 2000).

In a parallel with the Vatukaloko who refuse to accept non-ownership, here all ethnic Fijians are portrayed as intrinsically owners. In Qarase's political discourse, at the national level, ethnic Fijians are understood as landowners, as shareholders, vested with ownership of a powerful resource and as contributors of capital via their land. The capital of other investing corporations is discounted (and there are sound politics to criticism of the colonial and postcolonial capitalists who have made profits in Fiji). However, the poorly compensated labor of Indo-Fijian plantation workers and their unlanded descendants is also seen as secondary.[7] Therefore, there is little difference between local takeovers and national plans in their shared sense of the Christianized entitlement of ethnic Fijians. The questions ethnic-Fijian leaders seem to be addressing now are (1) how to articulate the Christianity of and in Qarase's blueprint and, most deeply felt of all, (2) how to synchronize the national takeover and local takeovers.

Finding the Christianity in and of ethnic-Fijian enterprise, conceived of as investment, seems to be a flourishing quest these days, from the *Daily Post*'s exultation in its "Thank You, Fiji Waters" editorial over the "God given resources" that will bring the Vatukaloko and the nation such returns, to the examples quoted below. Fully one-eighth of the text in a speech by Qarase to the new organization the Fiji Indigenous Business Association was devoted to Christian themes (*The Review* 2000b):

I am delighted to be with you today for the official launching of the Fiji Indigenous Business Council. Please accept my congratulations for taking an initiative which should strengthen our national effort to expand the role of the Fijian people in business and commerce....

The objectives of the Fiji Business Council are parallel to those of the Interim Administration—and I know they are shared by many right thinking people from all our Fiji communities....

I suppose some eyebrows might be raised initially by your belief that God the Creator and Sustainer is the key to Fijian entrepreneurship. At first glance, that reference did have a fundamentalist ring. Were you expecting to sit back and let God run your businesses?

I soon saw, however, that the context of your conviction is that Christian principles should form the basis for commerce. There can be no quarrel with that. Many businesses are managed in that way and some of them have been hugely successful.

We should never forget that Jesus Christ himself knew about commerce. As the son of a carpenter, who undoubtedly helped out in his father's workshop, he would have been familiar with many of the aspects of running a small business.

I can imagine the interest of Jesus in the quality of workmanship, on-time delivery, customer relations and trust, competition, purchase of materials, costing, pricing, selling, bookkeeping and careful handling of money.

As an extension of the religious ideals and principles you have adopted as a business creed, it is perfectly appropriate for you to regard profit as a reflection of good stewardship.... (Address at the official launching of the Fiji Indigenous Business Council by Mr. Laisenia Qarase, Prime Minister and Minister for National Reconciliation and Unity, October 19, 2000)

Even though Qarase here extols the compatibility of small business entrepreneurship with Christian practice, it is increasingly clear that his Fiji blueprint envisions ethnic-Fijian investment as the future of ethnic Fijians in business (see also Narube 1997). In both such cases, taking profit as a reflection of good stewardship is key. Consider the self-conscious use of Christian themes by the manager of Unit Trust (*The Review* 2000a:28) in an article titled "Tailor-Made for Small Investors: Unit Trust's Minimum Purchase Policy in Line with Its Socio-Economic Ideals":

> The phone call made Peter Mario's day. It was from a man in the Yasawas who had read the Unit Trust of Fiji general manager's interview in the Fijian language newspaper Volasiga. Mario was propagating the merits of saving, using the biblical story of the pharaoh whose dream about seven fat, healthy cows and seven thin, unhealthy ones foretold of seven bountiful years to be followed by seven years of famine.

> Heeding his interpreter Joseph's advice, the pharaoh ordered the granaries filled during years of plenty and this saw that no one in the country went hungry during the ensuing lean years. Mario likened investing in the Unit Trust, the government owned investment company, to loading the granary in preparation for possibly lean years in the future.

> The caller from the Yasawas told Mario he was struck by the story. So much so that he purchased 400 units soon after. What was particularly satisfying for Mario was that the caller was typical of the small, grassroots investor whom the Trust had been wooing, and for whom it was primarily set up for by the government in 1978....

We can even find nostalgia for Christianity in the words of Frank Bainimarama, the head of Fiji's military, whose forces underpin Qarase's government. Asked by an interviewer, "What's the answer to Fiji's deeply rooted societal problems?" Bainimarama responded, "Fiji needs well-defined visions and set goals to accomplish. Mottos such as 'Fear God and Honour the King' are no longer meaningful. We do things that are not supposed to be done in a Christian country. The values are gone. We need to instill values, have vision and goals. We need to renew our vows. The only way is through reconciliation and dialogue….We are doing a lot of public relations work in villages" (*The Review* 2000b:16).[8]

It is possible to imagine these comparisons as rhetorical flourishes. It is just as possible to imagine that the Vatukaloko demand that no water be bottled on Sundays is secondary to their desire to get a cut of the profits—until we remember how basic Jehovah and Jesus are in the history of ethnic-Fijian ownership, how Christianity participates simultaneously in defining Fijian separation from the market and in defining their ownership of "God given resources." What I think is going on here is a generalization of the "chiefs on the board of directors of the company" strategy, to turn all ethnic Fijians into shareholders who take profit from Fiji via their "God given" investments (see Kaplan n.d).

However, the bigger task now faced by Qarase and all the other ethnic Fijians who currently lead Fiji is to align national and local takeovers. Far more worrisome to ethnic Fijians than world opinion (largely condemnations of the coups as violations of human rights) is the problem of synchronizing the takeovers and uniting ethnic Fijians, a goal that is currently captured in the term "Reconciliation." In places such as South Africa, as the Comaroffs show, Reconciliation Commissions are a key to understanding colonial and postcolonial realities and, as they see it, the contradictions in neoliberal capitalism. For Fiji, we might thus expect that reconciliation work would focus on Fijian colonial history in total, with all of Fiji's peoples engaged. Laisenia Qarase's title is Prime Minister and Minister for National Reconciliation. Yet, it is quite clear from his use of the term and Bainimarama's that it is ethnic-Fijian reconciliation they seek. Many observers after Fiji's 1987 coups were struck by the way that ethnic-Fijian politics swelled to fill the space for discussion of national politics. The Constitution Commission then redirected the discussion toward a consideration of Fiji as a multiethnic nation. Now the 2000 coups have narrowed the space once more. The court-mandated elections created a new efflorescence of the ethnic-Fijian political contest.[9] Reconciliation is being narrowly defined as the need for ethnic Fijians to synchronize their takeovers.

LOLOMA AND LITIGATION

Contemporary events resonate with some of Gordon's first, most basic moves in ordering law in his new colony. They also resonate with the ongoing understanding of ethnic-Fijian self-nature and rights that posits the special relationship of ethnic Fijians and the Christian god. (Loloma, the term used in this section, means "kindly love" and "reciprocity" and an antimarket ethos. It is also the word used to translate "Christ's grace.") It is an open question in Fiji and for Fiji's future whether ethnic-Fijian claims of entitlement through loloma or claims to civil rights through litigation will shape national order and local events.

In November 2000, Justice Gates of the Lautoka High Court ruled that the 1997 constitution should not have been set aside. In 2001, the Court of Appeal upheld this decision and mandated new elections. However, following the November 2000 decision, Qarase and Bainimarama made it very clear in their public speeches that they did not consider the decision by the Court to be the basis for Fiji's future but rather that the future of the nation-state rests in ethnic-Fijian reconciliation, that is, loloma between Fijians.

Qarase, in his New Year's address (*The Review* 2000b:4) said this:

"The constitutional question will be at the forefront again in February. The Court of Appeal is to hear the State's appeal against the judgment by Justice Gates that the 1997 Constitution is still in place. The Gates judgment raises many profound questions that go well beyond the law in its implications. We must now await the outcome of the Court of Appeal hearing. The Interim Government will be guided at all times by the supreme importance of the collective interests and welfare of the people and the peace and security of the State. We must also take into account the views of the Great Council of Chiefs...."

The following excerpt is from the interview with Bainimarama (*The Review* 2000b:16):

[The interviewer] "We have a racial problem that the politicians are always using to divide people? Anyone who talks about unity is voted out of office."

[Bainimarama's reply] "Reconciliation is needed first among indigenous Fijians before we can reconcile with other races....There is this false unity when Fijians fight against the common enemy, Indians. But after May 19, the Fijians were back fighting each other. Then you have Justice Gates' decision, that again seemed to unify Fijians....

Both leaders assert that there are "deeper things" than law and, indeed, that ethnic-Fijian interests are united in opposition to decisions of courts and to constitutions. Therefore, as we have seen for the Vatukaloko, there is a sense of right that is god-given (Christ's loloma), which is more fundamental than elections, courts of law, or market contracts.

* * *

Let us recall the question of how colonial lawgiving, in ongoing intersections, shapes colonial and postcolonial histories. What entities constitute events in Fiji's colonial and postcolonial history? As John Kelly shows in Chapter 3 in this volume, Gordon's reliance on J. W. B. Money and Maine created a colonial order meant to deny competition, to create stability and security, to allow local elites to maintain their rank, and above all, to create separated racial spheres with differing legal ways and means for each, especially "Natives" separated from others. One might observe that Fiji's entire colonial history is one in which Gordon's original scheme is inhabited and routinized, yet also tested, challenged, and transformed.

It is not hard to trace active Indo-Fijian resistance and initiatives against the chilling consequences for "intermediate races" in Money's scheme, and it is not difficult to see ethnic Fijians historically inhabiting the role of Natives, not alienated by money and markets, insistent on their own system of status and honor, with highly elaborated etiquette. (Fijian society was "based not on contract and freedom but on consanguinity and status," wrote Secretary of Native Affairs Ratu Sukuna in his 1950 annual report [Sukuna (1950) 1983:1].) However, it would be truly mistaken to view ethnic-Fijian colonial and postcolonial agency as merely passive or conservative, especially when it comes to their appropriation, in effect, of Maine's Whig critique of political economy.

As Kelly (Chapter 3, this volume) shows, Maine was far less committed to tracking the triumphs of forces of modernization than to observing the realities of colonial complexities. Maine was not at all persuaded that Natives everywhere were on the edge of contract-dominated life. In embracing life without alienation—in the way of loloma—Fijians fashioned a Fijian-Christian world. In many ways, ethnic Fijians now encompass the history of progress in a universe of Fijian-Christian drama and possibility and cast themselves as specially positioned to avoid the evils of contemporary mammon while still reaping the profits from their god-given resources.

By understanding the ways in which Gordon was not simply setting up a social evolutionary narrative but instead, with Maine, a narrative of alternative possibilities, saving Natives from their fate elsewhere, we better understand the logic of today's ethnic-Fijian tenacious assertion of god-given entitlement to own and rule and to save and redeem themselves by that god's will. The key terms are *reconciliation* of ethnic Fijians and *redemption* as the end point of Fijian history. The logic of ethnic-Fijian takeovers, local and national, is based on a chronotope of redemption, not on colonial law per se. What is deeper than courts and constitutions is ownership of Fiji, the lands of God's promise. It is not that contemporary ethnic Fijians inhabit Gordon's scheme. They have taken it over, too.

Acknowledgments

I thank the Fiji Government for permission to conduct field and archival research in 1984 to 1985, 1986, 1991, and 2002. I acknowledge with particular thanks the sharing of historical knowledge and the friendship and research assistance of many people in Fiji and beyond. Responsibility for the analysis presented in this chapter is mine alone.

I am grateful for funding of the research drawn on for this chapter from the National Science Foundation, Fulbright-Hays Department of Education, the Institute for Intercultural Studies, the Wenner Gren Foundation, and Vassar College.

Notes

1. This chapter complements John D. Kelly's chapter in this volume. Chapter 3 sets out our argument concerning the inception of colonial rule in Fiji, including Cession, Sir Arthur Gordon's reliance on J. W. B. Money's colonial theory, and the legal entities of Pacific Islander Fijian separation and Indian contract plantation labor that Gordon established. We present a longer analysis of colonial lawgiving in Fiji in *Laws Like Bullets,* forthcoming from Duke University Press.

2. In Fiji, in a continuant of colonial discourse, the term *race* is generally used for "ethnic group" and is a political category. Since Independence in 1970, citizens have registered on communal voting rolls that reflect the social divisions colonially constituted as racial, especially "Fijian" and "Indian." "Europeans" are now included in the category "General Elector," along with people of Rotuman, other Pacific Islander descent, and East Asian descent, as well as so-called "Part-Europeans" of mixed ancestry. Communal rolls are in sharp contrast, for example, to the common roll practices in the US state of Hawai'i. Needless to say, I see *race* as a term in discourse, in no way tied to any essential or fixed nature of any group of people.

In the 1996 Census, with Fiji's population at 775,077, people identifying themselves as ethnic Fijians were 50.7 percent of the population, and Indo-Fijians were 43.7 percent. These two groups make up approximately 94.4 percent of Fiji's population. The remaining population includes the self-named Part-Europeans, comprising 1.5 percent (see Riles, Chapter 7, this volume), as well as other Pacific Islanders, Rotumans, Chinese, Europeans, and "All Others" (Fiji Bureau of Statistics 2001). Census figures, particularly post-coups census figures, are an interesting topic in their own right.

3. This vignette also appears in a footnote in Kaplan and Kelly 1999.

4. Elsewhere I have described four contesting ways in which Fijians came to imagine divine power and the fate of the gods of the land in relation to colonial power, the Christian God, and the Lands Commissions projects early in the 1900s (Kaplan 1988, 1995). First, in the coastal chiefly articulation, it was said that the true god had replaced heathen superstition, demanding rejection of old gods. Second, among those who continued to worship the ancestor deities, sometimes the old gods formed a secret mirror image of the top-down, centralized colonial order. Third, in other cases, the old gods became marginalized spirits, consulted in secrecy. Fourth, as Navosavakadua (and another important Fijian leader,

Apolosi Nawai) preached, some found that Jehovah himself was already a god of
the land.

On Fijian Christianity, there is substantial literature, beginning with the
archives and publications of missionaries Calvert 1858, Williams 1858, and
Waterhouse 1868, and including Garrett 1982, 1992; Niukula 1997; Kaplan 1990;
Toren 1988; Miyazaki 2000a; and Tomlinson n.d. My approach to understanding
the places of Jesus and Jehovah in Fiji's colonial and postcolonial history (see
Kaplan 1995) draws especially on Sahlins 1985:37–41 and on Rutz 1992, 1995.

5. See Miyazaki, Chapter 9, this volume, for an account of the Suvavou people's twentieth-century history of "Reports" to the Native Lands Commission in
efforts to establish land ownership. Interestingly, although bureaucrats and
lawyers pursued these efforts in the 1990s, none were taken to a court of law—
they addressed the Native Lands Commission directly or petitioned other ethnic-
Fijian leaders.

6. Questions about land ownership in the 1980s (and later) were raised in
the context of divide-and-rule tactics by ethnic-Fijian politicians and chiefs who
presented themselves as custodians of *taukei* rights in the face of purported Indo-
Fijian wishes to change the landholding laws. However, it is my sense that only
rarely were the individual inquiries so routinely managed by the commissioner
concerned with Indo-Fijian ownership of anything.

7. Indeed, the events told in this chapter and in Miyazaki's (Chapter 9, this
volume) look very different when told with a sense of the consequences of ethnic-
Fijian ownership claims for those Fiji citizens who, as non–ethnic Fijians, have no
claims to land. Vatukaloko desires for "their" land, or Suvavou peoples' demands
for higher compensation for the lands on which the national capitol is built,
reduce national revenues that could support social welfare projects. As ethnic
Fijians transform refusal of alienation to shareholding ownership in Fiji as nation
and as property, they can reconfigure ethnic Fijians as unalienated only by reinforcing alienation of labor and lack of hope for rights among Indo-Fijians.

8. There is much more to say about Bainimarama's language. One could
propose that he, and Qarase as well, represent a unique, new, globally constituted
modern bureaucrat-subject, with his language of "public relations work in the villages" and invocation of a now-global human rights discourse (much problematized) of "reconciliation and dialogue." Others would insist that he can be
understood only as a new form of "Fijian-global" bureaucrat. I prefer the second,
but I think that the periodizing of global connection needs care. We can also see

Bainimarama as part of a deep history of globally participating ethnic-Fijian leaders who linked themselves institutionally and discursively to empire and Christianity. His nostalgia for values lost is, in some ways, like the lament of colonial official/Christian high chief Ratu Jone Madraiwiwi, who in the 1880s minuted that the insubordinate people of Ra, who had had the opportunity to choose Christianity for decades, were "a land of black souls" (see Kaplan 1995:105). What comparison of such connections reveals is not one entry into some kind of modernity but a long history of changing articulations, including especially a post-World War II shift much resisted by Fijian leaders, from *imperial* globality to the formally egalitarian, rights-oriented United Nations globe of decolonized nation-states (see Kelly and Kaplan 2001).

9. In the past, coups and ensuing public political discourse have promoted and emphasized the paramountcy of ethnic Fijians (for example, see Rutz and Balkan 1992; Rutz 1995). Yet, we should note that elections themselves installed the multiethnic Fiji Labour Party in 1987 and 2000. Note also that in the 2001 election, mandated by the Court of Appeal, Qarase's victorious coalition refused to give Chaudhry's Labour Party any cabinet seats, a requirement of the 1997 constitution. This chapter cannot include an analysis of this decision except to suggest that it continues Qarase's position that Fijian institutions and rights supersede constitution and law.

7

Law as Object

Annelise Riles

From its inception at the hands of Fiji's retreating colonial government, Fiji's postcolonial era has been an era of groups. The first independence constitution gives political valence to a notion of racial groups by dividing voters into Fijians, Indians, and "General Voters," paving the way for both group-based politics and alliances across groups (Lal 1986). Since then, individual affiliation to these groups has been a crucial official and unofficial basis of legal entitlements. As the chapters in this volume collectively demonstrate, this notion of the group has its antecedents in concepts that defined the nineteenth-century colonial period, such as race, custom, and labor (compare Thomas 1991; Kaplan 1995; Kaplan 1998). It also has parallels in mid-century anthropology: The group-ness of Fiji as anthropological object has been perpetuated implicitly in ethnographic studies that largely take these groups as independent subjects of study. At the same time, recent work has taken as its point of departure the fact that this reified group-ness, in the hands of others, has come back to haunt us. At the moment of the failure of the group as an analytical category for anthropologists, the group enjoys a revival outside the academy such that anthropologists can now take a certain macabre fascination with others' ways of "doing what we used to do" (Miyazaki 2000b, following Strathern).

At the School of American Research advanced seminar, there was considerable discussion of current "crisis" in the Pacific. The crisis is familiar to anthropologists for other reasons as well. The failure of the group as an analytical tool is, for anthropologists also, one of an *excess* of knowledge, or signification, albeit of a slightly different kind—an exhaustion with denomination and identification, with endless questions of who belongs where, why, and for what purposes. The objectifications are not "theirs" alone, in other words. They are also ours, as evidenced by the charges and countercharges of essentialism within the discipline in the 1990s. The crisis to which this volume refers is as much a crisis of knowledge for anthropology as a crisis in the world. Indeed, that we experience analytical anxiety as a matter of a crisis "out there" is a paradigmatic example of how, as Roy Wagner (1981) described a quarter-century ago, anthropologists make their knowledge external to themselves, of how we make objects. In our collective understanding, "their" crises coincide with, cause, and are caused by "ours." Each is an instantiation of the other for us.

I invoke Wagner's work on objectification here because his arguments have powerfully influenced a body of literature that defined the moment preceding the theoretical present of this volume (and which this volume both extends and innovates upon), known as the turn to the "invention of tradition" (Thomas 1997:186). One of the principal interests of this literature concerned the nature of objectification— how the colonizer made the colonized into an "object" of knowledge and the dialogics of objectifications on the part of both colonizer and colonized that followed (Cohn 1987; Thomas 1997). As Miyazaki (2000b) has argued, this literature worked an implicit parallel between the objectifications of what it took as an outdated anthropology and the objectifications of the colonizer and colonized. The solutions to the theoretical problems this literature posed, as well as its understanding of colonial realities, instead emphasized anti-essentialism, the complexity of phenomena and their meanings, the proliferation of symbols instead of their constriction—in short, more signification, not less. Anthropologists responded to a crisis of excess by suggesting further levels, dimensions, and possibilities—by adding more rather than taking away.

If the discovery of crisis is an example of anthropologists' practices of object making, we have sought a solution to this crisis in our powerful critiques of objectification—until now. Recently, a new solution seems to have emerged to the crises we experience in our work and in the world. In the vocabulary of the invention of tradition literature, I want to suggest in this chapter that anthropologists have "objectified" law—we have imagined a phenomenon known as law as an essential object of contemplation, critique, or knowledge. This objectification is, at least at a theoretical level, curious, given the past decade's recurrent critiques of essentialism, attention to the effects of "invented" objectifications, and preference for arguments that emphasize complexity, hybridity, and other opposites of simple, essential wholes.

The editors of this volume encourage us to think about conditions of crisis in terms of the generative power of legal arrangements and, in particular, the legacies of legal institutions established long ago for current crises. Our collective project participates in a wider move afoot within the discipline to recenter law as fundamental to social analysis. The project builds on arguments about the generative power of knowledge made in the context of bureaucratic power (Foucault 1991a) and insights about the relationship of different kinds of actants in extending knowledge and constituting subjects (for example, Law 1994; compare Latour 1996). This focus is implicitly contrasted to an older anthropological interest in "informal" methods of social control, legal processes, and other approaches roughly glossed as "law in action" as opposed to "law in the books." It is a position taken self-consciously after the collapse of groups of various kinds (racial groups but also "clans," cultures, villages, and other anthropological workhorses) as legitimate or interesting subjects of ethnographic inquiry and *also* after a kind of collective exhaustion with studying "their" objectifications and their parallels to "ours." The recentering of law is seen to offer a respite from the theoretical quagmires that now plague the discipline: In disputes between materialist and symbolist approaches to anthropology, for example, law seems to occupy both positions and neither. Therefore, the editors suggest that law might serve in this volume as a "point of articulation" between the two (see the introduction). By recentering law, moreover, perhaps we hope also to recenter anthropological knowledge—to demonstrate its relevance to a new, postgroups, postculture world.

I want to confess some confusion about the law at issue here. To a lawyer, talk of law as an *entity* (a singular phenomenon that can be defined and imagined), such that it could be decentered or recentered, would make little sense. Lawyers view their world as consisting of various phenomena and stances—rights discourse, constitutions, procedures, bureaucracies, doctrines, private norms, and dispute settlement processes. There is no impetus to put these together into a singular actant, "the Law," whose consequences can be evaluated as a whole. Where lawyers see multiple legal phenomena at this moment, anthropologists see one singular phenomenon, albeit one that admits to being internally composed of the preceding elements and more (Strathern 1988).

The broad question I want to address in this essay is, What is the appeal or use of law as object at this anthropological moment? My answer concerns the very old anthropological subject of objectification, and in particular, the relationship between two kinds of objectification at work in the Anglo-American tradition of legal knowledge (in which Fijian law participates). The possibilities these two kinds of objectification provide, I argue, give legal knowledge the character of being both a reflection of the world and a thing in the world. This has enabled anthropologists to engage in one kind of productive conflation of these two kinds of objectification in the past and has enabled a conflation of an inverse kind most recently. I will explore the features of legal objectification with the use of a particular example, namely, the character of law as imposed on and experienced by so-called Part-Europeans (persons of mixed race) in colonial and postcolonial Fiji. I begin with one analytical framework for thinking about law as object that emerged from our collective discussions at the School of American Research seminar.

TWO GENRES

One comparative axis of this volume concerns the nature and effects of so-called dual legal systems, or legal systems that provide for separate bodies of "Native" and "European" law. Law in Fiji has consisted of two contrasting genres, which correspond roughly to distinct bodies of Native Law and European Law. Yet I want to suggest that it is crucial to understand both genres as present in almost every act of law-making, "Native" or "European." In other words, it is the genre of the legal act, not the group to which a body of law applies, that I want to foreground. The first genre is what I call an "expressive" genre. As I will explain, this was a genre of lawmaking carefully, and often purposely, crafted by colonial and postcolonial officials to effectuate meaning. Because of the explicit attention to meaning, the way this expressive form invites attention to itself as an object, and therefore the parallels to other objects of anthropological investigation, the expressive form has been the subject of a rich body of anthropological analysis, in Fiji and elsewhere. As anthropologists and cultural historians have shown, the expressive form of law makes *other* objects in the process of becoming an object of its own. As an object of the government's regard, Native Law in Fiji also objectified Fijian tradition, for example.

A second genre of legal knowledge, which I call an "instrumental" genre, has received considerably less attention in the anthropology and social history of the Pacific. As I will show, this form did not "mean" much of anything. Rather, the interest it provoked, and the effects it generated, concerned the particular kinds of ends it effectuated. Where the first form, in other words, directed attention at a law or act of lawmaking, the second form directed attention *through* the law to some further objective or state of affairs. It was this objective that was symbolically salient, and the evaluation of this second genre was possible only in relation to the ends it served.

Marilyn Strathern (1988:176) has defined objectification as "the way persons or things become the object of subjective regard or of their creation" and, glossing Marx, has pointed out that objectification is fundamentally a process of separating subjects from objects (1988:177). She emphasizes that this separation is achieved through a "constraint of form" and that this constraint may be *foregrounded* or *backgrounded,* made explicit or left implicit, from the actors' point of view (1988:180). This emphasis on the way a singular formal device can produce different kinds of objects, depending on whether it is rendered explicit or implicit, is a useful way of thinking about the distinction between the expressive and instrumental genres of legal act. In the expressive genre, the question of form—of *how* law and its object (Natives,

Europeans) come to be separate or of what makes an act of lawmaking distinct from other kinds of social activity—is not a question of concern. What is noticed, rather, is the separation of subject and object around which objectification occurs: Colonial administrators are not natives; a law is something quite different from the group to which it refers. In this sense, a law is a "referential symbol" in Wagner's (1981:xv) terminology; it sets up a "contextual contrast" between the symbol and the thing it symbolizes or signifies and therefore *refers* to its objects, the groups in the world it objectifies.

In practice, virtually every act of lawmaking, adjudication, or interpretation deployed both genres sequentially. The special quality of legal knowledge as both representation and object, I contend, derives from what Andrew Pickering (1997) has termed the "dance of agency" between the user of legal form and the form itself, enabled by the alternation between expressive and instrumental genres. I will return to this point later in this chapter in answer to the question of why anthropologists might choose, at this moment, to objectify law. For now, I will describe these genres independently in order to return later to the consequences of their coexistence.

Making Objects (1): The Expressive Genre of Legal Knowledge

Laws and acts of lawmaking take an expressive form when they mark groups. Consider the adjudication of land in colonial and postcolonial Fiji: As has been extensively discussed elsewhere (for example, France 1969), one of the colonial government's first acts was to prohibit the sale of land by "natives" and to return much of the land held by foreigners at the time of Cession to the *mataqali* (landowning units). According to the government's anthropological theory, the mataqali were the proper owners of the land. A Land Claims Commission established immediately after Cession to investigate the validity of every European title held hearings from December 1875 to February 1882 and ultimately disallowed more than half of all claims (Ward 1969:3). Those claims that were allowed became private property, or "freehold land." Since colonial times, therefore, land in Fiji has been spatially and legally divided into *Native Land*—defined as inalienable, held in trust by the government, and amounting to 83 percent of the total land of Fiji—and *freehold land*—land alienable at will and subject to a property law regime borrowed directly from English and Australian property law. These two categories of land rights refer expressly to two groups; they take Europeans and Fijians as their objects, and in the process of expressing the nature of these groups, they constitute them (compare Cohn 1987; Kelly 1989; Kaplan 1995; Merry 2000).

As this example suggests, the expressive genre makes objects such as social groups by producing significations about them. The objectifications of legal knowledge occur at a level of generality or abstraction that is a step removed from observations in the world: Fijian custom per se would be found nowhere for the administrator, except in European analyses and reflections on it. In the expressive genre, meaning is an infinite regress in which one representation stands behind another such that surfaces are always unstable and knowledge is relational. These objectifications are imagined as wholes constituted of internal parts—the population of Fiji is constituted of Native and European populations, for example—and to objectify in this way is to take an interest in the interrelationship among parts of the whole (compare Strathern 1992).

If the expressive genre creates objects of a particular kind, it also directs attention to itself—to the lawmaking at issue and to the implicit or explicit statements this lawmaking makes about its objects. The expressive genre is self-reflexive, in other words. Consider, for example, the following argument for the abeyance of law: As Sir Arthur Gordon, Fiji's first governor, wrote to Lord Carnarvon in the Home Office early in his tenure, "One of the most important questions which I have had to consider since my arrival here, is the degree and measure in which native laws and customs should be preserved in force, and how far English law should be at once generally introduced....What then is to be done?...Is the whole body of English Law to be imposed on all the population of the Colony alike, on the hundred thousand colored subjects of her Majesty equally with the white residents?" Of particular concern to Gordon was the discretion English common law vested in judges to make judgments about matters of value of the kind Gordon reserved to the administrators of native policy:

> Not only would the imposition in all respects of English Law
> be inequitable; but it would, I am convinced, be altogether
> impracticable to enforce obedience to it, and any serious

attempt to do so would, I have not the smallest doubt, cause an insurrection the limits of which it would be difficult to define....

Now, if there is one thing about the unknown and much dreaded law of the foreigners which the Fijians fear more than another, it is the uncertainty of its operation, of which they have already seen some striking instances, and nothing can be conceived more calculated to increase that uncertainty to the highest point, than a system of law to be administered, not as it stands written, or as it would be applied in the case of whites, but with such deviations as in each case the Court thinks just and expedient according to its own appreciation of native usages; and the degree of respect with which it may be disposed to regard them.

Gordon located his disdain for the common law in problems of custom: The danger was that the law, by hemorrhaging authority from the chiefs, "would degrade the chiefs and render them idle." His solution was a "recognized Native Code in addition to the General Law and subsidiary to it."[1] In so doing, the Governor drew attention to his own act of lawmaking and to the statement it might make about the difference between Europeans and Fijians. In other words, the expressive mode reflexively constitutes the legal act, also, as its object.

This objectification sets the stage for crisis of the kind this volume addresses: If the object at issue was the group, throughout the colonial and postcolonial periods, Part-Europeans have been officially defined and denigrated as "others" who do not belong to any group so constituted. At the time of Cession in Fiji, there were approximately 400 so-called "half-castes"—children of unions between foreigners and Fijians and their descendents (Ward 1969:9).[2] Throughout the colonial and postcolonial period, they posed a kind of objective challenge to the conceptual system.

From the outset, the colonial government alternated between willful ignorance of half-castes and open antipathy towards them.[3] Half-castes were the very products of Fijian contact with outsiders, in the government's view, and their interaction with Fijians only weakened the hold of custom.[4] Illegitimacy—cultural, personal, and legal—became the defining idiom in which the half-caste was constituted by the State, the question through which most aspects of government interaction with half-castes were framed. Administrative decisions concerning individual half-castes turned on whether the person in question was the child of a state-sanctioned marriage, where illegitimacy meant the exclusion from privileges reserved for Europeans.[5] This antipathy toward the liminal found itself supported by wider normative and regulatory schemes. Therefore, in the late nineteenth century, when the children of American and German settlers petitioned these governments for assistance, the Governor found the principles of private international law regarding citizenship squarely in his favor: "As regards half-caste claimants I took the position with [the US agent sent to Fiji to investigate the claims] at my first interview that they were (with one exception known to me), the offspring of polygamous marriages, or in other words the offspring of native concubines taken, or bought, at pleasure; and that until the contrary was shewn I must contend they followed the nationality of the mother and were therefore British Subjects. No attempt was made to show me that a valid marriage had taken place in any one case."[6] The difficulties the government encountered in defining and policing the "nationality" of Fiji's Part-Europeans will be familiar from the now-extensive literature on the forms and effects of colonial knowledge. For Fiji's colonial government, Part-Europeans represented a kind of excess, a remainder to the process of categorization (Douglas 1966; Butler 1990; Stoler 1995). This refuse provoked, and continues to provoke, periodic crises of governmental knowledge.

All that I have said so far about expressive knowledge rehearses the conclusions of a rich body of work on the objectifications of colonial law (Merry, Chapter 5, this volume; Kaplan, Chapter 6, this volume; Kelly, Chapter 3, this volume). Because the current volume is organized around a relationship of present to past, however—of historical legacy to contemporary crisis—I want to mention an even more commonsensical dimension of this expressiveness, namely, the way time and history are constituted as external to the objects the legal act makes for itself. In contemporary Fiji, the status of the freehold land is a salient political issue. In the years since the coups of 1987, politicians have periodically called for the government to confiscate or forcibly purchase this freehold land in order to return it to its "original owners"—the

descendents of the clans that sold it to the ancestors of its current owners. Land is an object of current political discourse, but one imagined
historically as existing in time. At the same time, the object of expressive action transcends the moment of the expression: Land, the
mataqali, the existence of Fijians and Indians, each becomes a constant
across time. The act of meaning making, in contrast, is imagined as a
historically contingent act and one that is only of the moment of the
expression. The effect is that the expression or meanings of law (such
as the constitution of one or another party as owner) can become
dated, decoupled from their objects. This evaluation of the expression
against the object, enabled by the differing temporalities of expressions
and objects, becomes a second source of crisis.

Making Objects (2): The Instrumental Genre of Legal Knowledge

What I have described so far will be familiar both from studies of
colonial law and from anthropological understandings of how knowledge constitutes its objects. The instrumental genre of legal act I discuss now will be less familiar, however. Why this might be so is a
principal concern of this chapter. I want to understand how this genre
and its artifacts go unnoticed by its various audiences and constituencies, as a site of contest, appropriation, or identity-making and as an
ethnographic subject.

The example I explore concerns the system of freehold land registration and its uses for Part-Europeans in the colonial era and at the
time of my fieldwork. If, as already mentioned, the status of freehold
land is politically contested in the postcolonial era, the system of producing and reproducing ownership—the land titles registration procedures—remains virtually the same as first designed by the colonial
government in the late nineteenth century. These procedures also
remain as unnoticed now as then: Although the decisions of the Land
Claims Commission were highly controversial and continue to attract
public and academic scrutiny today, once adjudicated, land claims
largely disappear from the historical and anthropological record, as
well as from the minutes of colonial officers and their dispatches to
London. Freehold land becomes a matter of its own record—the land
titles registration system—and requires little more from the legal ana-
lyst. Likewise, freehold land policy receives little more than a passing
reference or footnote in each of the major histories of Fijian colonial

government and land policy. Unlike land, which is essential in every sense of the term, land registration fails as an object; it is a means, not an end.

From the start, freehold land was an altogether different matter from Native Land to the colonial government. The architects of the freehold land regime sought to facilitate alienation with as much resolve as the architects of the Native Land regime sought to impede it. One of the colonial government's first acts was the introduction of a Real Property Ordinance, providing for all the forms of alienation deemed necessary for a modern capitalist land system.[7] Unlike the policies at issue in the regulation of native land, which sought to balance the protection of the native against the necessities of capitalism, the legal regime governing freehold land was aimed solely at fostering economic development through the efficient use of capital.

Many of the first Crown titles issued after the decisions of the Land Claims Commission were issued to the mixed-race children of original European settlers. Over the years that followed, land located in urban areas or valuable sugar plantation regions was often sold to corporations, recent émigrés, or foreign interests. Yet, in the rural areas Part-Europeans continued to own and live on their ancestors' freehold land. I was first forced to take notice of land title registration procedures by the Part-European inhabitants of the remote settlement of Kasavu, an hour by bus from Savusavu on the island of Vanua Levu. The inhabitants of Kasavu are descendents of David Whippy, an American seaman who arrived in Fiji around 1822, and their affines. The land they inhabit was acquired by their ancestor from the high chief of that region, Tui Cakau. The Land Claims Commission allowed David Whippy's sons claim for this land in 1880, and a Crown grant was issued for one-third of the total tract to each of David Whippy's three sons.[8]

If freehold land is defined by its alienability, the Whippys insisted that under no circumstance should land be sold "outside the family." In each generation, plots have been further divided in transactions of actual or approximated inheritance. At the time of my fieldwork, marriage between the Whippys and the Simpsons, descendents of David Whippy's friend and partner, for example, was most often discussed as a matter of division of land and of other interests, never as an accumulation of resources or alliance of groups. Nor was land imagined in the capitalist sense, as a source of productive wealth. It was inconceivable that the Whippys collectively might "amount" more (or less) to a quantity of land, wealth, or prestige in present-day Fiji than did their ancestor David Whippy 150 years ago (Riles 1998).

My hosts' distance from the principles and values underpinning Fiji's freehold land system did not alienate them from the devices of land transfer, however.[9] The title records make plain that from the first issuance of Crown grants, Part-European landowners transferred and partitioned their lands frequently. At the time of my research, even though many Part-European landowners could read their titles or transfer documents only with difficulty and were forced to engage lawyers in Suva at great expense in order to transact in land, they continued to use the system voraciously. The procedures surrounding registration were a constant topic of conversation, as people discussed the cost of surveying their land before registration, their visits to the Land Titles Office in Suva, or the activities and advice of their lawyers. Unlike European and Indian owners of freehold land, however, Part-Europeans rarely went to court over ownership disputes. In fact, my hosts in Kasavu insisted that they could think of no court case involving land until the present day.

Conversations in Kasavu invariably turned to title documents (fig. 7.1). Clan leaders maintained collections of legal documents and historical records concerning their land, and they took particular interest in poring over these with me in great detail. The survey diagrams and numerical measurements contained in the legal documents provided salient images of land and kin. This was made palpable in constant references to Certificates of Title (CT) numbers in daily discourse. When I proved unable to keep up with the chain of characters in a family story, for example, my hosts obliged me with schematic tree-shaped diagrams listing those who had inherited a share of the land, the amount of their acreage, and the CT number.

The system of land registration promulgated by Fiji's Real Property Ordinance that was so salient for my friends in Kasavu was very much a legal innovation (compare Hogg 1920). Unlike the land titles regime of England at the time, in which no centralized record of land ownership existed, or the land-recording system of the United States, in which deeds were recorded and indexed under the names of the transacting parties, Fiji borrowed the Torrens System of title registration

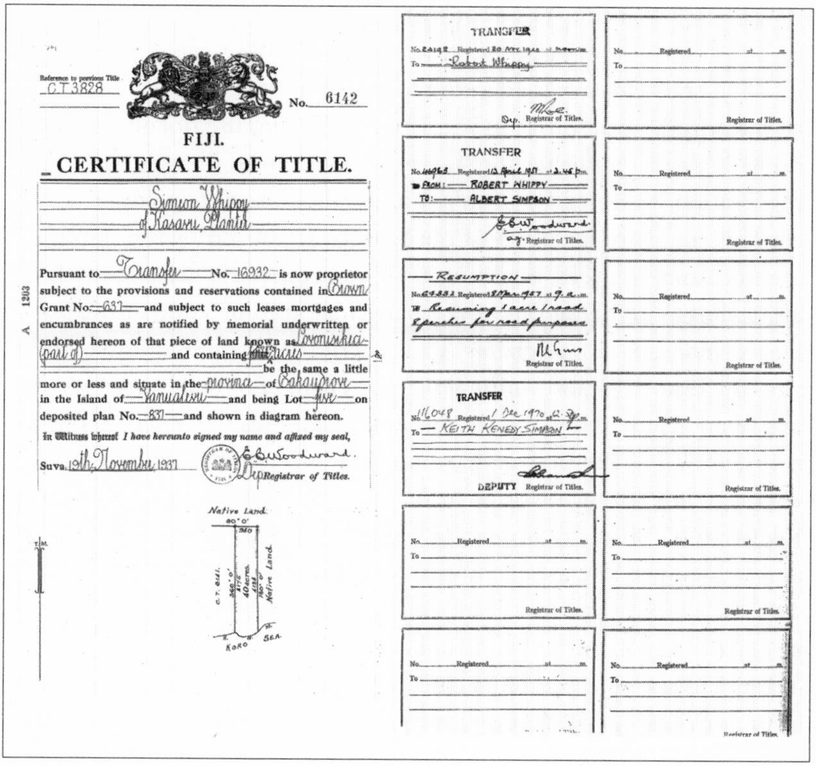
Reference to previous Title C.T. 3828

No. 6142

FIJI.

CERTIFICATE OF TITLE.

Simeon Whippy of Kasavu Planter

Pursuant to Transfer No. 16932 is now proprietor subject to the provisions and reservations contained in Crown Grant No. 637 and subject to such leases mortgages and encumbrances as are notified by memorial underwritten or endorsed hereon of that piece of land known as Lovonisikeci (part of) and containing forty acres be the same a little more or less and situate in the province of Cakaudrove in the Island of Vanualevu and being Lot five on deposited plan No. 637 and shown in diagram hereon.

In Witness whereof I have hereunto signed my name and affixed my seal,

Suva, 19th November 1937

E. G. Woodward. Dep. Registrar of Titles.

TRANSFER No. 24192 Registered 20 Nov. 1940 To Robert Whippy. Dep. Registrar of Titles.

TRANSFER No. 46963 Registered 13 April 1951 at 2.45 p.m. FROM: ROBERT WHIPPY TO: ALBERT SIMPSON. E. G. Woodward. ag. Registrar of Titles.

RESUMPTION No. 64883 Registered 28 Mar. 1957 at 9 a.m. Resuming 1 acre 1 rood 8 perches for road purposes. Registrar of Titles.

TRANSFER No. 116048 Registered 1 Dec 1970 at 2.50 p.m. To KEITH KENEDY SIMPSON. DEPUTY Registrar of Titles.

FIGURE 7.1

Certificate of Title 6142, establishing ownership of a portion of the estate known as Lovonisikeci in Kasavu, Vanua Levu (front and back sides). The back side records transfers of the tract to subsequent owners. (On file at Fiji Department of Land and Surveys)

from Australia, where it was first implemented in 1857 (compare Simpson 1976:68–90).[10] In this system, as one commentator has described it, "land is initially placed on the register as a unit of property, transactions are registered with reference to the land itself and not merely as instruments executed by the owner, and registration of transactions becomes essential to their validity and serves as a warranty of title and a bar to adverse claims" (Meek 1949:275). The goals of the Torrens System are purely instrumental: The system contributes to the value of land by making it easier to alienate land free of concerns about the validity of title because all relevant information about adverse claims, such as mortgages or encumbrances, is noted in the title document on view at the registry (Harvey 1910:187–188).

This transparency is achieved by isolating the title document from all interpretive questions; in the Torrens System, the document is the thing. This distinguishes the Torrens System from the system of land registration used in most American jurisdictions, for example, which consists simply of a record of purchasers organized by the names of grantors and grantees, made available to prospective grantees without any claims as to the validity of any particular grantor's title or the possible existence of adverse claims. The American system therefore emphasizes the historicity and contingency of a chain of ownership, conceived as a relationship of persons (as owners) to land (as the object of ownership), as well as the personalized and therefore indeterminate nature of the "truth" of ownership. In the Torrens System, in contrast, the Registrar of Title examines instruments presented for registration and can refuse any application that appears irregular (McCormack 1992:101). Thereafter, the State stands by the document, and its validity can be contested only in a very limited number of cases (Ruoff 1957:9).[11] The title is taken to present a true, complete, non-metaphorical representation of property. Nothing further need be known about title than what appears on the face of the document. For this reason, commentators often describe title in the Torrens System as a "mirror" of the land "which reflects accurately and completely and beyond all argument the current facts that are material to a man's title" (Ruoff 1957:8). In Fiji, the finality of the system was more absolute than elsewhere. Even when there were good reasons to doubt a claimant's right to a parcel of land, as long as the *form* of the title documents conformed to the prescribed formalities, the Registrar of Titles would honor them.[12]

The refusal to search for meanings beyond the surface of the document, this stopping of knowledge, is enabled by a turn away from people as owners—from property *relations*—in favor of a pure focus on land (Maurer 1997:209–211). The goal is "the transference of primary attention from the mobile, mortal, mistakable persons temporarily possessing or claiming rights over patches of the earth's surface, to the immovable, durable, precisely definable units of land affected and the adoption of these as the basis of record instead" (Dowson and Sheppard 1956:19). This focus is instantiated by a statutory requirement that each CT be accompanied by a schematic diagram of the land that depicts its contours and dimensions (Real Property Ordinance § 9-1). The diagrams in the Registrar's ledger are thin, two-dimensional schematic representations that purposely erase people, places, groups, histories, and other forms of context through which "meaning" might be made. The meticulous attention the government devoted to surveying freehold land in the early days of the colony—the team of surveyors sent from London, the instruments, the days of laborious work under difficult conditions (Lloyd 1968)—is particularly striking when juxtaposed against the government's utter lack of knowledge, its refusal to know, about the half-castes who owned and lived on many of these lands.

The refusal to know is also striking in contrast to the government's appetite for knowledge of all kinds about the customs and practices of Fiji's indigenous Fijians. This partiality of governmental knowledge is no doubt an effect of the meanings the colonial government attributed to custom, culture, labor, Fijian, and half-caste (Kelly 1989). Yet, it is also an effect of the genre in which knowledge of Part-Europeans as freehold landowners was effectuated. The instrumental genre of legal act differs from the expressive genre in its emptiness of meaning. The Torrens System expressly sets out to serve as a "mirror": Its ideological orientation is to refuse the opacities and complexities of signification in favor of a kind of perfectly stable surface that is not a step removed from the world and reflecting on it. The subjectivity of ownership is encompassed within the procedures and the documents; it is not distanced from the land registration procedures, so it is not objectified. This absence of a break with the world that would enable expression, however, is achieved by shutting out the world altogether. Commentators refer to the Torrens System also as a "curtain" that cuts off the inevitable complexities of property claims as a function of actual historical social relations and shields them from view (Ruoff 1957:25–31). Property is not a relationship between persons with respect to things here (Hann 1998) but rather an entry in the record, an internal feature of the document.

If, as we saw in the preceding section, the expressive genre backgrounded the constraints of form that make possible its own objectifications, the instrumental genre foregrounded the particular devices, practices, or orientations that constitute an act as law—what lawyers term *legal formalities*—at every turn. The Real Property Ordinance dictated a litany of formalities that would govern the disposition of freehold land in the colony. For example:

> 7. The Registrar shall have a seal of office with which he shall seal all certificates of title issued by him and stamp all instruments which have been presented to him for the purpose of authorizing an act of registration....
>
> The Registrar shall keep a book to be called the register of titles and shall bind up therein the duplicates of all grants and of all certificates of title to be issued...and each grant and certificate of title shall constitute a separate folium of such book and the Registrar shall record therein the particulars of all instruments....
>
> The Registrar shall also keep a book to be called the presentation book in which shall be entered by short description every instrument which is given in for registration with the day and hour and when that is required by the person presenting the instrument the minute of presentation and for purposes of priority between mortgages transferees and others the time of presentation shall be taken as the time of registration.

The ordinance paid particular attention to matters of aesthetics. It specified the precise format of the Certificates of Title and other transfer documents by literally drawing exemplars of these into the statute text. To succeed in registering his or her land, the applicant would have to produce a specimen in a particular genre. These formalities drew the grantor and grantee in to a set of actions distinguishable in genre from others and expressly marked as distinctive in this way (Fuller 1941).

From the point of view of Part-European titleholders, the land registration system was a frequently enacted ritual. The division of land proceeded according to the dictates laid out in the deceased's will, duly filed with the Probate Office together with a map delineating the necessary partitions. This filing followed other funerary practices in marking the passing of generations. Conforming to legal formalities, in turn, necessitated other social practices, activating other relationships. Those living on a parcel of land pooled their resources to engage a surveyor to chart the division according to legal specifications. They then sent a representative to Suva to file the necessary documents with the Registrar of Title. A group of siblings might work their land in common for an entire generation before saving enough money from copra sales to pay the surveyor's fee. The magnitude of such fees far eclipsed the amount of funds accumulated for funerals, marriages, fundraising for the settlement church or school, or the construction of new houses.

These actions had a particular effect: the production of an object, the title (and also the will, the probate document, the land transfer document), as something of a different order and distinct from the procedures themselves. This object was constituted by the formalities and therefore took on their formal attributes. This object, in turn, served as the "curtain" that shielded the complexities of the past from present view.

Once issued, moreover, the title document remained unchanged, except for the succession of names that filled the slots reserved for future owners. One effect of the record's internal production of spatial and temporal relations is a reconfiguration of the nature of the subjectivity of ownership. The title document is kept across generations: It exists outside and beyond the temporal horizon of its individual transactors. The parallel spaces in the title document in which the names of successive owners are recorded, each beneath the next, anticipate the coming into existence of particular kinds of persons—individuals contained within the historicity of the form as temporal functions of title.

Unlike the conceptual objectifications of law in its expressive genre, such as groups, for which history is an outside condition and constraint, therefore, the objects created by the Torrens System contain within themselves a particular temporality—spaces within the form for future generations to fill in (compare Miyazaki n.d.a). All moments after the initial creation of title are, in a sense, after the fact. Because of the way one name succeeds the next, the present of ownership encompasses, as it collapses into, the past. When properly transferred, the statute states that "each fresh certificate shall be as valid and effectual in every respect as if [its owner] had been the original grantee in the

Crown grant of the land contained in the certificate" (par. 13). And yet, unlike the objectifications of law in its expressive genre, such as "property relations" or "customs" that can only become out of date vis-à-vis current historical or political conditions, these objects of instrumental legal knowledge are artifacts of a historical moment (legal documents) and hence can actually be lost, stolen, and purposely or accidentally destroyed.[13]

From this point of view, it becomes easier to understand why the kinds of crises that now pervade the expressive dimensions of legal practice are largely absent in the sphere of instrumental legal knowledge. The document produced by the activation of the formalities of the Torrens System is an object in the world, not something apart from it (such as a concept or perspective). Objectification here is not a process of relating elements in the world, as for the production of meanings about groups, but rather an act that "seeks relational information within the object itself" (Danziger 1996:71). The question of the continuity between past and present—of the legacy of objectification—is already internally answered for the objects created by the Torrens System. For this reason, the instrumental genre does not become a problem or crisis of its own, for Part-European titleholders or anthropological critics of colonialism.

What is perhaps most salient about the land registration system at this moment of excess of signification is the way it goes unnoticed—how it deflects attention from itself. The instrumental genre fades into its target: Land registration documents, diagrams, and records become instantiations, not mere representations, of property rights. Wagner has contrasted "referential symbols" such as the artifacts of the expressive genre to what he terms "non-referential" symbols, symbols that "assimilate, encompass what they symbolize" (Wagner 1981:xv) and therefore "stand for themselves" (Wagner 1986). Borrowing this vocabulary, we can understand the Torrens System as encompassing property rights within its own symbolic qualities and ceasing to be available as an object of its own. This very mundanity of the registration procedures— the system's already known quality—functions as a kind of stopping point for the appetites for knowledge and the excesses of signification that characterize the crisis to which this volume refers.

Yet, from whose perspective is the individual an object? It is not from the administrator's or the system's users', although each certainly acts with this objectification in mind. To return to this volume's project of recentering law, it is from the perspective of the formalities themselves that documents and persons emerge as parallel objects in the world. The legal formalities achieve this centrality by the way they encompass all they represent. The document's perspective is really no perspective at all.

Sequenced Genres

From this ethnographic example, we can hypothesize in more general terms that legal practices involve two distinct kinds of knowledge and two kinds of objectification. Although I have separated the two genres analytically in this discussion, it will be apparent that every act of lawmaking and encounter with legal procedures entails both expressive and instrumental genres (compare Wagner 1981:45). Even in the admittedly extreme example of land registration procedures presented here, where the State explicitly disavows an interest in meaning making, the establishment of the Torrens System certainly expresses the distinctiveness of a capitalist sphere of ownership, as against Native Land, for example. Even the refusal to know at the heart of the system can be understood to make a statement about the primacy of ownership. Indeed, it is this statement—the State's preference for individualized and anonymous identities of ownership over group-ness—that served Part-Europeans so well in weathering the colonial administration's antipathy (Riles 2004).

The centrality of documents, and of this instrumental genre of legal knowledge for Fiji's Part-Europeans, moreover, was precipitated by the existence of other legal norms that clearly expressed Part-Europeans' illegitimacy in the polity. Because half-castes, as illegitimates, could not rely on the rules of inheritance that provided for land to pass to one's heirs in the absence of a will, their mastery of the instrumental effects of legal title transfer became a matter of survival. And the instrumentality of the Torrens System, in turn, also enabled further acts of expression. The rules forbidding the State from inquiring into the substantive legitimacy of a transfer as long as the transfer conformed to form opened up to Part-Europeans the possibility of using legal documents for expressive purposes of their own. Early on,

Part-European wills filed in title transfer cases emerged as a site for family members to make statements about themselves. Many wills allude directly to practices, such as polygamy, that served as the target of colonial administrators' denigrations of Part-Europeans. A clause in what the Whippys of Kasavu termed the "master will" of David Whippy Sr., states, in direct contravention of the capitalist principles governing freehold land, that "the land should not be sold to strangers. But if anyone leaves the land for good it shall belong to those who stay on the land, and it is my wish that they sell none of the land nor deny anyone related to the Whippy family the use of as much land to plant on, as well as feed on."

The case of Part-Europeans' uses of the land registration system therefore suggests how actors alternatively engage the expressive and instrumental genres of legal knowledge. These two genres of legal knowledge produce two kinds of reifications—the objectifications of expressions and the objects of instruments. Another way of describing this is to say that legal knowledge is alternatively in the world and a reflection of it, alternatively knowledge and its own object. What is important, however, is that the two forms of objectification are not engaged and apprehended at once but sequentially, in alteration. The moment a will is created as an expressive statement about the nature of "Whippy family" is not the same moment that will is filed with the Registrar of Lands. Actors alternatively share objects with one another and constitute themselves and others as objects. As with the case of the Whippy will, the latter objectification is achieved with the help of the former.

LAW AS ANTHROPOLOGICAL OBJECT

This brings us to the present character of law as an object of anthropological knowledge. If one defines the distinctiveness of law ethnographically, that is, as the *fact* of being noticed as distinctive (by anthropologists of law, colonial administrators, Part-Europeans, or anyone else), what renders law distinctive, what makes it a separate subject and field of action, is its instrumental side. This is because, as we saw, the instrumental genre of knowledge foregrounds the particular constraints of form (the legal formalities) that distinguish an act of filing documents from other actions a person might take and that result in the production of particularly legal objects, such as title documents, distinguishable from other objects in the world.

In the past, most anthropological studies of law have made legal texts and practices their object by foregrounding their expressive dimensions—by conflating or collapsing the two genres I have described into the expressive (for example, Thomas 1991). In contrast to the instrumental genre, this expressive genre backgrounds the distinctiveness of legal practice relative to other social practices because, as we saw, the constraints of form at issue in the expressive genre remain opaque to the actor and observer. In the anthropology of colonialism, for example, law was just another set of significations, alongside others the colonial government might produce. Sometimes, this obviation of the unique features of law found expression in anthropologists' insistence that what lawyers call "law" is just a set of practices anthropologists are accustomed to thinking about under other rubrics, such as "social control" (for example, Malinowski 1966) or "local knowledge" (Geertz 1983). Law was not more or less interesting than other social practices, nor was it distinctive.

This focus on the expressive also implicitly obviated the distinction between the significations of law and of anthropological knowledge. As noted at the outset of this chapter, the anthropology of colonialism drew an implicit parallel between what "they did" and what "we used to do." Like the expressive genre of law, much anthropological knowledge backgrounds its own constraints of form and instead emphasizes the distance between subject and object, or between anthropological knowledge and the world it describes. The parallel between anthropological and legal practice, this analytical kinship between the anthropologist and the colonial administrator, enabled anthropologists to critique their colonial subject in a way that had become untenable with regard to other ethnographic subjects. One implication, however, was that the critiques anthropologists leveled at legal objectifications were always implicit but powerful critiques of anthropological practices of meaning making as well.

The focus on the expressive dimensions of law was achieved only by creating a kind of blind spot to the instrumental dimensions of legal knowledge, however. The objects of instrumentalism—the documents, the individuals—remained inaccessible to the anthropologist's own objectifications; anthropologists could treat law as text only by ignoring its concrete effects. Of course, because the instrumental and expressive genres coexist sequentially, these concrete effects were always right before us. They were simply uninteresting from the anthropologist's point of view.

This brings us back to my original question: Why, after the careful critiques of essentialism and objectification of culture, groups, identities, or societies, would anthropologists choose at this moment to recenter and objectify law? The preceding discussion suggests that we must first consider what kind of objectification law is for anthropologists now. If the expressive dimension of law backgrounds law's distinctiveness, when anthropologists talk about "recentering" law, that is, foregrounding it, they necessarily turn to its instrumental dimension— to the side that makes law apprehensible as a distinctive subject and therefore capable of being recentered.

Yet, as we have seen, the artifacts of the instrumental genre of legal knowledge are of a different character than the artifacts of the expressive genre. Unlike the latter, they do not take the form of a conventional anthropological subject; they cannot be analyzed for their meanings. Thus, when anthropologists confront the artifacts of law's instrumentality, from human rights doctrines to constitutions, they now often treat these not as ethnographic subjects but as concrete objects in the world, with uses. Anthropologists often turn to possessing and using law, in other words, in much the same way as the Whippys possess and use their documents. The recentering of law emerges as a solution to the problem of the privileging of ideas in anthropology precisely because the law at issue here is not an "idea" but a concrete and instrumental object. This distinction, in turn, frequently inspires a different kind of response from the anthropologist: It is now commonplace for anthropologists to seek to participate, as representatives or agents of local people, in acts of legal reform or implementation (for example, Riles 1997b) or to critique legal artifacts such as constitutions or laws, again, as implicit or explicit spokespersons for others (for example, Kaplan and Kelly 2001). What these two responses—participation and critique—share is a desire to do something with or against law, as an object the anthropologist now understands herself to confront, and use, in the world.

The preceding discussion is meant to demonstrate that this move from a concern with the expressive modalities of law to a concern with law's instrumental modalities is enabled, in part, by the particular features of legal knowledge itself. Where a prior anthropology of law took the expressive side of law as its sole subject, some recent anthropological objectifications of law, such as the Whippys' use of documents, simply engage another moment in the sequence, law as object.

Yet, if these analyses are enabled by the nature of legal knowledge, they must also be understood as responses to what has happened to anthropology's objects after the critique of objectification that characterized the anthropology of the 1990s. In the aftermath of anthropological objectifications of others' objectifications, which, in the process of exposing the features of colonial law, also problematized anthropology's own devices of objectification, anthropologists have been forced to search for new forms of objects altogether. In particular, anthropologists have been searching for a means of obviating the break between the anthropological observer and the world in two senses. First, in the aftermath of the critiques of the us/them distinction, many anthropologists seek a subject position that is at one with their (former) subjects. These anthropologists seek a kind of object that is no longer differentiating, in Strathern's terms, as between anthropologist and informant. Second, many anthropologists seek a renewed connection with their publics; they want anthropology to be connected and relevant to the world they imagine that anthropologists have too often kept at a remove (for example, Nader 2000; Di Leonardo 1998). Some anthropologists now want to share with the likes of the Whippys a set of *tools* and thus become potential allies, critics, or adversaries, in sum, actors engaged in a singular plane by virtue of shared objects. The move to recenter and objectify law represents a kind of obviation of its own—a reaction to a certain exhaustion with the more traditional anthropological device of knowledge making through differentiation.

The wider point of this extended discussion of instrumental and expressive genres of knowledge is that there are consequences to this imagination of law as an instrument, as a means toward some other end, whether the end is social justice (for example, Kelly and Kaplan 2001) or economic efficiency (for example, Posner 2003). To take law as object in this sense is not to "know" law but to work through law. The object has a studied opacity in these accounts. What law "is" is too often given in these accounts; it is not open to ethnographic reimagination. What interests these anthropologists about law, rather, are the ends law serves and how anthropologists and their indigenous subjects-turned-collaborators might *use* legal objects. One sometimes hears this glossed with the statement that events in the world guide one's work (for example, Kaplan and Kelly 2001).

There is another possibility for the anthropology of law, however, and it is to open up the instrumental dimension of legal knowledge to ethnographic investigation. To do so will require a refiguring of the character of anthropological inquiry because, by definition, this dimension of legal practice does not provide meanings for the anthropologist to interpret. An ethnography of the instrumental genre of law and its objects would therefore, by definition, engage a postinterpretive anthropology. It would also demand ethnographic attention to how the formal features of these instruments beguile the anthropologist as much as the colonial administrator or the indigenous activist. I intend this chapter as an initiation of such a project.

Acknowledgments

This chapter is based on eighteen months of fieldwork in Suva and Kasavu, Fiji, from 1994 to 1996. I owe my deepest thanks to the Whippy family and the many other Part-European families who took time to teach me about questions of family and land. I thank Sally Merry, Don Brenneis, and the participants in the School of American Research advanced seminar for much stimulating conversation. I also thank Gregory Alexander, Don Brenneis, Sally Merry, Hiro Miyazaki, and Marilyn Strathern for their thoughtful criticism. This chapter draws upon material collected in the context of advocacy work (Riles 1997b), as well as on a companion piece to this one, written for a legal audience (Riles 2004).

Notes

1. "A Despatch from Sir Arthur Gordon to the Earl of Carnarvon enclosing the Minutes on question of native law by W. C. Carew, Commissioner to the Kai Colos, and by Rev. F. Langham, head of the Wesleyan Mission. March 6, 1876." On file at the National Archives of Fiji.

2. *Half-castes* was the universal appellation for those who were not full Fijian, European, or Indian. In 1936, the term was officially replaced with *Persons of*

European and Native Descent (after the terms *Anglo-Polynesians, Anglo-Fijians, Euro-Polynesians,* and, later, *Euronesians* were considered.). (See file C.S.O. F114/1, on file at the National Archives of Fiji.) In the 1940s, this term was replaced by *Part-Europeans.*

3. In essence, there was no government policy toward half-castes. In fact, the government remained as utterly ignorant of half-caste social practices as it was knowledgeable about the intricacies of Fijian customs and politics. For most of the period of colonial rule, it was not even clear who in the government held responsibility for liaison between the government and the half-caste community. In 1892, Acting Native Commissioner Basel Thomson held a meeting with heads of Part-European families and subsequently urged the government to do something on their behalf:

> The half-castes alone of all the classes in the community have had no one charged with the protection of their interests. They have been classed by the Executive and the law as Europeans, though in reality in their mode of life and thought they are more nearly allied to the Fijians than the race of their fathers. The majority of the children are growing up without any sort of education or restraint, and unfortunately their natural disposition is not inclined to respectability nor to influencing the native for good.... The Fijian half-castes seem now to have awoken to the fact that they have no status at all in the Colony, and they evince a strong wish for some sort of organization among themselves. (C.S.O. 1386/1892)

4. Government officials displayed great anxiety about married Fijian women running away from their Fijian husbands to live with Part-European men, for example, and even considered suggesting to the *Rokos* that Fijians use physical force to take back their women in such cases. (C.S.O. 274/1885; C.S.O. 2883/1885; C.S.O. 3389/1885; on file at the National Archives of Fiji)

5. C.S.O. 2027/1902 (Assault on Half Caste; Status of Half-Castes in Native Courts). May 2, 1902. On file at the National Archives of Fiji.

6. John B. Thurston, "Despatch to Colonial Office re: US Land Claims. September 2, 1896." On file at the Office of Public Records, London.

7. "An Ordinance to Provide for the Transfer of Land by Registration of Titles, No. 6 of 1876 (March 1, 1877)." The importance the government attached to this ordinance is evidenced by its almost continual revision over the decades that followed. Amendments were introduced in 1877, 1883, 1892, 1895, 1913, 1923, and 1924, and the entire ordinance was ultimately redrafted in 1933.

8. Land Claims Commission Report No. 875, Claim of Samuel and Peter Whippy to Lovonisikeci (1880). On file at the National Archives of Fiji.

9. Indeed, what is perhaps surprising about Part-Europeans' own engagement with the titles registration system, from the point of view of the cultural history of colonialism in Fiji, was their lack of discourses or practices of resistance to the daily exigencies of colonial rule—their lack of effort to find a position outside the concerns and practices of the colonizer as embodied in that system

10. *In re West* [1890] 1 Fiji L. Rep. 227 (following the practice of the Colony of Victoria concerning the registration of under-leases).

11. *Caldwell* v. *Mongston* [1908] 2 Fiji L. Rep. 1 (even when a Crown grant may have been issued in error, the Court will not go "behind" the grant); Ram *Kali* v. *John Percy Bayly and Santa and the Registrar of Titles* [1954] 4 Fiji L. Rep. 139.

12. *Gaspard* v. *Colonial Sugar Refining Co.* [1904] 3 Fiji L. R. 57, 58. *Re The Estate of H. Maughan*, re *The Estate of W. A. Scott* [1929] 3 Fiji L. Rep. 123, 125.

13. Practical details in the ordinance attested to the problems raised by the title's object quality: "As soon after the passing of this Ordinance as practicable the Governor shall provide at the public expense and shall thereafter maintain in proper repair a building of stone or brick to serve as the office of the Registrar and the place of deposit and preservation of the registers duplicates instruments and documents connected with the registration of titles and shall fit up the said office with such fireproof safes and other secure places as may be necessary."

8

Kū'ē and Kū'oko'a

History, Law, and Other Faiths

Jonathan Kamakawiwo'ole Osorio

On February 23, 2000, the United States Supreme Court issued a decision that has had a significant effect on Native Hawaiians and their seventeen-year-old movement to reclaim self-government. Chief Justice Kennedy articulated the opinion of the Court finding that Hawai'i's denial of petitioner Harold Rice's right to vote in the trustee elections for the Office of Hawaiian Affairs violates the Fifteenth Amendment of the US Constitution. However, Justice Breyer's concurring opinion that Hawaiian people have neither political nor cultural claims to distinct treatment by American law promises to transform Hawaiian civil society and provides powerful motivation for Hawaiians to seek independence from the United States.

As a result of this decision, a handful of Hawai'i residents are seeking to dismember more than eighty years of federal and state legislation that has set aside land and created two major state agencies for the benefit of legally defined Native Hawaiians. Several historic cases *(Bartlett v. Department of Hawaiian Homelands and Arakaki v. Office of Hawaiian Affairs)* filed in federal courts argue that entitlements to Native Hawaiians, set up under federal and state legislation, are violations of the equal rights protections of the US Constitution. In response, the state and *Kanaka Maoli* (people of Hawaiian ancestry) individuals and agencies have been working to secure federal legislation that recognizes Hawaiians as Native Americans. Another sovereignty initiative, the Council of Regency (COR) of the Kingdom of Hawaiʻi, managed to obtain a hearing before the Permanent Court of Arbitration (PCA) at The Hague, Netherlands. This group solicits international recognition that the nation-state status of the Kingdom has not been extinguished despite a century of US occupation.

The history of sovereignty movements in Hawaiʻi provides a framework for understanding the discursive trends that sustain and alter cultural identity. Ultimately, the confrontation between cultural identity and social-political frameworks such as law provides the clearest understanding of how institutions, especially colonial institutions, are translated and adopted.

To discuss how American law and international law address political questions of ethnic and national identity, I will compare two distinct legal avenues through which the aboriginal people of Hawaiʻi are seeking self-government—Ka Lāhui Hawaiʻi (KLH) and the Council of Regency. I will describe how these two strategies are employing distinct and mutually exclusive interpretations of nationhood. While Ka Lāhui has struggled to secure recognition as a Native nation within the larger American nation, the Council of Regency has pursued the re-establishment of the independent Hawaiian Kingdom. The differences between these two initiatives, I contend, contribute to the confusion over definitions of nationality, race, and self-determination, which cannot be solved by juridical decision at either the national or international level. Indeed, they can barely be addressed at the level of local politics because of certain important and historic ideological differences that separate Hawaiians.

A BRIEF AND CONTEMPORARY POLITICAL HISTORY

The liberal franchise extended by the 1900 Organic Act in Hawaiʻi defined Hawaiians as American citizens, despite their widespread opposition to the American takeover (Coffman 1998; Silva and Minton 1998). Yet, from 1902 until the decade before the Statehood Act, political control was maintained by the Republican Party, which successfully recruited thousands of Native Hawaiian voters, in part, through a carefully managed system of patronage. Territorial and county government positions were routinely dispensed to loyal Republicans. Labor union- ism, associated with the Democratic Party, was stigmatized as antitheti- cal to Hawaiian interests because it would primarily benefit the largely Asian plantation workforce.[1]

Under Republican control, a few powerful *haole* (Caucasian) cor- porations and families were able to manipulate all the important sectors of the economy, including finance, shipping, wholesale dis- tribution, and, most importantly, cheap access to the Crown and Government Lands of the Kingdom, which made up nearly one-half the total land area of the archipelago. The labor movement grew stronger, and on the eve of statehood the Republicans surrendered political supremacy to the Democratic Party without, however, surren- dering their control over land and wealth (Kent 1983).

The first fifteen years of statehood under Democratic Party control did not favor the economic or political aspirations of Hawaiians in gen- eral. Considered by many to be a failed minority in American society, Hawaiians demonstrated classic symptoms of an underprivileged minority: high levels of arrest and incarceration, alcoholism and increasing drug abuse, low levels of education and upward social mobil- ity, and a virtual nonparticipation in what many saw as the economic miracle of the state's transformation from an agricultural to tourist- dominated economy (Kent 1983:180–185). In fact, many Hawaiians began to see their economic position erode after the 1930s, as well as into the 1960s and 1970s, when large estates began to evict Hawaiians from their homes and farms to make room for new and much more profitable urban developments (Trask 1999:66). At the same time, Japanese and Chinese Democrats replaced the Native Hawaiian Republicans in the legislatures, marginalizing Hawaiians politically.

In the mid-1970s, several issues converged: a Native-led opposition to the US military bombing of Kahoʻolawe Island since 1941, outrage at the rising number of evictions from the land, and public discussion of the failure of the Native Hawaiian Trusts, especially the Department of Hawaiian Home Lands. In 1977, two young Hawaiian activists were killed trying to prevent the US Navy from bombing Kahoʻolawe, believ- ing that the *ʻāina* (land) was sacred, conscious, and an elder sibling to the Kanaka Maoli themselves.

In that same year, a federal-state task force investigating the Department of Hawaiian Homes found a history of gross mismanagement of the trust, with only a few thousand leases awarded to qualified beneficiaries. More than half of the lands were leased to people and companies who were not Hawaiian. Thousands of acres were simply appropriated by the state and federal governments. Nearly 20,000 claimants languished on waiting lists, some for as long as thirty years. The task force recommended a half-billion-dollar expenditure to create sufficient infrastructure to implement the aims of the program, calling on both the federal and state governments to share the expense. Neither would.

Disgust with American promises and priorities, combined with a cultural renaissance in Hawaiian music, dance, art, literature, history, and language, fueled the nationalist movement. In 1978, future governor John Waihe'e led a group of Native delegates to the State Constitutional Convention to draft and secure the inclusion of laws that would protect Hawaiians and their culture. The new constitution mandated the teaching of Hawaiian history, language, and culture in all public educational institutions, included Hawaiian as the second official language of the state, and created the Office of Hawaiian Affairs to receive and distribute funds from the ceded lands for the benefit of Native Hawaiians. In 1978, the Hawai'i Supreme Court ruled that Native Hawaiians were entitled to 20 percent of the ceded lands' revenues because these represented one of five uses mandated by the Organic Act. The Office of Hawaiian Affairs, with special voting provisions allowing only Natives to participate, became a source of self-rule that was, nevertheless, limited and tightly controlled by the legislature and governor's office, which appropriated money for its operation.

Under the first elected Native Hawaiian governor, John Waihe'e (1986–1994), there was much publicity about native affairs but little substantial improvement in Hawaiians' economic standing. Politically, Hawaiians began to filter back into the legislature, usually as Democrats, and numerous grassroots organizations, including the original sovereignty movements, began to agitate for recognition. These organizations, some of them cultural and academic, such as the Hawaiian Language Immersion programs and the Center for Hawaiian Studies, strengthened Hawaiian resolve for sovereign control of Kanaka Maoli resources.

After reaching a high point of widespread discussion and acknowl-
edgment in 1993 with the well-publicized centennial observation of the
overthrow, the sovereignty movement has suffered a backlash of legal
challenges: *Rice v. Cayetano,* state government intrigues under the current
governor, and more internal disagreements among Native Hawaiian
groups over strategies and goals.

In 1996, the State Attorney General began an investigation of the
largest and richest Hawaiian private trust, the Bishop Estate, which
employs a multibillion-dollar land and investment portfolio for the support of the *Kamehameha* schools and for scholarship and outreach programs affecting tens of thousands of Native Hawaiian children, who are
the primary beneficiaries. This investigation ultimately ended in the
replacement of all the trustees appointed during the Waihe'e/Cayetano
years and the convening of grand juries against three trustees, two of
whom had been powerful Democratic Party legislators in the 1980s.[2]
Although the investigation was sparked when concerned Native educa-
tors protested the trustees' micromanagement of the school, the very
public examination of every single member shamed and alarmed the
Hawaiian community at large, which feared that the most powerful
Hawaiian institutions surviving from the Kingdom would be torn apart
and devoured by the State of Hawai'i.

For Hawaiian nationalists, the Cayetano administration has not
been kind. The governor has gone out of his way to threaten Hawaiian
entitlement programs. When his original appointee to head the
Department of Hawaiian Home Lands became too effective, securing
the return of more than 16,000 acres appropriated by the state from the
Hawaiian Homes inventory, Cayetano replaced him—the week after the
governor won a closely contested re-election. After his re-election,
Cayetano became even more vocal about his opposition to Hawaiian
entitlements, arguing that he himself is Hawaiian at heart but that, as
governor, he cannot protect the interests of one group over any other
group of citizens. He has even insisted that the revenues due the Office
of Hawaiian Affairs are an unfair obligation the state cannot afford
to pay.

As Hawaiians have amplified their calls for self-government, the
State of Hawai'i has ratcheted up the political stakes by threatening
Native Hawaiian resources through a discourse on American principles

of equal protection and access under law. Certainly, the broken promises and failed protections of the trust relationship between America and Native Hawaiians have contributed to the rise of the sovereignty movement, as has the relative political displacement of Native Hawaiians with the rise of the Asian Democrats in the 1960s. However, as much as the sovereignty movement has focused on redressing past grievances with America, it has also insisted on defining what it means to be Hawaiian.

THE SOVEREIGNTY MOVEMENT IN HAWAIʻI

Ka Lāhui Hawaiʻi (KLH), the elder organization in the sovereignty movement at sixteen years, is, in 2003, also the largest, with close to 20,000 citizens. KLH's constitution is based on a nation-within-nation model similar to that of several Native American governments that have treaty relationships and federal recognition with the United States. At the same time, KLH has sought international support through the Unrepresented Peoples Organization (UNPO) and has worked together with other Natives to craft a Declaration of the Rights of Indigenous Peoples within the United Nations (Trask 1999:75).

Assessment of KLH's political success is difficult because KLH appears to have more influence and credibility outside Hawaiʻi than within. KLH representatives to world and indigenous councils enjoy recognition and respect for carrying on a determined, non-violent sovereignty movement for more than a decade, but, surprisingly, KLH has never been much of a political force within the Hawaiian Islands. This is surprising not only because KLH boasts a comparatively large membership but also because its political aim—to create a sovereign Native government within the United States—has legal precedence and addresses the fears of many Hawaiʻi residents that Hawaiian sovereignty threatens their rights as American citizens. From its inception, KLH has limited its land claims to former Crown and Government Lands of the Kingdom. In the minds of KLH citizens and sympathizers, the return of these lands would be a significant first step in repairing the relationship between the United States and the Hawaiian people, would provide a suitable land base for the Native nation, and would steer clear of any threat to private land holdings in Hawaiʻi.

Those ceded lands, however, represent more than 90 percent of

the lands in the state's possession, and many politicians besides the current governor have insisted that the state is financially dependent on
the revenues those lands generate. Critics of the state's land use have
long asserted that the State of Hawaiʻi does not employ those lands
judiciously, allowing certain favored corporations and individuals to
lease highly productive properties at bargain rates (Faludi 1991). Be
that as it may, few people in the sovereignty movement imagine that the
State of Hawaiʻi will surrender its control of ceded lands without some
kind of legal or political challenge.[3]

Perhaps for that reason, not many public officials even acknowledge the existence of KLH. Clearly, the organization possesses few of
the attributes (a disciplined cadre, overwhelming numbers, or even the
ability to influence a public election) that mark a political player.

If citizenship in KLH offers something other than an opportunity
to be politically active and empowered, it is a sense of identity based on
ancestry rather than on the nation-based citizenship created by the
Kingdom of Hawaiʻi during the reign of Kamehameha III. As such,
KLH follows a logical, historical pattern of Native Hawaiians' identifying as an ethnic group or race.[4] The political treatment of Hawaiians as
a race is traceable in the development of American law and administration in the Hawaiian Islands, beginning with the 1920 Hawaiian Homes
Act and ending with the Apology Law in 1993.

In fact, the proposed federal legislation known as the *Native
Hawaiian Federal Recognition Legislation* (S-344), before the US Congress
in 2003, is also a part of this historic process designed, in part, to protect previous federal and state laws administering trust benefits on
behalf of Native Hawaiians. Those who supported this bill generally
view Hawaiians as an ethnic group whose identity is fostered by and
through ancestry. Those who opposed the bill made up a large spectrum of political opinion, from people who oppose anything resem-
bling affirmative action in America to Hawaiian nationalists who insist
that nothing short of the reestablishment of the Kingdom will resolve
the ongoing dispute over Hawaiian self-determination.

THE RIGHTS OF HAWAIIAN NATIONALS

On November 8, 1999, a Hawaiian national, Lance Larson, initiated arbitration proceedings against the Hawaiian government with

the PCA at The Hague. Hilo police arrested Larson in 1998 and incarcerated him for nearly a month after he objected to his arrest for driving an automobile that was not registered and licensed under state law. Larson had been ticketed and fined on numerous occasions and had refused to appear in court because he "does not recognize the laws of the United States or its political subdivision, the State of Hawaii, as valid within the Hawaiian Kingdom" (Parks 1999:11).

Larson's attorney, Ninia Parks, filed an original complaint for injunctive relief in the United States District Court for the State of Hawaiʻi, alleging that the Hawaiian government was allowing the unlawful imposition of American domestic law within the territorial jurisdiction of the Hawaiian Kingdom over his person. Federal Judge Samuel King dismissed the case on February 5, 1999, submitting all issues to binding arbitration "between the Hawaiian Kingdom and Mr. Larson at the Permanent Court of Arbitration at The Hague in the Netherlands" (Sai et al. 2000:116).

Eventually, Larson's action brought the Council of Regency of the Kingdom of Hawaiʻi, represented by David Keanu Sai, into a plea before the PCA asking the Court to define the duties and obligations that the Kingdom, through its Council of Regency, has toward its subject, Lance Larson. Both parties in the arbitration, held in December 2000 at The Hague, stipulated that Larson's rights had been violated by the actions of the occupying power, the United States, and the appeal for arbitration was to enable an international tribunal to direct the Kingdom's government concerning the scope of its obligations to its subject under the laws of occupation.

The Council of Regency of the Kingdom of Hawaiʻi has been in existence since 1996. Its creation and membership came about subsequent to the formation of the Perfect Title Corporation in 1995, a Native-owned land title abstracting company.[5] Perfect Title alleged that all land conveyances had to be legal under the laws of the Kingdom of Hawaiʻi, originating with the legislative establishment of the Board of Commissioners to Quiet Land Title on December 10, 1845. Subsequent legislation (the Mahele and Kuleana Act) in 1848 and 1850 devised the method for determining and awarding title among the people, chiefs, and Mōʻī (King) of Hawaiʻi. Perfect Title maintained that American occupation had initiated new policies and laws inconsistent with

Kingdom practices and that land conveyances after 1886 were legally unsound.

In essence, the Council of Regency asserts that there was no over-throw of the Queen in 1893 and no legal annexation of the islands in 1898. Rather, the Kingdom of Hawaiʻi, a recognized state in the "Family of Nations," has been suffering a prolonged occupation that, according to international law, binds the occupying United States to uphold and honor the laws of the Kingdom. Believing that it was obligated to follow Kingdom regulations wherever possible, Perfect Title found that because it could not register land claims and title changes with a Registrar for the Bureau of Land Conveyance under the Department of the Minister of the Interior, as called for by statute, it was "necessary and logical" to create an Acting Minister of the Interior, or Regent. Keanu Sai, one of the original partners in Perfect Title, assumed this position and appointed an acting Council of Regency. It is this council, along with the attorney for Lance Larson, that appeared before the PCA in December.

The PCA's willingness to hear the case gives credibility, if not stand-ing, to the Council of Regency.[6] More importantly, because the World Court in The Hague does not concern itself with non-nations or the rights of indigenous peoples, the PCA appeared to believe, on some level, that the Kingdom has standing as well. This is significant because the Council of Regency's principal claim is that law has created a legitimate Hawaiian state and that only law or conquest can extinguish that state. In short, the Council of Regency seeks to protect the rights of Hawaiians as nationals, not as colonized indigenous peoples. Thus, it is tracing a Hawaiian national identity that is also based on a particular read of history, one in which nation-states are founded and survive not only by the existence of a people and their sovereignty over a national territory but also by the formation of law and recognition by other nations.

SELECTING HISTORICAL EVENTS

KLH and the Council of Regency rely on different historical events to elaborate their legal positioning. For KLH, the significant historical event centers on the overthrow of the Queen in 1893, the formation of the republic in 1894, and the subsequent annexation by the United States in 1898. According to KLH's read of history, the United States participated in the conspiracy against the Queen and her subjects and therefore owes reparation for the damage done to Native Hawaiians by the Americanization of the Hawaiian Islands. The fact that annexation changed the political status of every ethnic group in Hawaiʻi is not particularly important to this analysis because the real harm was done to Native Hawaiians, to their language, to their education and economic prospects, and to their sense of identity. In effect, annexation improved the political status of both American and Asian residents by the awarding of full citizenship, although this occurred immediately for the Americans and only eventually (and begrudgingly) for the Asians.

American, European, and Asian immigrants achieved something from annexation that they did not have before, American citizenship, but Hawaiians "achieved" that same citizenship at the expense of being forced to forsake their own. Accordingly, the very formation of a national entity in 1840 under the rudiments of Euro-American constitutions victimized the Native Hawaiians, consigning them to unfamiliar and inferior roles as wage laborers. Caucasian newcomers proceeded to transform the economic and social systems, marginalizing the Native both demographically and symbolically.

The Council of Regency reads the legal history of Hawaiʻi quite differently and centers its attention on the legal formation of the Hawaiian Kingdom in 1839 and 1840. It argues that Kamehameha III enunciated the essential rights of the Hawaiian subject to land and participation in government and solidified the Native position by securing international recognition of his government in 1843. In fact, the Council of Regency holds that the last legitimate lawmaking body in the Kingdom was the legislature of 1886, before a small group of armed Caucasian nationals and foreign residents forced the Bayonet Constitution on King Kalākaua in 1887.

The Council of Regency also holds that the subsequent overthrow in 1893 and annexation in 1898 did not actually occur, citing international laws addressing the recognition and rights of nation-states at the turn of the century. In sum, the Council of Regency believes that annexation did not occur because it did not *legally* occur and that the descendents of Hawaiian nationals have a case to make before the World Court that its sovereignty can and should be restored.

Between these two very potent yet oppositional points of view are numerous disagreements not only on strategies for obtaining sovereignty but also in what exactly constitutes the Hawaiian nation and what role law plays in legitimizing and protecting nationhood. The ideological differences between these two formulations make fruitful discussions between them extremely difficult and compromise most improbable. One very important difference concerns the definitions of *nationality*.

NATIONALS OR RACE?

The KLH constitution declares that citizenship is bonded to ancestry. No person without Hawaiian blood can be a citizen in KLH. Even though non-Natives may apply for honorary citizenship, they are not allowed to vote or to run for office. For historical reasons, KLH has, from its inception, also had to deal with the issue of blood quantum. Because many original citizens of KLH were also actual or potential beneficiaries of the Hawaiian Homes Act of 1921 (HHA), citizenship in KLH is defined by two categories, Native Hawaiian and Hawaiian. Native Hawaiians, with a blood quantum of 50 percent or more, must be represented by one half the KLH legislature, and the other half can be represented by citizens of any blood quantum (Ka Lāhui Hawai'i 1993:15).

There is no indication that these categories have ever presented any sort of problem for KLH citizens. One reason may be that although the vast majority of people of Hawaiian ancestry do not qualify for HHA benefits, they have never begrudged the entitlement to those who do, especially because, in many cases, beneficiaries are close relations and because of the view that those who do qualify tend to suffer the most from poverty (De Cambra 1993:114). In 1993, Mililani Trask, a founder and former *Kia'āina* (governor) of KLH, acknowledged that the federal government did not have the right to determine who was a Native Hawaiian with the 1921 legislation. However, having done so, it has no right to undo the blood quantum requirement without Native consent. KLH's position is that because the federal government provides land for fifty-percenters based on a qualification it had no right to make, it must now provide land for the rest of the Hawaiians as well, rather than insist that all Hawaiians share the 200,000 acres set aside in the act.

KLH has consistently sought to protect Hawaiians from the ravages of federal and state laws, which, as Mililani Trask put it, "have always had assimilation as their primary goal" (DeCambra 1993:114). One important ideological foundation for Mililani Trask and KLH is that the melting pot policies seeking to undermine a Native identity and replace it with a homogeneous society need to be resisted at every turn. Natives are natives by blood, location, to a lesser extent by language, and by less quantifiable criteria as social values. Hawaiians must feel Hawaiian, necessitating a demonstration of *aloha* and *kōkua* (helpfulness) to other Hawaiians. They cannot be selfish, self-aggrandizing, or bent on capital accumulation without attracting a certain suspicion that they are not completely Hawaiian. As long as one has the blood, the *koko,* no one is beyond remission. Therefore, Hawaiian is also a behavior, although ancestry is paramount.

Assertions of Hawaiian cultural behavior are scattered throughout the KLH constitution, from the preamble statement that Hawaiians are strong believers in the *Akua* (gods or God) to the sections on land that identify Hawaiians as taro growers and fishermen and pledge the government to the protection of *heiau* and other sacred sites (Ka Lāhui 1993:10–12; Trask 1999:39). The constitution, therefore, not only asserts a Native-Hawaiian claim to sovereignty but also seeks to defend what the framers felt were fundamental Hawaiian codes and values. This defense is not purely ideological. State laws dealing with issues such as *ahupuaʻa* (land segments from mountain to sea) gathering rights proclaim Native rights to access public land, through private lands if necessary, for subsistence of all kinds, including fishing and shellfish gathering and flower, timber, and herb gathering in the forests. Since 1996, several legislative bills have sought to challenge and compromise the exercise of these rights in favor of more western legal notions of private and public property.

The Council of Regency defines its citizens or subjects as descendents of actual Hawaiian subjects in 1886. For the council, it is a simple matter of law. The descendents of those who conspired against the Queen and government in 1893 are as fully enfranchised (although theoretically landless) subjects of the Kingdom as a full-blooded Native Hawaiian whose family never left the archipelago.[7] The Kingdom, the council argues, was a multiethnic government, even though subjects of Hawaiian ancestry were clearly in the majority. A wide ideological chasm separates the council from KLH because neither ancestry nor behavior exclusively defines the Hawaiian subject. Kingdom law was unflaggingly liberal, allowing residents of any country the right to apply for full citizenship. As such, it is doubtful that such a model of nationhood could have much appeal to those Hawaiians who believe that "being Native" needs to be defended from an overwhelming "mainstream" culture (and from its laws).

For KLH citizens, such a formula had already proven a historic disaster for Native Hawaiians. After all, haole subjects had initiated and maintained the laws and plantation economy that had weakened the traditional culture. Also, haole subjects led the conspiracies in 1887 and 1893 to overthrow the government. Not only do their descendents not deserve a place in a Native nation, many believe, but also their very presence would always be potentially dangerous for Native citizens. According to one writer, haole should never again take leadership roles in the nation (Kame'eleihiwa 1992:326).

The council would say that the subject's ethnicity is irrelevant as far as the law is concerned. Interestingly, though, the council's news organ, *The Polynesian,* took the time to calculate the number of Native Hawaiians versus non-native descendents of Kingdom subjects, pointing out that under Kingdom law Native Hawaiian voters would enjoy as overwhelming a majority today as they did in 1886 (Goodhue and Sai 2000). Presumably forewarned by their painful political lessons with Americans over the past century, Hawaiian subjects today could easily control legislation and political appointments and even change the requirements of citizenship to make it more difficult for anyone but Native Hawaiians to exercise political power. It would simply be a matter of making law.

One can easily see why these two groups talk past each other; indeed, they barely speak to each other. Both groups believe substantially disparate histories. It is not as simple as a disagreement over strategies for achieving sovereignty; they see much more essential things very differently. Furthermore, their disagreements over strategies stem from and lead to very separate claims. Whereas KLH aims at recovering the ceded lands and is willing to settle for controlling those lands within the American federation, the council stands for nothing less than what the law (in its view) allows. It demands independence.

KŪʻĒ / KŪʻOKOʻA: RESISTANCE AND INDEPENDENCE

Ironically, the Council of Regency can proffer a sovereignty argument very conservative in its claims and still be viewed as the most radical of activist groups. In truth, little is radical about asserting that the rights of a people can be best protected by a national government framed by constitutional law and recognized by other states. This assertion was first made in Hawaiʻi by the visiting British captain Lord Byron, who addressed a gathering of *Aliʻi Nui* (Great Chiefs) in Honolulu in 1825. Lord Byron recommended that a system of laws commensurate with those of civilized nations be adopted, including recognition of the King as the head of state, a system of taxation, and jury trials. Over the next fifteen years, missionary advisors to Kamehameha III, Rev. William Richards in particular, devised a code of laws that Kamehameha approved in 1839 and 1840, establishing constitutional government in the Kingdom.

Over the next half-century, the Kingdom's government moved quickly to transform the traditional subsistence-based culture of the Kanaka Maoli to a plantation economy thoroughly dominated by haole landowners and investors, many of them former missionaries and their descendents. As the Kanaka population imploded in the nineteenth century from perhaps 200,000 in 1800 to fewer than 40,000 by 1896, the survivors lost ground economically because of legislation and judicial decisions favoring the sugar agribusinesses over traditional subsistence. Not only land but also water resources gradually accrued to the sugar planters, to the detriment of Native taro growers and subsistence farmers.

The Kingdom's foreign policy also favored the growth of sugar through the government's active recruitment of Asian labor (the Masters and Servants Act) and reciprocity treaties with the United States to ensure a spectacular demand for sugar in the 1870s and 1880s. The legislatures that passed the Masters and Servants Act in 1850 and the Reciprocity Treaty in 1875 were composed entirely of native-born and naturalized subjects of the Kingdom. They were signed into law by Hawaiian kings whose every stated intention was to preserve the nation's independence. Even more startling is the fact that even though Native Hawaiian electors outnumbered Caucasian electors by more than five to one in this period, they generously elected haole candidates. In the 1880s, Caucasians were never less than 50 percent of the legislative assembly (Osorio 2001:369–370).

Such a history prompts various responses from KLH and the Council of Regency. For the council, this history demonstrates a true nation-state at work, with a thriving economy, a high rate of literacy (78 percent by the 1880s), an independently minded electorate, and a legal system protecting the rights of all its nationals. This was a democratic nation with liberal naturalization laws that, until 1887, did not discriminate on the basis of race. Even more telling is that Natives evidently were willing to vote for haole candidates, even over Native ones. Most important to the Council of Regency, the Kingdom had codified laws that protected the economic rights of the ancient makaʻāinana (subsistence farmers and fishermen), even while the government approved policies enabling the growth of sugar and haole control of lands.

Furthermore, the Council of Regency's position is that Kingdom law, if scrupulously followed, could result in a massive redistribution of land to Native Hawaiians. Contrary to popular understanding and scholarly analysis (Chinen 1958; Kameʻeleihiwa 1992), the 1848 *māhele* (division and sharing) of the Kingdom's lands did not permanently dispossess the vast majority of makaʻāinana (people of the land, non-chiefs). The māhele set out to divide the vested interests of the three "estates" of the nation. The first two estates—the King's (Mōʻī) and the Chiefs' *(Konohiki)*—were divided between 1848 and 1850. At the same time, the Kuleana Act of 1850 encouraged the Native tenants (makaʻāinana) to claim allodial title to the lands they inhabited and farmed. Although the Kuleana Act expired in 1850, with makaʻāinana land awards at that point totaling less than 1 percent of the Kingdom's 4.2 million acres, the Council of Regency claims that the right of makaʻāinana to receive fee-simple titles to their vested rights in the land was unequivocal in Kingdom laws and continued after the expiration of the act (Sai et al. 2000:19).

In 1894, the Supreme Court of the Republic of Hawaiʻi declared that makaʻāinana who failed to make claims during the two-year act had surrendered any further right to land *(Dowsett* v. *Mt. Kaʻala).* The Council of Regency asserts that this Court's finding contradicted Kingdom law and practice because every deed issued during and after the mahele bore the caveat "subject to the rights of Native Tenants."

Therefore, the descendents of makaʻāinana who did not make land claims, or whose claims were either lost or denied by the Land Commission in 1850, are still eligible, the council believes, to divide out their interest in the lands of Hawaiʻi and claim allodial title. This can only happen, they say, under the laws of the Kingdom of Hawaiʻi. Furthermore, this distribution would involve all lands, even those purchased or awarded as fee-simple lands, because all "interests were subject to the rights of native tenants to divide their vested interest in fee-simple" (Sai et al. 2000:19).

At a symposium at the Center for Hawaiian Studies following The Hague arbitration hearing, Keanu Sai, one of the Council of Regency's acting ministers, praised the work of Rev. William Richards for helping to create the nation's legal framework and successfully pursuing international recognition, which are the bases for Native Hawaiian legal claims today. Believing that the laws themselves substantiate the essential and historic rights of the Hawaiian subjects, Sai and the Council of Regency do not seem particularly concerned with what shape the nation would take when the laws of the Kingdom are reestablished. However, they are clear that under foundational Kingdom law, the Native subject would have land rights that would not be legally available to subjects who are not descendents of the aboriginal race. They see no other distinction between Native and non-native subjects.

Such distinctions are much more important to KLH supporters and citizens. The analysis of historian Lilikalā Kameʻeleihiwa, a citizen and outspoken supporter of KLH, is that western laws contributed to the confusion Hawaiians had about themselves and the foreigners' world, a confusion encouraged by American missionaries whose racist views of Hawaiians continually asserted the Kanakas' inferiority to Caucasians.

The issue of racism is a central departing point for many Hawaiians who seek a sovereign nation that is exclusively native. Religious and political conversions, they believe, were fulminated by a people who conceived of themselves as racially superior to Natives throughout the world and whose "service" to Hawaiians in the nineteenth century cannot be separated from their ambitions to govern them.[8] Although American law and social discourse today may contradict the notions of the nineteenth century, many indigenous writers and political leaders feel that conceptions of racial superiority are masked by the more recent assumption that western ideas should be adopted as universal (Trask 1999; Meyer 1998).

A wide range of Native writers insist that Euro-American discourses on indigenous ways come preequipped with certain assumptions that make their discourses untenable. One is a presumption of Euro-American cultural superiority. Only the most insensitive of white people (and who will listen to them?) will baldly assert that superiority, but western ideas and values dominate the cultural and social landscape of contemporary Hawaiʻi. KLH citizen and university professor Haunani-Kay Trask has devoted much of her scholarship and teaching to questioning the hegemony of the western academy over Hawaiian history, politics, economics, and social analysis. Her essays include provocative subjects such as the prostitution of Hawaiian culture (especially hula) by the tourist industry in Hawaiʻi, the ongoing economic imperialism of western nations in the Pacific, the assumption of expertise by haole academics on Native subjects, and the denial of Native-Hawaiian rights to self-determination (Trask 1999:113–122). Trask also fiercely defends the notion that Hawaiians and other Native peoples have powerful cultural connections to the land and nature that are antithetical to rampant capitalism. On this, she and fellow professor Kameʻeleihiwa agree.

These cultural connections, coupled with the doubt that haole could really appreciate living in a society that encourages consensus and community over naked self-interest, is one reason for KLH's insistence that only Kanaka Maoli be enfranchised. Their perspective rests on the belief that Hawaiians are unique, that their uniqueness is a positive addition to the diversity of human races and cultures, and that maintaining this uniqueness requires resisting (kūʻē) assimilation into America.

The Council of Regency seems unconcerned about whether Hawaiians are culturally distinct. It is enough, they argue, that their nation be independent (kūʻokoʻa). Independence, in the style of any other state in the world, would guarantee that the citizens of the Hawaiian nation could structure their society as they pleased. With control of the Government Lands from the māhele and with Native Hawaiians renewing their claims to private lands, an independent government could allow Hawaiians to live as they want.

How independent, though, is any government today? One criticism of the nation-state model is that, as a political entity, it seems designed to facilitate things such as international trade, capital expansion into previously "underdeveloped" regions, and rapid transformations of the environment. The idea that it protects the wealth and the distinction of a national group may be truer in some cases than in others. In the case of Native peoples, national governments have yet to demonstrate either the ability or willingness to protect a society that does not want its lands mined and drilled, its forests penetrated with highways, and its people educated to fulfill a destiny as wage laborers.

Furthermore, is it a good idea for Hawaiians to claim a kind of immunity from colonialism based on a nineteenth-century constitution and a few words of recognition by a British diplomat and a French diplomat? Should not national identity mean more than that? Should we Hawaiians acquiesce to the colonization of other Native peoples because they themselves did not perform these legal rituals?

SOME INITIAL CONCLUSIONS

The strategies of both KLH and the council require their own articles of faith. One side places that faith in the rituals of law; the other believes in the power and importance of ancestry and ethnic distinction. Their opposition to each other strongly resembles the opposition of makaʻāinana to legislation in the 1840s that made room for foreigners to become citizens, secure political office, and purchase land (Kameʻeleihiwa 1992; Osorio 2002).

Between 1845 and the 1850, the Kingdom's legislature and the Privy Council received and stored dozens of petitions from their Kanaka subjects. A few score individuals signed some, but other petitions bore the signatures and marks of thousands. Essentially, all the petitions said the same things. They appealed to the King and the legislature not to allow foreigners to become subjects, not to make them councilors and chiefs in the Kingdom, and not to sell them lands. Many petitions expressed the makaʻāinana's fear that the foreigners would replace their chiefs and them as the Lāhui (the nation) and they would be left to "drift from one place to another" (Osorio 2002).

The makaʻāinana fears have certainly been justified in history. One could say that their perspicuity means little, a simple recognition that they were doomed. After all, the government's response, signed by Kamehameha III and Minister of the Interior Keoni Ana (John Young Jr.), dismissed the maka'āinana, saying that little could be done to prevent foreigners from coming ashore. The only government strategy that made sense was to incorporate haole into the Kingdom by allowing them to become citizens, own land, and share a stake in the Kingdom's future.

This is where we find the heart of the disagreement between KLH and the Council of Regency. Allowing haole citizenship did not make haole loyal to the Kingdom in the same way that Natives were loyal, and for the maka'āinana of the 1840s, that loyalty was important, not just politically but also socially and culturally. One petition drafted by a Native representative in the 1845 legislature put it very succinctly: "We are divided among ourselves. An independent race according to our own nature, the foreigners despise us and we hear them revile us to our faces. Who indeed would agree to making ali'i of the white-skinned people? We are as God made us, brown skinned, as was his wish. He furnished this race with the mind and the land, the chiefs and the people, and all things. These things remain that we should seek with all our strength" (Kingdom of Hawai'i 1845).

The maka'āinana 150 years ago saw and appreciated the distinctions between themselves and haole. That is no less true today. Although intermarriage, loss of language, and myriad changes as a result of western education, commerce, and consumption may have transformed the Native culture, a strong sense of uniqueness persists. Moreover, despite the very powerful and popular notion in contemporary America that racial distinctions are unsavory leftovers from nineteenth-century Euro-American imperialism and slavery, Hawaiians are insistent that those racial distinctions used by Europeans and Americans to justify their political control have nothing to do with indigenous people determined to maintain some semblance of national identity.

This is why the Council of Regency's model of independence, basically re-creating a 130-year-old kingdom, raises an important issue. What, after all, is the point of resurrecting a government that did not address the most critical issues of its people? On the other hand, the Council of Regency is quite correct that nothing short of a national government can protect Hawaiians from lawsuits, judicial review, and future federal legislation and review that could as easily withdraw entitlements as award them and reverse federal recognition at any time.

Between these two initiatives for sovereignty exists, perhaps, some common strategy, but this is difficult to see. It appears that the Council of Regency is looking for an easy solution to a terrible cultural knot. The problem is, what connections do race, nationhood, and law have to one another? The Council of Regency thinks that the issue can be easily settled by making the other two subject to nothing more than the law. By dividing ancestry from national membership, the law does not need to speak to the issue of racial difference. KLH, however, understands that for Native Hawaiians that racial difference is and always has been paramount. Few Hawaiians think that their own government victimized the Native people when the Queen surrendered to the overwhelming strength of the United States. Most Hawaiians understand that a very small number of haole, using the unwitting power of a large nation and the faith that Kanaka had in law (Osorio 2001), succeeded in convincing the Queen and most of her people not to fight in 1893 or in 1898, when America "annexed" Hawaiʻi.

Perhaps our faith in laws, constitutions, and the right of nations to exist betrayed our people at the turn of the last century. Perhaps we should have fought then. Perhaps we should fight now. Perhaps the fight is all we have left to demonstrate our kinship and devotion to our Lāhui. If that is the case, the nation shall have to continue to strengthen itself, by struggle and by sacrifice, if it is to demonstrate to its people that it is worth defending. It will also need to show that a Hawaiian nation would be different and would construct a different society than the one we presently occupy. Otherwise, what is the point of spending one's life in pursuit of Lāhui rather than simply looking for ways to make wealth?

Clearly, a simple change in government will not create the nation. That nation is created of people who are today testing themselves against the most potent, omnipresent culture of materialism ever seen in the world. Perhaps we would have a less vulnerable state if we brought back the Kingdom, but without a Lāhui of determined, educated, and loyal individuals, what would be the point of an independent Hawaiʻi? The Council of Regency may be successful in its appeal before the World Court, but it will never secure an independent government without its Native citizens, and it will never secure those citizens until it demonstrates that it can and will fight for them to be Hawaiians.

LAW, HISTORY, AND OTHER FAITHS

Perhaps it is inevitable that the differences among Native Hawaiians should become more apparent at the moment American ideological and legal opposition to reparation to Kanaka Maoli is reaching new heights. After all, we Hawaiians can hardly be unaffected by portrayals of us as unreasonable and whining, looking for a handout, and refusing to cooperate with the rational globalism dominating modern American ideology. To return to the *Rice* v. *Cayetano* case, Keanu Sai is apparently not alone in his belief that the problems of race and ethnicity in the United States can be dealt with as a matter of law. Like Sai, the US Supreme Court counts the law as the most important, most sacred of institutions, more crucial than justice and transcendent over history. In other words, history is background to the fundamental practice of making and interpreting law because, in the Justices' minds, only law truly protects the nation.

Of course, history can be made and interpreted too. Moreover, history is a necessary context for understanding law. That America has had to amend its constitution specifically to protect its citizens' civil rights is revealing of America's own racist past. Without those amendments, could the republic have survived the social traumas of slavery and apartheid? Does not the continued intercession of the Supreme Court imply an ongoing need to mediate between Caucasian and other Americans? Is it not ironic that in the last census almost 98 percent of the American people continued to identify themselves as a single ethnic group and in Hawai'i more than 20 percent of its people counted themselves as multiethnic (*Advertiser*, 20 March 2001), yet the Supreme Court feels the need to speak to the issues of race and fairness here?

Hawaiians have had a remarkably different experience with race than Americans. In fact, Americans wrote the first laws in Hawai'i discriminating against Asians, disenfranchising them in the Bayonet Constitution of 1887 and continuing that policy of exclusion under their republic. For us Hawaiians, who have willingly (and lovingly) mixed our genes with every ethnicity that has ever visited these islands,

American fascination with race and determination to legislate and adjudicate ethnic relationships are curious, even bizarre.

This may be what really distinguishes Hawaiians from Americans. Americans look to law to define and protect their nation's fragile sense of racial diversity. Hawaiians have never needed laws to promote racial diversity and cannot now place their faith in law that discounts ancestry as either an irrelevant or unwarranted emblem of identity. To do so would entail relinquishing the last vestige of that which makes us Hawaiian in the first place. As to the necessity of law's existence, there is, perhaps, less disagreement. Even as the Council of Regency proclaims the importance of recognizing Kingdom constitutions, few other sovereignty groups will contest the importance of having a constitution in the first place.

The Reinstated Hawaiian Government, with at least 4,000 members under the leadership of long-time activist Henry Noa, elected representatives and nobles in 1999, following the laws of the 1887 Bayonet Constitution. Noa argues that because the Queen swore to uphold this constitution in 1892, it was, and continued to be, the law of the land until the 1999 Legislative Assembly amended it. Noa challenges the Council of Regency and its right to represent the Hawaiian nation without being elected. KLH, too, has always contended that rival sovereignty initiatives have no legitimacy without constitutions and elected officials. If we are to understand how a Hawaiian national being has managed to survive, surely we must begin by understanding how virtually every nationalist group uses and argues law in presenting its particular political case, but also how omnipresent law is in those sensitive areas that most determine our values and identities.

Something is remarkably optimistic about the ways in which small, patriotic Native groups vulnerable to many things, including hopelessness, grasp the mechanics of law and the potions of history and contend with one another for shaping the national spirit. We have certainly changed in many ways, but in our rapt absorption with, and our refusal to concede, either law or history to anyone, we demonstrate how very like our nineteenth-century ancestors we are.

This means that some common ground may exist after all. Certainly all the major sovereignty initiatives have proclaimed a faith in law and the electoral process. This, in itself, is a telling reminder that our world has changed, and significantly. One crucial aspect of law is that it enables contending and competing groups within a society to coexist, compensating for the lack of faith between them by requiring that they place their faith in law instead. Even if law may betray the weak and helpless more often than it does the powerful, it may be the only platform from which one group, no matter how small, may fearlessly stake out its right to exist and to endure.

However, placing faith in law requires that we acknowledge a layer of authority other than custom and tradition. This is an ideological razor's edge for nationalists who see sovereignty as a protector of "the Hawaiian culture." Law involves compromise, and tradition can be so uncompromising. Nevertheless, Hawaiians have already made the concession to trust in law. Perhaps that should be the first thing on which we can agree. We will certainly dispute many things: our read of history, the importance we attach to ancestry, how we will live, and how we will treat Americans and foreigners. Because we do not see these things the same way now, let us fashion laws that will enable us to act together in spite of it all.

Among all the conversions the Kanaka Maoli accepted from America, the one that proved most unreliable was the implicit promise accompanying the introduction of western laws—that justice is possible. More than 160 years later, our willingness to drape our future onto a legal frame demonstrates profound understandings of law and history. Regardless of the fact that law has changed the Native and may have created a being that is not entirely like his ancestors, law has also been made a part of our being, adopted and adapted to our view of ourselves and the world. Our experience with colonialism makes us wise in our understanding of the limits and promise of law. We do understand the significance of bending to its authority. In a world where other faiths are so carelessly deployed against one another, humanity itself should prefer that a genuine faith in history and law be desirable, useful, and meaningful to all. That the imperialist can convey this message as credibly as the conquered is doubtful.

Notes

1. This requires context. Many Hawaiians belonged to and led labor organizations, especially among longshoremen and teamsters' unions in the 1930s and

1940s. Few Hawaiian Republican families did not have active union members by the late 1930s.

    2. A circuit judge dismissed indictments for the fourth time in the case on grounds that state lawyers had presented evidence in a way that prejudiced the indicting grand jury (*Advertiser,* 26 November 2000).

    3. I am a plaintiff in the *Office of Hawaiian Affairs* v. *Housing Finance and Development Corporation et al.* in the First Circuit Court. This suit, continued since 1996, seeks to enjoin the State of Hawaiʻi from selling or exchanging 5F trust lands, also known as Ceded Lands, until the sovereignty over those lands can be determined. In 1995, the state sought a summary judgment from Federal Judge Healy and was denied.

    4. Using the term *race* for ethnicity may strike some as offensive. I do not use *race* to imply a different species, but as an interchangeable term with *ethnicity* or *ancestry.*

    5. Perfect Title was formed on December 10, 1995, to investigate (and confirm or reject) all claims to fee-simple titles consistent with Kingdom law for its clients and to register valid titles with the Kingdom's Bureau of Conveyances. All the partners in Perfect Title agreed that the business would be operated in "strict compliance to the business laws of the Hawaiian Kingdom as noted in the Compiled Laws of 1884 and the Session Laws of 1884 and 1886"(Sai et al. 2000:66).

    Noting that a legitimate Bureau of Conveyances was in absentia because of more than a century of American occupation, a second company, the Hawaiian Kingdom Trust Company (HKTC), was formed on December 15, 1995, to act for and on behalf of the Hawaiian Kingdom government until the absentee government was reestablished and fully operational. Acting for the absentee government, the trustees of the HKTC have gradually assumed the roles of agencies and ministries of the Kingdom's government. In its memorial to The Hague, the Council of Regency states, "The 1880 Co-partnership Act requires members of co-partnerships to register their articles of agreement in the Bureau of Conveyances and that a Registrar shall superintend said bureau. This statute places an obligation on members of co-partnerships to register, and at the same time this statute places a corresponding duty on the Department of the Minister of the Interior to assure compliance with the statute. Logic and necessity dictated that in the absence of an executor of this department that a registered co-partnership could assume the department's duty" (Sai et al. 2000:69).

    In this manner, the trustees of the HKTC, the only registered company representing the interests of the Kingdom, appointed David Keanu Sai to the Council of Regency on February 27, 1996, one day after he formally relinquished all his interests in HKTC and Perfect Title. On March 1, 1996, Regent Sai formally proclaimed that the Office of the Regent and its delegates would replace HKTC as the agency empowered to issue patents in fee-simple or enter into lease negotiations between the government and qualified individuals.

6. In April 2001, the PCA declined to continue its involvement, citing the absence of the United States in the proceedings and pointing out that the Court had no power to proceed without the presence of all the parties. The Court did not deny the legitimacy of either the Kingdom or the Council of Regency as its representatives.

7. The penalty for treason or conspiracy to commit treason was forfeiture of lands (Compiled Laws of the Kingdom of Hawai'i, 1884).

8. My own work in this area (see Osorio 2002) clearly indicates that the triumph of the Bayonet Constitution in 1887 was part of a steady, systematic process by which an overwhelming and racist discourse devalued and diminished Native culture, voters, legislature, and finally, the King.

9

Delegating Closure

Hirokazu Miyazaki

Bernard Cohn and others have drawn attention to the effects of colonial documentation projects such as the collecting of census data (Cohn 1987), the codification of customary law (Moore 1992), the registration of native land titles (France 1969; Rappaport 1994), the surveillance of religious movements (Kaplan 1995), and the recording of ethnological information more generally (Dirks 2001; Thomas 1992). Many of these studies have focused on how documentation projects objectified aspects of colonized societies and, in the process, profoundly shaped colonized populations' modalities of knowing and modes of resistance (see Comaroff and Comaroff 1991; Merry 2000). In this sense, these studies reflect a larger emphasis in the anthropology of colonialism on the unintended epistemological and ontological consequences of colonization (compare Foucault 1991b).

The emphasis on *unintended* consequences and effects reflects a broader assumption in contemporary social theory about the profoundly indeterminate nature of reality. This assumption, in turn, renders indeterminacy as the condition for acting and knowing. From this perspective, for example, Sally Falk Moore (1978:50) has drawn

attention to the way actors "use whatever areas there are of inconsistency, contradiction, conflict, ambiguity, or open areas that are norma-
tively indeterminate to achieve immediate situational ends." Of course,
the nature of indeterminacy at stake in these analyses varies widely,
from an indeterminacy of cause and effect (Hayek 1980 [1948]) to an
indeterminacy of rules (Bourdieu 1977; Comaroff and Roberts 1981;
Moore 1978; Wittgenstein 1953) and of meaning (Geertz 1973). Yet, as
the philosopher of social science James Bohman (1991:6) has suggested, there is broad consensus among social scientists that a commitment to indeterminacy should replace a commitment to determinacy
as the common goal of the social sciences: "The social sciences are
indeed 'sciences of indeterminacy' whose theories do not succeed by
predicting unique and determinate outcomes."

This chapter suggests that, from actors' point of view, indeterminacy is not always a given condition and that indeterminacy, as well as
determinacy, may be a product of carefully orchestrated strategies.[1] I
focus on the strategies deployed by Fijians to invoke indeterminacy in
their efforts to define their knowledge about their origin place (that is,
where they came from) and therefore, metonymically speaking, their
knowledge about who they are. I argue that Fijians' efforts to produce a
condition of indeterminacy surrounding their knowledge derive from
a specific regime of truth surrounding Fijian land. Early in the twentieth century, the government collected each Fijian social unit's migration narrative through the sworn testimony of elders. These narratives
were declared final evidence of landownership and were closed to
future revision. The government since has maintained this regime of
truth by rendering these records as sacred documents and strictly controlling access to them. In this regime of truth, the production of the
indeterminacy that enables postcolonial actors to redefine who they
are on the basis of their present knowledge is experienced as an
achievement. In this chapter, I examine various strategies Fijians have
deployed to create moments of indeterminacy out of this condition of
extreme determinacy.

My focus is on a series of petitions Fijians from the village of
Suvavou wrote to the government during a period of approximately
one hundred years, from 1898 to 1995, requesting that inquiries into
the legal basis of the confiscation of their land be reopened. The

authenticity of the underlying claims is not my concern. Rather, following Natalie Zemon Davis's analysis of letters of remission in sixteenth-century France, I seek to situate these petitions in a wider regime of document production. The petitions are quintessentially heterogeneous documents (compare Hanks 2000:13) that draw on diverse genres of knowledge practices, including bureaucratic, academic, and ritual practices. In many cases, the documents are also products of collaboration between the petitioners and their scribes, "researchers," "consultants," and lawyers (compare Davis 1987:5). Therefore, they cannot be reductively analyzed in terms of either their cultural specificity or their adherence to the technicalities of bureaucratic form. Nevertheless, the documents deploy a variety of strategies deriving from, and in dialogue with, a genre of official documents produced by government officials to record Fijian social systems and migration narratives. As mentioned earlier, these official documents, generated in the course of the colonial administration's evidence-taking from Fijian witnesses in the early twentieth century, have long been declared uncontestable. In this chapter, I draw attention to strategies these petitioners deployed to challenge the finality of the knowledge about them contained in these official records. I argue that while the strategies deployed in these petitions have changed over time in dialogue with the government's responses, one element has remained constant: The self-knowing effectuated by these petitions is overwhelmingly indeterminate.

My larger goal here is to contribute to an understanding of the work of indeterminacy in knowledge production, ours as much as theirs.[2] William Hanks and others have sought to use the notion of the dialogical to understand what they perceive as the fundamentally indeterminate character of reality (Hanks 2000:182; compare Bakhtin 1981). For example, John Kelly and Martha Kaplan (2001:6) state, "We support an anthropology more dialogical in the Bakhtinian sense. For Bakhtin and others, history as a dialogical process is an open series, with neither absolute priorities of level nor finite numbers of subjects and objects involved. In a dialogical account, even global history is a series of planned and lived responses to specific circumstances that were also irreducibly constituted by human subjects, creating not a single vast chain of 'the subject' changed by 'the object' and vice versa, but a dense, complex network of individual and collective subjects continually responsive to one another." From this perspective, the production of postcolonial actors' knowledge about who they are, as well as administrative and academic knowledge about them in postcolonial Fiji, is a dialogic process, an interplay of past and present, of colonial legacies and current interests open to undisclosed future possibilities (see Kaplan 1990:128, 144–145, 147, n. 16; Kaplan, Chapter 6, this volume; Kaplan and Kelly 1994:128–129, 146; Rutz 1995:87–88).

I want to suggest, however, that Fijians have sought to create the condition of indeterminacy out of the overdetermined regime of truth in which they find themselves through a very similar invocation of dialogicality. If the goal of this volume is to theorize emerging uncertainty and indeterminacy in the intersections of the colonial past and the postcolonial present, my objective in this chapter is to draw attention to and therefore question the very device that enables our efforts to invoke such indeterminacy. This may lead us to question whether what is really needed is yet another layer of dialogical analysis on the part of the anthropological observer.

CLOSED KNOWLEDGE

In 1880, the Fiji government established the Native Lands Commission (NLC) to register Fijian titles to land according to an official model of Fijian social structure in which Fijians were organized into *itokatoka* (subclans), *mataqali* (clans, or sets of itokatoka), and *yavusa* (sets of mataqali).[3] The NLC meticulously recorded the names and kinship of local landowning units and also each unit's narrative of migration from its origin place to the land it then occupied, as "evidence" of land ownership (see also Kaplan, Chapter 6, this volume). By the end of the 1910s, the NLC had adopted a standardized form of evidence taking. At each hearing, NLC members summoned representatives of each yavusa to give statements regarding their yavusa's migration to its present site of residence and to provide an account of the current composition of the yavusa, including the ceremonial duties or standing *(itutu)* of each mataqali within the yavusa. When the NLC obtained these statements, it summoned other representatives of each mataqali within the yavusa and asked them to swear to the validity of these stories. The main text of the ensuing migration narratives was recorded in *Ai Tukutuku Raraba* (literally, "general statements"). The testimony of the collaborating witnesses was recorded in what the NLC called its "Evidence Book." Whereas many anthropologists have drawn attention to the importance of narratives about origin places as charters for cultural identity in Austronesian societies (for example, Fox and Sather 1996; Parmentier 1987), the NLC's taking of migration narratives on oath clearly established this narrative form as the most important form of self-knowledge for Fijians.

At the time of my fieldwork (1994–1996), government records produced before 1960, other than these NLC records, were available to local researchers and overseas research permit-holders at the discretion of the government archivist at the National Archives of Fiji. Access to NLC records, however, was generally very difficult for both Fijian and non-Fijian researchers to obtain. Fijian researchers had trouble accessing even those NLC records that concerned their own *vanua*. When I sought access to these records, for example, an NLC official instructed me to present a bundle of *kava (yaqona)* roots to the chief of the vanua (place or land) whose records I wanted to consult, to obtain his written permission. The NLC official explained that the records belonged to chiefs and that one must first seek their permission.

The NLC has not only restricted access to its records but also has sought to cultivate among Fijians a sense of their finality, closure, and incontestability. For example, the NLC has repeatedly told Fijians that their ancestors' statements on oath were sacred texts *(ivola tabu)*. Closure in this sense is the foreclosure of the possibility of going back to question the validity of statements made in the past: Fijians are encouraged to accept their ancestors' testimonies as final statements about their land. This has resulted in many contemporary Fijians' shared sense of alienation from knowledge about their origin and land and, therefore, metonymically from their knowledge about who they are.

This, of course, does not mean that the NLC has dictated Fijian social organization. Many anthropologists of Fiji have repeatedly shown that the standardized form of segmentation used by the NLC for registration of native land was a pure colonial construct and that the NLC's "rigid" model diverged from more "flexible" realities. For example, Rusiate Nayacakalou (1965:126) has noted that "while I have the highest regard for the records of the NLC and for the competence of the men who compiled them, I believe that the commission has erred in its conception of the basic structure of Fijian society. I believe that the compilation of these records was inspired by a conception of Fijian society which was too rigid, tying down the constitution of Fijian social groups to descent alone, thus robbing the system of much of its flexibility" (see also France 1969:174; Rutz 1978:23, 26–29). As Henry Rutz (1978:24) has pointed out, however, administrative documentation based on the NLC's official model of Fijian society certainly has shaped the character of Fijians' engagement with the government. The official model has also been an important subject and basis of debates and disputes among Fijians themselves.

Most Fijians living in the village of Suvavou are descendants of the original landowners of Suva, Fiji's capital city.[4] Suva's original landowners were relocated from the Suva Peninsula, where Suva stands today, to the present village site in 1882, when the Fiji government established its colonial capital at Suva. As compensation, Suvavou people have received a nominal annuity every year since 1882.[5] Over the past century, Suvavou people have repeatedly petitioned the government for larger amounts of compensation, and the colonial and postcolonial governments have mobilized considerable legal and administrative resources to defeat their claim.[6] It is important to note that within the village, Suvavou people have not been always united about their strategy. Especially since the last surviving member of the original chiefly line of Roko Tui Suva died in 1918, different factions of the village have fought over the chiefly title and the accompanying entitlement to the largest share of compensation (if and when it is ever granted by the government).[7]

In what follows, I focus on a report submitted to the government in 1994 by a mataqali in Suvavou regarding its claim to the chiefly title. I compare this with other Fijian "letters of request" *(ivola ni kerekere)* that Suvavou people sent to the government during a period of approximately one hundred years, from 1898 to 1995. Some of these letters concern Suvavou people's request for compensation for the loss of Suva land; others concern disputes among villagers over the distribution of shares of annuity and other rent monies from the leasing of Suvavou village land. The focus is on the development of this genre of writing as a particular form of self-knowing over time.

A REPORT

In 1994, Mataqali Koromakawa, a mataqali in Suvavou, submitted a "report" to the NLC.[8] The report concerned the mataqali's long-standing claim that it should hold the chiefly title of the village Tui Suva. The title had been held by another mataqali of the village, Mataqali Kaiwai, for some time. Since the mid-1980s, Mataqali Koromakawa men had repeatedly written to the NLC to challenge the legitimacy of the current chiefly mataqali. The NLC had rejected Mataqali Koromakawa's claim to the chiefly title on the basis that NLC records showed Mataqali Kaiwai as the legitimate holder of the title. Soon after a Mataqali Kaiwai man became the new chief of the village in 1989, for example, the chief *(turaga ni mataqali)* of Mataqali Koromakawa wrote a letter of protest to the NLC. The chairman of the NLC replied by sharply reminding the chief of Mataqali Koromakawa that their ancestors *(qase)* had given sworn *(bubului)* statements and that it was the NLC's "duty" *(itavi)* to protect *(taqomaka ka maroroya)* these statements. In other words, what their ancestors had already confirmed could not be altered.

In Mataqali Koromakawa men's opinion, however, their challenge to the NLC had not been entirely ineffective. In 1991, they succeeded in obtaining a response from an NLC official that confirmed a portion of their longstanding claim. The official migration narrative recorded by the NLC in 1921 listed Mataqali Koromakawa's standing *(tutu)*, or ceremonial duty in the chiefdom of Suva, as that of *bete* (priest). Yet, the chief of Mataqali Koromakawa pointed out in his 1991 letter to the NLC that when his grandfather had been asked by the NLC to swear to the validity of the migration narrative in 1921, he had contested that portion of the narrative by claiming that his mataqali's standing should be *sauturaga* (the installer of the chief). This claim was predicated on the fact that, as sauturaga, Mataqali Koromakawa would have the right to select and install a legitimate chief. Indeed, this Mataqali Koromakawa man's objection had been recorded in the NLC's Evidence Book. The NLC responded by admitting the error and altering its record to change the status of Mataqali Koromakawa from bete to sauturaga. Although the NLC's confirmation that the mataqali's standing should be sauturaga did not seem to be endorsed by other clans in the village, for Mataqali Koromakawa men it served as proof that the government would accept their claim if they could support it with documentary evidence. The report Mataqali Koromakawa men submitted to the government in 1994, therefore, was a product of their renewed hope.

The report as a genre of Fijian writing seems to have emerged in the late 1980s. Its emergence coincided with the appearance of Fijian consultants and lawyers as mediators between rural Fijians and the government. These consultants' and lawyers' principal role was to prepare documents for submission to the government on their clients' behalf, in return for a portion of any compensation later gained. They frequented the National Archives of Fiji and other government offices to consult administrative records. Typically, most of the consultants were retired government officials well versed in the language of bureaucracy. All the Fijian lawyers engaged in this business had recently returned from Australia or New Zealand, where they had studied law on Fiji government scholarships reserved for ethnic Fijians after the 1987 coups. In other words, the emergence of the report reflected the increasing bureaucratization and legalization of the terms of engagement between Fijians and the government.

Many such lawyers and consultants had approached Suvavou people in hopes of obtaining a portion of the large amount of compensation villagers might some day receive from the settlement of their claim. Some had presented villagers with documents they thought would win their case, such as old lists of the original landowners of Suva obtained from research at the National Archives of Fiji. Suvavou people also had contacted lawyers and consultants on their own. In the late 1980s, for example, Suvavou people commissioned a retired Ministry of Fijian Affairs official to prepare a report on the history of the Suva land case. This man collaborated with Anare Matahau & Associates, one of the most successful and controversial Fijian consulting firms at the time, and completed a 222-page report titled *Suva State Land: "Land of My Fathers"* in 1991.[9] The chief of Suvavou signed the report and submitted it to the president of Fiji. Separately from this villagewide project, in 1988, Mataqali Koromakawa commissioned a young Fijian lawyer to prepare a report on a piece of land in Suva that it claimed as its ancestral site (yavutu).

The report that Mataqali Koromakawa submitted to the NLC in 1994 was unique, however, in that it was prepared without the assistance of such consultants or lawyers. Although the report was submitted in the name of the mataqali chief, its actual author was a Mataqali Koromakawa man who had no experience working in government offices. He was assisted by his categorical brothers, a medical technician and a telecommunication consultant, with the use of their personal computer. Nevertheless, this report contains all the stylistic features commonly deployed in reports prepared by consultants, lawyers, or government officials. For example, paragraphs in the report are numbered, and there are frequent references to serial numbers of government records in the text.

Although the stylistic features evoke the technicality of bureaucratic and legal work, giving this report a very different look from other letters of request written by the mataqali, the report is not simply an appropriation of bureaucratic and legal technicalities. Rather, I understand the report as the culmination of Suvavou people's hundred-year project to produce a document that finally would reopen and set in motion the government's closed knowledge about Suva's original landowners and resolve their conflict with the government once and for all.

APPENDICES

The Mataqali Koromakawa report consists of three parts. In the first section, it presents a narrative of the mataqali's migration route from its origin place. The second section lists a series of questions regarding the details of NLC records concerning the three yavusa of Suvavou. The third section consists of appendices containing copies of archival records. Each section draws on old and new strategies that have evolved in dialogue with the government and its records over the past hundred years.

The appendices in the third section of the report reproduce archival records such as documents contained in the Colonial Secretary's Office (CSO) files and NLC records. The practice of attaching copies of past government records as evidence seems to have emerged as common practice in Suvavou people's letters of request during the 1970s. For example, in 1973, when fifty Suvavou people objected to the NLC's registration of Suvavou village land as the common property of the three yavusa of Suvavou, the villagers enclosed in their letter of request a copy of a letter dated December 27, 1905, and written in Fijian by Native Land Commissioner David Wilkinson.

This letter details the locations of pieces of land held by each mataqali in Suvavou village as evidence that, in Suvavou, mataqali and not yavusa should be landowning units.[10]

This increase in the uses of government records as documentary evidence in Fijian letters of request since the 1970s was the result of the introduction of photocopying technology and the increased access to government records. The government's efforts to preserve administrative records and make them available to the public began during the mid-1950s (Crozier 1958, 1959; Diamond 1978), but I do not know precisely when Fijians began to consult government records at the National Archives of Fiji to prepare their letters of request. By the 1970s, however, judging from Suvavou people's letters, a fair number of government records seem to have been in Suvavou people's hands. In 1994, for example, I found a copy of Wilkinson's letter among other old government records a Suvavou man kept in his briefcase. He told me that he had inherited these records from his mother's brother. At the time of my fieldwork, many of those who held leadership positions in *tokatoka* (subunits of a clan), mataqali, or yavusa kept collections of government records concerning their own tokatoka, mataqali, or yavusa. These records usually consisted of NLC lists of tokatoka and mataqali membership (*vola ni kawa bula,* or native register).[11] Others kept copies of other kinds of government records, such as old maps of Suva, NLC records concerning the genealogy of Bauan chiefs to whom the original chiefly line of Suvavou people was related, and government records relevant to their mataqali's specific claims.[12]

The appearance of appendices in Suvavou people's documents coincided with the emergence of village "researchers," villagers who devoted much of their energies to archival research. Suvavou people repeatedly told me that they were not allowed to see all the relevant government records about Suva's original landowners and their land at the National Archives of Fiji and the NLC because the government wanted to hide the truth from them. At the time of my fieldwork, however, at least two people in Suvavou had conducted extensive research at the National Archives and other government offices. One was the author of the Mataqali Koromakawa report, and the other was the daughter of a Suvavou woman who claimed to be a descendant of the original chiefly line. This woman had conducted extensive research at government departments and had written numerous letters to the government regarding her mother's claim. Given their exposure to the style of bureaucratic writing at the archives, perhaps it is not surprising that both researchers used appendices in the documents they submitted to the government. In 1989, for example, when the woman sent a letter to the Minister for Fijian Affairs regarding her claim to the chiefly title of her clan, she attached a series of internal memoranda between government officials concerning her case, as well as all correspondence between herself and the government, all in chronological order. The 1994 report continues this use of appendices to demonstrate inconsistencies in the government records. This exhibition of government records as appendices reflects a more general strategy that an examination of the report's other two sections will make explicit.

QUESTIONS

In the second section of the Mataqali Koromakawa 1994 report, the author of the report directs questions at the government. The NLC records that the report challenges consist of the recorded answers by Fijian witnesses to government officials' questions. Therefore, this move to ask questions of the government reverses the participant roles in those records. Such reversal of participant roles was one of the oldest strategies deployed by Suvavou people in their letters of request. To illustrate the significance of this strategic move, I now turn to Suvavou people's earliest letters of request.

In 1898, Suvavou people expressed their discontent for the first time with arrangements regarding Suva Peninsula land.[13] This letter did not include a single question. The government, however, responded sharply with a series of questions: The chief of the village and other villagers who signed the letter were summoned by Colonial Secretary W. L. Allardyce. In his memo, Allardyce described a meeting with nine Suvavou people in which he first confronted the villagers by reading aloud their letter. "I read them their letter enclosed and asked them if they really intended me to take the matter up seriously. They said they did to which I replied 'Very well but you will first of all answer me the following questions.'" Allardyce then asked them his question:

Why have you waited for the last 20 years and not brought
forward your claim until now? You have had many opportunities of doing so. You admit to receiving and having
received for many years past the sum of £200 annually on
account of the lands within the yellow mark [including the
entire area of the Suva Peninsula] on the accompanying
sketch exclusive of lands granted to Europeans.[14]

In 1904, a group of Suvavou people again requested more compensation for the taking of their land. This time, however, the villagers
asked the government a number of their own questions:

We...hear it said that the land was given and that the land
was sold. We ask you whether you know anything about the
land having been given or sold?

1. Who was the owner of the land who gave it away?
2. To whom was the land given?
3. For what reason or in payment of what was the land given?
4. In payment of whose debt was the land given?
5. Who arranged for the land being given?
With reference to the alleged sale of the land
6. Who was the owner of the land who sold it?
7. To whom was it sold?
8. What was the price of the land?
9. Who divided the money?
Every year £200 rent is paid for the piece of land on which
the Governor lives, but we get nothing for our land.
Why is this?[15]

By asking the government questions, Suvavou people reversed the
questioner-respondent relationship. These questions, along with the
sophisticated legal argument presented in the letter, led one government official to doubt the authenticity of the letter: "I doubt if there is
more than one writer in this case, or perhaps I should be more correct
in saying 'inditer,' and that one person is not a Fijian."[16] The effectiveness of this strategy was evident in the way it prompted the government
to investigate the legal grounds of its possession of the Suva land.

Ultimately, the government's conclusion was that "the question which was settled so long ago cannot now be reopened."[17] Nevertheless, Suvavou people's questions had triggered an internal debate among government officials about the Suva land case.

The author of the 1994 report, writing in the late twentieth century, was better positioned to ask questions. Unlike his ancestors, he had gained access to some of the government's own records. Questions in the Mataqali Koromakawa report challenged head-on certain technical details of the NLC records about Suvavou people and their land. The report's questions focused on the incompleteness and inconsistencies of information in the NLC records. The NLC had conducted two inquiries into the status of Suvavou people and their land. The first inquiry was conducted by Native Lands Commissioner David Wilkinson in 1902, and the second inquiry took place between 1919 and 1921. At the time of my fieldwork, the NLC regarded the result of the 1919–1921 inquiry as the final record concerning Suvavou people and their land. This was not unusual. In the 1920s, in response to the development of a standardized method of recording, the NLC had decided that the work of the original commission was inaccurate.[18]

The Mataqali Koromakawa report seized on apparent discrepancies between the NLC's 1902 and 1919–1921 findings. The report described the discrepancies between the two inquiries as evidence of the baselessness of the NLC's findings. The report notes, for example, that whereas in 1902 the NLC found nine mataqali in Suvavou, in 1919 the NLC found four yavusa and twelve mataqali. The report then asks its reader a question: Why this difference? The report also points to the incomplete nature of the information recorded by the NLC in 1921. The NLC recorded three statements made by three elders of Suvavou, representing each of the three yavusa of the village. The Mataqali Koromakawa report points out, for example, that none of the three narratives mentions its respective yavusa's place of origin. The report then simply asks where these yavusa originated. Furthermore, the report notes inconsistencies and contradictions among the three yavusa's narratives. For example, according to one narrative, during a mid-nineteenth-century war between the powerful rival chiefdoms Bau and Rewa, the chief of Suva, Ratu Ravulo, stayed in Rewa. According to another narrative, Ratu Ravulo stayed in Bau (see Sahlins 1991; Wall

1920). Again, the report simply asks, why do these narratives disagree?

Of course, the NLC has never claimed that the basis of the finality of the NLC records is their logical coherence. In fact, in the late 1910s the NLC abandoned all the results of its earlier inquiries. The finality of the NLC records, rather, is temporally defined: The NLC simply denies the retroactive contestability of its records. In other words, whether or not information given on oath at NLC hearings is logically incoherent or simply "wrong," it must be treated as final.

From this standpoint, it is probably not so much the act of pointing to the logical inconsistencies of the NLC records as the act of asking questions that is threatening to the integrity of the NLC records. The strategy to reverse the participant roles in the questioner-respondent relationship seeks to engage the government in discussion and reopen inquiries into land. Although access to government records in the 1980s opened up for Fijians a new manner of engagement with the government, namely, a substantive critique of government records, the effectiveness of this new form of engagement depends on an old strategy of asking questions from their standpoint.

This strategy of asking questions invokes two aspects of the act of questioning. On the one hand, questions asked of the government are manifestations of a search for information and are designed to solicit a response (Goody 1978:23). On the other hand, the questioners do not always expect a response, partially because whether they will get a response is ambiguous and partially because their main concern may not be whether they will get a response (Goldman 1993:198). The goal of asking questions may be simply to "pose" questions (Goldman 1993:198). I suggest that these "open" and "closed" potentials of the act of questioning (Goldman 1993:199) can coexist in a single set of questions. The subversion of the questioner-respondent relationship, therefore, creates an interesting effect of both openness and closure at once.

This is true from another perspective as well. Judging from the internal discussion within the government triggered by Suvavou people's questions, the strategy did work and the government began to investigate Suvavou people's concerns. It failed, however, in that Suvavou people did not succeed in reopening the case; almost always, the government categorically denied the contestability of past government decisions concerning Suvavou people's land. For both sides, these questions opened and closed the possibility for revising the official record about Suvavou people. To understand the full significance of the interplay of openness and closure embedded in the act of questioning, I now turn to another subversive strategy deployed by the report.

MIGRATION STORIES

The first section of the report presents an alternative migration narrative of Suvavou people that, according to the author of the report, is more logically consistent and complete than the migration narratives recorded by the NLC in 1921. According to the report's migration story, Suvavou people originated from Nakauvadra, a mythic origin place that many contemporary Fijians would identify as their ultimate origin place. The mentioning of Suvavou people's origin place contrasts with the lack of such information in the migration narratives recorded by the NLC. The narrative ends with a schematic representation of the allocation of ceremonial duties among three brothers, who were Mataqali Koromakawa's ancestors. According to the narrative, the eldest of the three brothers installed the youngest of the three as the chief of Suva. The eldest of the three installed himself as sauturaga, and the other became bete. This self-contained structure of the chiefdom of Suva contrasts sharply with what the 1921 NLC records seem to suggest. Information given in the migration narratives recorded by the NLC in 1921 suggests, instead, that Suva had three chiefs, one for each yavusa.[19]

This effort to present an alternative form of a ritual polity should not be understood simply as a move to create an alternative sense of closure through logical coherence. Rather, the notion of a self-contained ritual polity challenges the direction of the logic behind the notion of the chiefdom of Suva presented in the three migration stories recorded by the NLC in 1921. These focus on how several parts gathered together to constitute the chiefdom of Suva. In these accounts, the focus is on the present. In other words, as one traces the migration stories back toward the past, one finds the place where each yavusa used to reside. In contrast, the narrative by the chief of Mataqali Koromakawa focuses on how the original entity was divided at different points along the route. For example, when Suvavou people's ancestors reached a place called Delaitoga, they divided into two groups. One group remained in Delaitoga, and the other sailed down a river and eventually reached Suva. Whereas the migration stories recorded by the NLC seem to validate the composition of Suvavou people at the time of the NLC inquiry as a historically constituted entity, the Mataqali Koromakawa chief's story draws attention to the fragmentation of an entity from which Suvavou people originated. If one traces the migration route presented in the Mataqali Koromakawa report, one encounters other parts of the original entity of which Mataqali Koromakawa still considers itself to be a part (see Miyazaki n.d.b).

Like the reversal of the questioner-respondent relationship, the reversal of the relationship between a ritual polity and its parts in the migration narrative also creates an effect of openness and closure. Unlike the NLC's historically constituted and inclusive entity created by gathering disparate groups, the Mataqali Koromakawa's self-contained chiefdom defined by an act of division privileges formal closure and exclusivity. However, the reversal of the relationship between a ritual polity and its parts in the NLC's official migration narrative instantiated in the Mataqali Koromakawa report also reveals a new horizon of openness. This openness is defined by an interactional method of proof: Mataqali Koromakawa men pointed out to me that they could prove the truthfulness of their story by going back to Delaitoga, where their ancestors divided themselves into two groups, according to their migration story. The descendants of the other half of the original entity still lived in Delaitoga, and the stories of these two groups would "correspond" *(sota)* such that each would prove the other. Although open, this aspect of Mataqali Koromakawa's migration narrative equips the report with a potential for triggering an ontologically based interactional closure of its own (see Miyazaki 2000a).

Spurred by this claim, I visited Delaitoga in January 1995 in hopes of learning what villagers knew about Kai Suva. Although I spoke to the chief of Yavusa Suva and other people in Delaitoga, I could not obtain much information about Mataqali Koromakawa's migration story. At first, Mataqali Koromakawa men were disappointed when I returned to Suvavou without any substantial story. They were looking forward to the tape-recorded stories I might bring back from Delaitoga. However, their disappointment soon turned to a kind of confirmation that only they could get such information. "If we go there to sit down with them and talk," they told me, "our stories will 'meet' (sota)." Naturally, I could not gather the stories, they surmised, for to know the facts was not enough; the possibility of correspondence depended also on a particular form of ritual interaction known as *veiqaravi* (attendance) (see Miyazaki 2000a). Here, closure was defined ontologically. The seemingly open character of the migration narrative was accompanied by a narrowly defined method for its own closure.

DELEGATION AS A METHOD

As far as knowledge about Fijian land is concerned, indeterminacy is not a given condition but a condition to be achieved. The indeterminate character of acts of knowing contained in the petitions to the government I have described is strategically created. As we have seen, the Mataqali Koromakawa report contains multiple devices for creating an effect of indeterminacy. These include the open-ended questions that appear in the second section of the report and the migration narrative presented in the report that, by its form, suggests its own method of proof.

What these devices have in common is their dependence on acts of delegation or indirection (compare Brenneis 1986; Keane 1997). The reversal of both the questioner-respondent relationship and the form of the NLC's migration stories ultimately delegates closure to a third party. By asking questions of the government, the Mataqali Koromakawa report invites the government to answer those questions. The migration narrative likewise calls implicitly on another mataqali, the part of the original entity that was left behind, to prove the truthfulness of the narrative. The strategy of listing government records as appendices also reflects this delegation of proof elsewhere.

Acts of delegation produce an effect of indeterminacy because they situate acts of knowing in an interactional terrain. The indeterminate nature of interaction arises from the way it invokes a recursive relationship between an initiating act of interaction and its response. Whether questions will be answered, for example, depends not so much on the content of the questions as on the way they are posed. Likewise, whether stories will correspond and therefore prove one another's truthfulness depends on the character of the encounter between the parties involved. In the same way, whether access to documents is granted at the National Archives and other government offices depends on the identity of the parties and the nature of the relations between the bureaucrats and clients. Interaction is radically indeterminate because one side's response depends on the other's manner of attendance (see Miyazaki 2000a; compare Miyazaki 2000b). Here dialogicality emerges as a device to create a moment of indeterminacy.

In light of my observations of some Fijian actors' efforts to construct indeterminacy as a condition for knowing, the move to emphasize indeterminacy through the deployment of dialogics in anthropology and related social theory needs to be reconsidered. I suggest that anthropologists' move to emphasize indeterminacy parallels Fijians' efforts to create indeterminacy as a condition for the production of knowledge. For both anthropologists and Fijians, indeterminacy is an achievement. In fact, the wider anthropological move to emphasize indeterminacy, as opposed to earlier positivist emphases on determinacy, can be understood as an example of a common alteration between the production of determinacy and indeterminacy as effects of knowledge. From this perspective, what is needed at this moment is not so much a dialogical framework of analysis as a framework from which one can observe the work of the dialogical framework in both Fijian and anthropological knowledge production.

Notes

1. My argument echoes Elizabeth Povinelli's claim (1993:680) that Australian Aboriginal women strategically invoke the "language of indeterminacy" in their efforts to "negotiate and interrelate" different domains of knowledge.

2. Here I am following Marilyn Strathern and others' deliberate efforts to examine the parallel uses of certain devices in knowledge practices of anthropologists and those of their subjects (for example, see Maurer 2002; Riles 2000 and Chapter 7, this volume; Strathern 1991, 1996).

3. The work of the NLC proceeded very slowly and was not completed until the 1960s (see France 1969:102–148, 167–175; Nayacakalou 1971).

4. The Suva Peninsula was originally sold in 1868 by the most powerful chief of Fiji of the day, the Vunivalu of Bau, Ratu Seru Cakobau, to the Polynesia Company of Melbourne, Australia. At the time, Cakobau's pre-Cession government was in debt to the US government for damages of $42,248 caused by some

Fijians to some US citizens. The Polynesia Company had offered to pay Cakobau's debt to the US government in exchange for the Suva Peninsula and other large tracts of land, which amounted to approximately 90,000 acres in total. However, even after the Polynesia Company had subdivided approximately 27,000 acres of the Suva Peninsula land for sale to individual European settlers, the Fijian inhabitants of the peninsula remained and resisted some European settlers' attempt to occupy the tracts of land they had purchased.

Subsequently, the government paid back $9,000 to the Polynesia Company and annulled all property transactions between the Cakobau government and the Polynesia Company. Acting on the recommendation of the Land Claims Commission, the government upheld the claims of settlers who could show that they had occupied and made use of land regardless of the conditions of the sale. However, many of these claimants had debts to James McEwan & Company. Later, the government negotiated with the company and acquired approximately half of these claimants' land (see Derrick 1943: 207). All other claims based on Polynesia Company land warrants were rejected.

Upon the Land Claims Commission's rejection of claims to Suva land, though, the land was not returned to its Fijian owners, as were lands everywhere else in Fiji. Instead, the government kept for itself all Suva land except those tracts already occupied by European settlers, as well as approximately 300 acres of land that the Polynesia Company had set aside as "Native Reserve." In fact, the government began to construct public facilities in Suva. The government also subdivided the land acquired from James McEwan & Co. and sold some of it to government officials. All these facts suggest that the government never intended to return the land to the people of Suva. When the capital of Fiji was relocated to Suva in 1882, all the inhabitants of the "Native Reserve" known as Old Suva Village, or Naqasiqasi, were removed to Narikoso, a tract of land located diagonally across the Suva Harbour from Suva, where Suvavou village is located today. The new village was named *Suvavou* (New Suva).

5. The original sum of £200 was increased to F$4,000 in 1972 and to F$9,400 following the 1987 coup. See "Annuity Payments for Crown Land at Suva Peninsula," Cabinet Decision 128 of 1972, 2 August 1972, in Cabinet Paper (72) 121, in F 36/92/7 (National Archives of Fiji, Suva); "Suvavou to Get More for Domain," *Fiji Times,* 23 March 1988.

6. The government has conducted numerous internal inquires into the Suva land case to confirm the legitimacy of its claim to the Suva land (see Miyazaki n.d.b).

7. Annuity and rent monies were divided equally to the ten mataqali of the village after the chief of the village, the three yavusa heads, and ten mataqali heads took their shares.

8. All mataqali names are fictitious.

9. A former Ministry of Fijian Affairs official, Anare Matahau, studied law and land management in England before returning to Fiji. He became a controversial figure in the 1990s, after founding the Foundation of the Indigenous People of Fiji, commonly known as *Yavutu* (origin place or foundation) among Fijians. The organization's principal demand was the return of all state land to its original landowners. Its founding in 1993 coincided with the International Year of Indigenous People. That year, Matahau organized a march through Suva that attracted chiefs from western Viti Levu and other lesser chiefdoms who were not content with the post-coup political situation.

10. Letter to Minister for Fijian Affairs, 24 May 1973, F 36/92/7 (National Archives of Fiji, Suva).

11. All mataqali chiefs within two yavusa of Suvavou possessed NLC lists of tokatoka and mataqali members. None of the mataqali chiefs in the other yavusa had NLC records about their own mataqali membership. Even Mataqali Koromakawa did not possess the list of its own membership. This might have resulted from the reluctance on the part of Mataqali Ikalevu, the present chiefly and leading mataqali of this yavusa, to distribute these NLC records within the yavusa. At the time of my fieldwork, government officials, as well as villagers, were under the impression that only the chief or leader *(iliuilu)* of the vanua (chiefdom) could request these records from the NLC.

12. For example, the chief of a Suvavou mataqali kept a record prepared by Native Lands Commissioner David Wilkinson in 1899. The record shows that his mataqali was registered as a landowning unit in another peri-urban village near Suva. He had kept the record as evidence of his mataqali's entitlement to shares of rent arising from leased properties in that village.

13. Letter to Colonial Secretary, 19 November 1898, in CSO 4655/1898 (National Archives of Fiji, Suva).

14. W. L. Allardyce to Assistant Colonial Secretary, 8 December 1898, in CSO 4655/1898 (National Archives of Fiji, Suva).

15. Letter to Native Commissioner, 25 January 1904, in CSO 562/04 (National Archives of Fiji, Suva).

16. Commissioner of Works to Native Commissioner, 29 January 1904, in CSO 562/04 (National Archives of Fiji, Suva).

17. Henry Jackson to Colonial Secretary, 18 February 1904, in CSO 562/04 (National Archives of Fiji, Suva).

18. For example, see CSO 2690/23, CSO 2689/23 (National Archives of Fiji, Suva).

19. It is evident that the three witnesses who testified at the 1921 NLC inquiry also strove to show that each yavusa was a self-contained unit forming a ritual polity for itself. In other words, the 1921 NLC record was a result of the witnesses' effort to present their yavusa as an independent polity as defined by the NLC's official model.

10

Heartbreak Islands

Reflections on Fiji in Transition

Brij V. Lal

Peace, peace is what I seek, and public calm:
Endless extinction of unhappy hates

—*Matthew Arnold*

Fiji is a paradox and a pity.[1] A paradox because this island nation is endowed with wonderful natural resources, a talented and multiethnic population with a high literacy rate, and a sophisticated (but now crumbling) public infrastructure where drinkable piped water was once guaranteed, public roads had few potholes, poverty and crime and squatters were visible but contained, hospitals were uncrowded, children went cheerfully to schools, and respect for law and order was assured. But this nation is tragically prone to self-inflicted wounds with crippling consequences. One coup is bad enough for any country, but three in thirteen years—two in 1987 and one in 2000—staggers the imagination. Fiji is a pity because no genuine resolution of the country's deep-seated political and economic problems is in sight as its leaders dither and the country drifts divided. The battle lines are clearly drawn in a deadly zero-sum game. The militant nationalists, happily unconcerned about the destructive implications of their actions, threaten violent retribution if their agenda for political supremacy is marginalized in mainstream public discourse. Compounding the problem, on top of all this is a manifest lack of collective political will to exorcise the country of the demons that terrorize its soul.

The tragedy of modern Fiji politics has been that rosy rhetoric for global consumption has always won over the hard realities on the ground, blinding its people to the deep-seated problems that beset the country. At the least, this has caused them a sense of slight unease about probing too deeply into the darker recesses of national body politic, lest they discover some discomforting truth about themselves that they would rather ignore (Lal 1992; Scarr 1984; Sutherland 1992). If the emperor had no clothes, it was better not to find out. Fiji therefore portrayed itself as a model of functioning multiracial democracy, largely free of the ethnic tension and conflict that plagued many developing countries—the way the world should be, as Pope John Paul II intoned after a fleeting visit to the islands in 1985. Few publicly acknowledged inter- and intraethnic tensions, the deep reservations the different communities had about the structure of power relations in the country, and the deeply contested struggle for a definition and clarification of Fijian political identity that preceded independence. The illusion of harmony and amicable understanding in the post-independence era was just that, an illusion, and just as misleading and fraught and dangerous as the impression of balance and equilibrium and harmony conveyed by an earlier metaphor of Fiji as a three-legged stool (Sukuna 1984).

RACE AND PUBLIC MEMORY

The brutal truth, of course, was that Fiji never had a genuinely shared sense among its citizens about what kind of constitutional arrangement was appropriate for it. It was an issue that had bedeviled the country's politics since the late 1920s. Indigenous Fijian and European leaders, with active official support, argued for separate racial representation. For them, primordial loyalties were paramount. The Indo-Fijians, on the other hand, championed a non-racial common roll, privileging sectarian ideology over ethnicity. The issue dominated political debate throughout the 1960s, leading to boycott of the Legislative Council and tense elections and by-elections (Lal 1992; Norton 1990; Mara 1997). The communal voice won in the end, largely because of Fijian and European opposition but partly also because of the Indo-Fijian leaders' lack of genuine commitment to the idea, following the death of A. D. Patel, the tireless advocate of common roll

(Lal 1992). Their compromise—in truth, compromised—agreement was enshrined in the secretly negotiated independence constitution, which retained ethnicity as the principal vehicle of political participation while making a halfhearted commitment to non-racial politics as a long-term national objective (Lal, ed. 1986; Ali 1977).

Unsurprisingly, race dominated post-independence politics. The two main political parties, the Alliance and the National Federation, were essentially race-based, the former among Fijians, Europeans, and a sprinkling of Indo-Fijians, and the latter predominantly among Indo-Fijians. In time, virtually every issue of public policy came to be viewed through racial lenses: affirmative action, poverty alleviation, allocation of scholarships for tertiary education, opportunities for training and promotion in the public service. The intent to create a level playing field, to assist the indigenous community to participate more effectively in the public sector, was laudable, but race-based instead of needs-based policies inevitably corroded interethnic harmony. Public memory was racially archived even though the plain reality of daily life questioned the salience of race. Citizens were asked (as they still are) for their "race" when they opened a bank account, applied for a driver's licence, and left or entered the country. "Race is a fact of life," Ratu Sir Kamisese Mara, Fiji's first and longest-serving prime minister, kept reiterating. Under his administration, it almost became a way of life. Political leaders on both sides opportunistically championed moderate multiracialism but privately—and not so privately—played the race card on every occasion to secure power.

With time, other realities intruded, questioning the legitimacy and value of a political edifice constructed on the foundations of ethnic compartmentalization. Forces of change, rapid in their pace and bewildering in their implications, were fast eroding old, exhausted assumptions of public discourse. The television and video brought new and strange images into people's homes. Urbanization proceeded apace, spawning problems that transcended race, and attenuated traditional social and cultural links and attachments. Improved roads speeded up communication, and cash cropping fostered individualistic values. As R. G. Ward (1987) put it, "the combined introduction of new skills, new technology and money have weakened the functional cement which binds native Fijian village society. This does not mean that the structure has collapsed, or will do so in the near future. It does mean that the risk of disintegration exists if other factors shake the edifice." Decades earlier, O. H. K. Spate, R. F. Watters, and C. S. Belshaw, among others, had made essentially similar points but were dismissed by traditionalists afraid of change and were ignored by a colonial government too timid or too tied down to orthodoxy to embrace potentially progressive ideas (Spate 1959; Watters 1969; Belshaw 1964). An opportunity was thus missed to enable and empower the Fijians to embrace the forces of modernity engulfing their lives, largely on their own terms and at their own pace. For this failure, they would pay heavily later.

COUP AND ITS CONSEQUENCES

Things came to a head in 1987, the year of the first two military coups, when a democratically elected, nominally left-leaning, Labour-led coalition was ousted after a month in office. Some commentators saw the crisis as a straight-out "racial fight" between the Fijians and Indo-Fijians (Scarr 1988). Others saw the conflict fundamentally as a class struggle between the haves and the have-nots, Fijian commoners and Indo-Fijian working class joining hands against the dominance of chiefs and the Indo-Fijian business elite (Robertson and Tamanisau 1988). The importance of both race and class is acknowledged, as it has to be, but the coups were also an effort to turn back the clock, to fortify old structures and values that sustained them against forces of change, to shore up the importance of rural areas as well as the power of traditional leaders at a time when the new government was determined to democratize elements of the traditional order (Lal 1988). As Dr. Timothy Bavadra, the deposed Labour prime minister, told his campaign rallies in 1987, the individual's democratic right to vote did not mean a compulsion to vote for a chief. It was a free choice. "By restricting the Fijian people to their communal way of lifestyle in the face of a rapidly developing cash economy, the average Fijian has become more and more backward. This is particularly invidious when the leaders themselves have amassed huge personal wealth by making use of their traditional and political powers" (*Fiji Times,* 17 November 1987). These were revolutionary words in the context of the time and the place, a call to action (by an indigenous Fijian, no less) against a system already feeling itself under siege. This had to be nipped in the bud quickly.

The traditionalists rallied to restore the status quo. The post-coup 1990 constitution, decreed by presidential edict and prepared without widespread consultation, predictably privileged rural Fijians over their urban counterparts, allocating thirty of the thirty-seven Fijian seats to them and only seven to urban and peri-urban areas, even though nearly forty percent of Fijians were urban dwellers. Moreover, a candidate had to be registered in the *Vola Ni Kawa Bula* (Register of Native Births) of the constituency in which he or she was standing, further entrenching provincialism in Fijian politics (Lal 1998; Robertson 1998). Provincial and regional affiliations, often opening up precolonial social cleavages and questioning the structure of power distribution in traditional society, acquired an unprecedented public and symbolic significance that tested the colonially created notion of an overarching Fijian cultural and social identity. It also had the seriously deleterious effect of weakening the operation of political parties among Fijians. Candidates were selected by the provincial councils, so their first loyalty was to their provincial power wielders. Leaders of political parties had limited influence over the selection of candidates and even less power to discipline them for insubordination or breach of party discipline. The predictable result was an undisciplined proliferation of political parties among Fijians, formed by disgruntled or discarded candidates flying regional flags or conveniently camouflaging their private agendas under the guise of "Fijian interests."

To prevent fragmentation, Fijian leaders had the Great Council of Chiefs sponsoring a single political party to unite disparate indigenous opinion and interests under one umbrella (Lal 1998). That party, the Soqosoqo ni Vakavulewa ni Taukei (SVT), was launched in 1990, but the hope for unity was predictably stillborn. Many openly questioned the wisdom of a chiefly body becoming embroiled in party politics and the highly contestable assumption that Fijians were of one mind on all things political. Would a Fijian opposed to the SVT be any less "Fijian" than one who supported it? In an ironic twist, a commoner, albeit an uncommon one—Sitiveni Rabuka—was elected president of the party over one of the highest-ranking chiefs of Fiji, Adi Lady Lala Mara. Unsurprisingly, dissension built up, opposition emerged, rival factions developed, and alternative parties were launched—such as the Fijian Association Party, privately supported by Mara; the All National

Congress; and later the Party of National Unity in western Viti Levu, formed by Apisai Tora, the perennial chameleon of Fiji politics. The SVT was dislodged from power in 1999 because of several factors, but among the most important was the political fragmentation of the Fijians (Lal, ed. 2000). That trend, which shows little sign of abating, will continue to hobble party politics among the Fijians, especially now that provincialism is back in business and flourishing and Fijian leaders are seeking to institutionalize provincial administration along the Melanesian model. "We are still coming out of provincialism," Rabuka says, "and having that form of system will be counter to creating national cohesiveness" (*Sunday Post,* 20 April 2003). He is right but, sadly, in a marginalized minority.

INDIGENOUS RIGHTS AND THE CONSTITUTION

The party presently in government, Soqosoqo Duavata ni Lewenivanua, launched after the 2000 coup on an explicit nationalist platform to woo the supporters of the coup, was able to win power by adopting a fiercely pro-indigenous platform and by outbidding other moderate Fijian parties, which failed miserably at the polls. Its efforts to consolidate its position included a promise to review the constitution to entrench Fijian political control and a promise to pursue race-based, pro-Fijian, affirmative action policies in commerce, education, and the public service (Lal 2002b). It also bought off potentially troublesome opposition with diplomatic postings and other employment opportunities: Ratu Inoke Kubuabola, a key nationalist and coup supporter, is now Fiji's high commissioner to Papua, New Guinea. Isikia Savua, police commissioner at the time of the 2000 coup and allegedly involved in it, is Fiji's ambassador to the United Nations, and Adi Samanunu Talakuli, a known Speight supporter from the Kubuna Confederacy, is Fiji's high commissioner to Malaysia. Berenado Vunibobo, a George Speight sympathizer, has recently handled several diplomatic assignments for the government, and several people publicly known to have supported the coup—Apisai Tora, Ratu Josefa Dimuri, Ratu Inoke Takiveikata, Reverend Tomasi Kanailagi—are in the Senate. Ratu Jope Seniloli, coup leader George Speight's choice for president, is vice president. Political patronage has yielded the government much needed short-term benefits, but what will happen when the well runs dry, when there are no more perks to be distributed, or when the purchase price for silence or compliance rises beyond reach? How will the disgruntled elements be pacified then?

The present government has made review of the constitution a key plank in its political platform. Indeed, while heading the interim administration set up soon after the 2000 coup, Laisenia Qarase established a constitution review committee to recommend changes, headed by Professor Asesela Ravuvu, a known nationalist-leaning, former University of the South Pacific academic (Ravuvu 1992). This committee, created without public consultation, criticized from the beginning, and filled with handpicked men of dubious credibility (certainly in the Indo-Fijian community), lacked legitimacy and was unceremoniously disbanded after a few months.[2] A summary of its report—the full report, although taxpayer-funded, has not been released—suggested a hard-line nationalist position requiring *vulagis* (guests, foreigners such as Indo-Fijians) to accept the primacy of the *taukei* (the indigenous people, the first settlers) in politics. The fundamental nationalist argument is that Fiji "belongs" to the indigenous Fijians and its political leadership should therefore always be Fijian. Others can live in Fiji and work and pay taxes but should never aspire to political leadership. That acceptance, the nationalists argue, is an absolute, non-negotiable precondition for political stability.

Although that position is unpalatable to liberal democrats, it will, I suspect, be broadly embraced by many indigenous Fijians as a symbolic recognition of the indigeneity of the country. There was political stability in Fiji from independence to 1987 because a Fijian, who had the confidence of his people, was at the helm, many Fijians say. When his hold on power was threatened, as in 1977 and again in 1982, retribution was threatened. When he lost power in 1987, violence was sanctioned to reinstate him. In other words, democracy is viable only with an indigenous Fijian at the helm. Perhaps. But Ratu Mara led the country under a constitution forged through consensus, flawed though it was in many respects. Astute and skillful manipulation of the electoral system put the Alliance Party in power, not a constitutional requirement for an indigenous Fijian as head of government. Any constitution that breaches human rights conventions embraced by the international community will be rejected outright. That much is absolutely certain. A constitution that sanctions racial discrimination is doomed from the start, dead before the ink has dried.

There are other issues as well. Fijian society is much more diverse now than ever before. It is crisscrossed with a host of class, regional, provincial, and rural-urban interests that contest the claim of unity (Dakuvula 1992). No one leader commands the respect and loyalty of all Fijians as Ratu Mara once did, or Ratu Sir Lal Sukuna before him. The question is not really whether the head of government should be Fijian but rather which Fijian leader would be acceptable to a particular group of Fijians at any given point in time. Dr. Timoci Bavadra was a Fijian, and he was ousted by Fijians in a military coup. Rabuka was a Fijian, and he was defeated by indigenous Fijian votes, first in 1994 and again in 1999. Ratu Mara was a high chief—paramount chief of the province of Lau—and he was turfed from office after the 2000 coups by a group of Fijians. Commodore Frank Bainimarama is a Fijian, but his leadership of the armed forces was challenged by Fijian members of the military in a bloody mutiny in November 2000. George Speight claims indigenous ancestry (he now prefers to use his Fijian name, Ilikini Naitini), and he is languishing in jail for a crime whose beneficiaries are ruling the country.

Fijians of all ranks and backgrounds talk wistfully about the urgent need of forging indigenous political unity, but as the Reeves Commission argued, that goal is now unattainable, if it ever was. In the past, Fijians lived in villages, for the most part isolated from other communities and dependent on subsistence agriculture. They had their own "Native Regulations" and programs of work under the leadership of traditional leaders. But Fijian society has changed dramatically in the years since independence. Now, more than forty percent live in urban or peri-urban areas, participate in the cash economy, enjoy the benefit of tertiary education, and are well represented in the professions and the public sector (Prasad, Dakuvula, and Snell 2001). A sizeable and rapidly growing, self-made, Fijian middle class is an undeniable social fact in contemporary Fiji. It is therefore unrealistic to expect one political party to accommodate and represent a whole multiplicity of complex and competing interests.

The emphasis on unity also constrains the choices available to Fijian people, who cannot vote a Fijian government from office if it does not deliver on its promises. Fijians, like other citizens, have the same regard for effectiveness and efficiency. "The idea that a Fijian government must be maintained in office at all costs has grave consequences for political accountability," the commission argued. "It requires setting aside the normal democratic control on a government's performance in office. This is bad for the Fijian community as well as for the country as a whole" (Reeves, Vakatora, and Lal 1997).

Perhaps, as Stewart Firth (1989) suggests, Fijian politics increasingly is not about delivering on promises but rather about taking turns at the helm balancing regional, provincial, and social interests by virtue of traditional power calculations rather than competence or merit (private communication). In this equation, non-Fijians matter little. Demographic reality dictates that the future direction of Fiji politics will be influenced predominantly by indigenous concerns and calculations. The projected population of Fiji in 2002 was 824,596, of which indigenous Fijians numbered 441,363 (53.5 percent) and Indo-Fijians, 328,059, constituted 39.8 per cent (Fiji Bureau of Statistics). This trend will continue with accelerating Indo-Fijian migration and a lower birth rate in the community. Provincial and regional calculations will, as they already do, determine appointments, promotions, and other opportunities in public life. Commodore Bainimarama, from the Kubuna confederacy, was appointed commander of the Fiji military forces in part, people say, because the two previous commanders, Sitiveni Rabuka and Ratu Epeli Ganilau, were from Tovata. Rabuka complained how, bound by the 1990 constitution, under which Fijian members were elected to parliament from the provinces, he had to ensure the presence of all the provinces in the cabinet, irrespective of ability and talent. Not to do so would have been interpreted as a slight on a province's name and would have incurred its wrath. As Fijian numbers increase, however, the Fijian people will realize that good governance and not the calculations of provincial representation will serve their interests better. Many Fijians privately do but are fearful of expressing dissent when the strident talk of "Fijian interests" fills the air.

THE PROBLEM OF LEADERSHIP

Leadership is a problem for both the Fijian and Indo-Fijian communities. Among Fijians, the era of the dominance of paramount

chiefs with overarching influence across the whole spectrum of indigenous Fijian society, tutored for national leadership by the British in the
postwar years, has ended. The paramounts are gone: Ratu George
Cakobau, Ratu Edward Cakobau, Ratu Penaia Ganilau are all dead, and
Ratu Mara is in ailing retirement. These Fijian leaders brought with
them practical experience of public service—Mara was a district officer
in the predominantly Indo-Fijian sugar district of Ba—and a broad educational background in Fiji and overseas (Mara 1997). Whatever else
may be said of them and their politics, they generally believed in the
principles of good, accountable governance, no doubt a legacy of their
experience in the colonial civil service. They also had a multiracial cir-
cle of friends. They were committed to the principles of democracy,
even if it was on their own terms.

Their successors lack their broad experience and background.
Many latter-day Fijian leaders went from racially exclusive provincial
primary schools to predominantly Fijian secondary schools, such as the
Queen Victoria or Ratu Kadavulevu schools, their formative years unin-
formed and uninfluenced by any meaningful exposure to the cultures
of other communities (Dean and Ritova 1988; Sharpham 2000). They
are thus culturally ill-equipped to meet the leadership challenges of
building a multiracial nation, embroiled as they often are in provincial
and regional politics to carve out an inclusive, more embracing national
personality for themselves. In civil administration, too, senior military
leaders, facing dead-end careers but politically well connected, were
plucked from the armed forces to become district commissioners. They
served in areas and among people whose culture and way of life they did
not understand, unlike their colonial counterparts, who were expected
to have some fluency in the dominant language of the area (Hindustani
or Fijian, as the case might have been). That trend is likely to continue in
a public culture dominated by the politics of racial patronage.

Indo-Fijians have leadership problems of their own. Over the years,
there has been a marked shift in the social and educational background of Indo-Fijian leaders. At the time of independence—and
before—the majority of Indo-Fijian politicians were lawyers, businessmen, or landlords. Now, the base has diversified, with increasing numbers coming from the trade unions, academia, and the ranks of retired

schoolteachers and civil servants looking for second careers. They, too, for the most part, are handicapped by cultural limitations similar to those of the Fijians. Few politicians, for instance, are fluent in the indigenous language, more specifically Bauan, although those from rural areas with a substantial Fijian population, such as Bua, Savu Savu, Taveuni, Levuka, and Nadroga, do speak the local dialects. Not many of them have a direct experience of Fijian culture. Those who do are few and are not always appreciated. When a Labour parliamentarian made his maiden speech in his Nadroga dialect, there were disapproving voices among his own colleagues. The present minister of multiethnic affairs, George Shiu Raj, is a fluent Fijian speaker, at ease in both the cultures, but his cross-cultural skill is sadly derided. The message seems to be that you cannot be an "authentic" Fijian or Indo-Fijian if you are cross-culturally fluent or transgress ethnic and cultural boundaries. Such is the nature of public discourse in a racially segregated society.

The trade union culture, at least the way it has evolved in Fiji, muddies the already troubled currents of national politics. That was one of Mahendra Chaudhry's most severe handicaps as prime minister. Few disagreed with his prognosis of the problems facing Fiji, but they disliked the manner in which he articulated them: Forthright, testy, even confrontational, he did not appreciate that the Fijian mode of both private and public discourse is allusive and tempered by protocol. In trade union politics everywhere, ends often justify the means, but in national politics, the means, articulated in the glare of intense, unrelenting public scrutiny, are probably just as important as the end, if not more important. Chaudhry often chanted the mantra of electoral mandate to justify his uncompromising pursuit of his election promises. To be sure, he had the mandate from the voters, but that, he discovered to his enormous cost, was only one mandate among many. The Great Council of Chiefs had its mandate for the indigenous community, the Native Land Trust Board had its mandate, and the Fijian-dominated army its own. The art of political leadership in such a situation lay in negotiating one mandate among many competing and often incompatible mandates. Chaudhry's tragedy was that he ignored this crucial fact or at least showed an insufficient appreciation of it. This did not cause his downfall but did contribute to it.

MISCOMMUNICATION AND MULTIETHNICITY

Multiethnic societies, with divergent traditions of discourse, are prone to miscommunication and misunderstanding among the people and their leaders. Fiji is no exception. Indo-Fijian politicians revel in open, robust public debate often conducted without subtlety or irony. Their sledgehammer approach is direct, frontal, and confrontational and applauded by supporters drunk on the rhetoric of polarized politics. The Fijian tradition of public discourse, on the other hand, is generally the opposite: allusive, indirect, and hedged in by cultural protocol and a sensitive sense of person and place. In that context, sometimes what is not said is probably as important as what is. The gap is accentuated by the colonial legacy of racial compartmentalization, the absence of shared cultural traditions and language (except English), attachment to different faiths, and, more recently, the corrosive effects of the coups. Leaders talk at one another rather than to one another, and that, too, through the media. Of course, Fiji is not alone in this, but its peculiar history compounds the problem.

Misunderstandings are not only linguistic but also cultural. Let me illustrate. Most Indo-Fijians routinely assert that Fijians have more than eighty percent of all the land in Fiji. That is statistically true, but only a small percentage of it is economically useful. Moreover, land is not owned by one monolithic entity but by thousands of social units scattered throughout the islands. Thus, some Fijians have ample land, but others are effectively landless. These internal facts of uneven patterns of native landownership and land distribution escape Indo-Fijian comprehension beyond the most generalized understanding of their complexity. There is something more. Sir Vijay R. Singh (1995) wrote: "To most non-Fijians, land is an item of economic utility, a basis for an income, to be acquired, used and disposed of, if the occasion arises, without much emotional wrench. To most Fijians, on the other hand, and almost every rural Fijian, it is part of his being, his soul; it was his forebears' and shall be his progeny's till time immemorial. And the Indian sees large stretches of land between Suva and Sigatoka and Nausori and Rakiraki lying idle and can't understand it. He even becomes angry and bitter when he sees [what] his former flourishing farm is now after he was denied renewal of his lease—bush and scrub. The Fijian does not see it that way. Sufficient for him that it is there" (see also Overton 1988; Kamikamica 1997). Singh's characterization of the problem may have an element of deliberate exaggeration to underscore the difference in perception between the two communities, but the larger truth holds about two essentially competing and often incompatible notions of land as commodity and as cultural inheritance.

Just as Indo-Fijians do not grasp the Fijians' almost mystical attachment to their vanua (Ravuvu 1985), indigenous Fijians have little understanding of the deeper cultural and philosophical impulses that inform the Indo-Fijian mindset. The two most crucial concepts in Indo-Fijian thought are *izzat* (honor) and *insaf* (justice) (Gillion 1977; Mayer 1973; Lal 2000a). "Do what is right, not what is opportunistic," the *Bhagvada Gita* teaches. Islam sanctions jihad in the face of oppression. Death is preferable to dishonor. "A no muttered from the deepest convictions is better and greater," A. D. Patel told his rallies in the 1960s, quoting Mahatma Gandhi, "than a yes muttered merely to please, or worse, to avoid trouble," because in the end, truth will triumph *(Satyame Vijayte)*. I believe that Indo-Fijians would accept an outcome, even if it was politically disadvantageous to them, provided that it was transparently fair and did not affront their sense of dignity, honor, and self-respect. Indo-Fijian leaders pushed for a common roll of voting in the 1920s, when they were a minority in the population. As H. L. S. Polak told the Colonial Office in 1929, "everywhere they [Indians] stand by the principle of the common franchise as symbol of equal citizenship" (Gillion 1977:138). In the 1960s, the overwhelming majority rallied to that cause because the cause was just, not because it was politically advantageous or, indeed, achievable. Privately, many Indo-Fijians would probably accept a Fijian head of government if that outcome were achieved through political negotiation, but never as a constitutional right. In 1997, for example, Indo-Fijians put aside their longstanding demand for political parity with the Fijians and accepted proportionality in the reserved seats (twenty-three Fijian and nineteen Indo-Fijian) because the allocation was based on the demographic size of each group. It is difficult to convey how deeply offensive the words *second-class citizenship* are to the Indo-Fijians' sense of honor and self-worth.

INTERETHNIC DIALOGUE

Many Fijians feel that the Great Council of Chiefs (GCC) should play a more active role in national politics (Madraiwiwi 2002). Since its formal establishment after Cession in 1874, it has been the principal advisor to colonial and postcolonial governments on matters relating to the indigenous community. In the 1970 independence constitution, its nominees in the Senate enjoyed the power of veto over all legislation touching indigenous Fijian interests and concerns. The 1997 constitution, for the first time, recognizes the GCC as a constitutionally established institution (as opposed to one established by an Act of Parliament). Its fourteen nominees in an upper house of thirty-four members enjoy veto powers similar to the provisions of the 1970 constitution. The GCC also nominates the president and the vice president of Fiji. In short, its role and authority are an important political as well as constitutional fact and, perhaps more important, are beyond dispute or debate.

The GCC's supporters see it as an important force for good in restraining ethnic chauvinism, facilitating ethnic accommodation, and bridging the ethnic divide (Norton 1999). Perhaps, but the actual evidence is contestable. In 1987, the GCC convened to legitimize the overthrow of the Labour Coalition government, its proceedings dominated by its more hard-line, violence-threatening elements. Rabuka was hailed as a cultural hero and inducted into the GCC as a life member. In 2000, it similarly convened, at the behest of Speight supporters, to demand changes to the 1997 constitution—the very constitution it had unreservedly blessed—to accommodate the nationalist Fijian demand. Such inconsistency or blatant opportunism undermines the GCC's moral authority and legitimacy among non-Fijians. The current chair of the GCC, Ratu Epeli Ganilau, says that he is "keen to involve Indian leaders in the chiefs' council to discuss sensitive issues such as land" (*Fiji Times,* 14 April 2003). That is a welcome gesture in the right direction, but it would require a consistent effort to ensure that the Indo-Fijians are able to make genuine representation of their concerns, interests, and aspirations. Some Fijian chiefs, such as Adi Litia Cakobau, however, have argued that the chiefly council should represent the concerns of the indigenous community exclusively and that anything else would detract from its central purpose and mission.

Unfortunately, few avenues are available for interethnic dialogue outside the political arena, where talk is inevitably shrill and antennas are tuned to ethnic partisanship and sectional advantage. Religious organizations have few opportunities for regular interfaith conversation. The Methodist Church, to which the majority of Fijians belong, has been strongly nationalistic since the 1987 coups, except briefly, when it was led by Dr. Iliata Tuwere. In 2003, the church was pleading for the pardoning of the soldiers involved in the 2000 mutiny, as a part of the reconciliation process. In the mid-1990s, the various faiths—Hindu, Muslim, Christian—were able to overcome their differences to establish an Inter-Faith Search to seek common ground to pave the way for national healing and reconciliation, but corrosive effects of ethnic and religious politics have eroded its foundations (Hurley 2000). Fijians have their traditional avenues for intra-Fijian dialogue and dispute resolution, through district and provincial councils and through the machinery of the Fijian administration, but these are closed to the Indo-Fijians. The Girmit Council, an organization of various Indo-Fijian social and cultural groups formed in 1979 to mark the centenary of Indian arrival in Fiji, is virtually defunct. The Indian Summit, convened in the aftermath of the 2000 coup, has vanished without a trace. Indo-Fijians have their village committees and voluntary social and cultural associations, but these are ill-equipped to facilitate cross-cultural, interethnic dialogue. What is urgently required is a proper and properly equipped forum—outside the political arena—for an exchange of views between the two communities (Vakatale 2000).

Perhaps in this context, one recommendation of the Reeves Commission is worth revisiting. A number of Indo-Fijian organizations and community leaders asked the commission to recommend the creation of a representative Indo-Fijian umbrella body similar to the Great Council of Chiefs. The commission reported: "We endorse the principle behind the suggestion, but think that, initially, it should be taken up informally by the Indo-Fijian community. If there is agreement about the basis for the selection of the members of such a body, and it is able to meet and work in a way that demonstrates broad support for its composition and role, consideration should then be given to providing it with a statutory constitutional base" (Reeves, Vakatora, and Lal 1997:263). The Fiji Labour Party has already rejected the idea. An Indian council, it says, would "only serve to further divide the people [and] compartmentalise through the creation of racial institutions"

(*Daily Post*, 24 April 2003). That is true, just as it is true that a properly functioning council could also conceivably challenge the party's power base in the Indo-Fijian community. Be that as it may, the prospects look bleak.

The one bright light in an otherwise dim scene is the work of various multiethnic, non-government organizations. The Fiji Women's Rights Movement and the Women's Crisis Centre have done much to educate the public about issues of gender and domestic violence, even though both are urban-based. The Ecumenical Centre for Research, Education and Advocacy has sponsored important research on sensitive issues of social justice (Ratuva 2002). The Fiji branch of Moral Rearmament plays its part in trying to build cross-cultural bridges. Perhaps the most important, certainly the most controversial, has been the multiracial Citizens Constitutional Forum (CCF). Formed in the mid-1990s, it has convened numerous meetings and sponsored conferences, workshops, and publications to educate the public about its constitutional and human rights (Ghai 2000; Griffin 2001; Cottrell 2000). The CCF successfully challenged the abrogation of the 1997 constitution and, most recently, sought a Supreme Court ruling on the legality of the Qarase government's unwillingness to form a multiparty government with the Labour Party, as provided for in the constitution. The CCF has consistently been a sharp critic of the government's race-based affirmative action policies. Stung by CCF's criticism, the government deregistered it, but the organization's spirit remains undaunted, and it continues its battle for a non-racial, democratic Fiji. I believe that organizations like these, which seek non-violent resolution to the country's deep-seated problems through non-racial means, have much to contribute to the difficult task of nation building.

Recent crises have severely tested the fabric of race relations in Fiji. On the surface, things look calm. People play and work together, mingling in the markets, and children attend mixed schools—but the underlying tone is one of apprehension and anxiety. The government's affirmative action for indigenous Fijians, approved in some form or other by many Fijians, is resented by most Indo-Fijians because it is not transparent and is based on assumptions that defy the experience of daily life: Large sections of the Indo-Fijian population live in desperate poverty. They look in dread at the glass ceiling in the public sector.

Sugar cane growers, for the most part uneducated and unskilled, are forced to relocate and start over again as leases expire and their formerly productive fields revert to bush, generations of effort vanishing at the stroke of the pen or because of an official edict. The talk of reviewing the constitution to further entrench Fijian control causes them deep anxiety. I asked a prominent Indo-Fijian lawyer married to an indigenous Fijian what the future held for the Indo-Fijians. Her response was this: "There is little future for them here unless the present government changes its policies." That looks unlikely in the short term. Unwanted and uprooted, Indo-Fijians leave. Since 1987, more than 80,000 have left, and more will leave if they can, draining the country of skills and resources Fiji can ill-afford to lose (Mohanty 2002; Bedford 1989; Gani 2000). Now, more and more indigenous Fijians are leaving as well, to give themselves and their children a better future. The Indo-Fijians are caught in a bind. They are leaving because they do not see a future for themselves, and especially for their children, and the government is reluctant to spend money on training and educating a group it knows will one day go. A tragic catch-22 situation if ever there was one.

RECONCILIATION

To heal the wounds, the government has set up the Department of National Reconciliation and Unity to promote racial harmony and cohesion through social, cultural, educational, and sporting activities. Interethnic reconciliation, however, is only one part of the government's effort. An important role for the department is to "promote greater unity within the indigenous Fijian community through various programmes and activities at village, tikina, provincial and national levels." Political self-interest and survival instincts drive the reconciliation effort, for the government knows that its chances of electoral success depend crucially on Fijian unity, however elusive that prospect might be. Precisely for this reason, however much the government may wish it (and I know that members of the government at the highest level want justice done), the government cannot afford to be seen as proactive in pursuing the perpetrators of injustice. For this reason, the government reportedly asked the military to be lenient on those convicted of mutiny. For this reason, coup supporters have been dealt with lightly, and the government is loathe to reprimand ministers who utter racist remarks under the cover of parliamentary privilege.[3] Having aroused Fijian expectations with ambitious but costly promises, the government recognizes that it cannot now retreat. To appear to be compromising in the national interest would be seen as a sign of defeat. In short, the government is riding a tiger it cannot dismount at will.

True and enduring reconciliation, which all the people of Fiji want, will come only when the truth of the past is confronted honestly and dispassionately. In 1987, opportunistic leaders looked the other way when the coup took place. Sitiveni Rabuka was hailed as a cultural hero of the Fijian people—"Steve: The Hand of God," the T-shirts proclaimed. Which interests and concerns supported the overthrow of the Labour Coalition government were never investigated. Fiji is again reluctant to look too deeply into the heart of its problems. Thirteen years later, Fiji experienced another, and more violent, overthrow of a democratically elected government. If the causes of the present crisis are not investigated, Fiji will, as surely as night follows day, encounter more violent turbulence on its ill-fated journey into the future. The politicalization of the military, the police force, and the public service will have to cease. The culture of corruption and nepotism nourished after 1987 will have to be confronted; the political ambitions of the "Children of 1987" will have take the front seat as a matter of ethnic right curtailed. Regard for law and order will have to be reintroduced to groups of people, often young, unskilled, marginalized in the march to modernization, and vulnerable to emotional exploitation by would-be politicians. Only then will a solid base for economic development and investment be built.

Beyond that, the people of Fiji will have to reexamine the foundations of a political culture they have inherited. It is my firm view that a very large part of Fiji's problems derives from having a political system based on race (see also Naidu 2000). An obsession with race encourages ethnic chauvinism, poisons multiethnic discourse, and hinders the search for solutions to Fiji's deep-seated social and economic problems, which have little to do with race but everything to do with color-blind forces of globalization. I am not saying that ethnic sentiments are not authentic or deeply felt or that it is a "false consciousness" that will disappear with "modernization." Ethnicity has its proper place in public discourse. But I do have a problem with a discourse that sees an individual as nothing more than the sum total of his or her ethnicity, to the exclusion of every other formative influence. I do have a problem when the central pillars of state institutions are constructed solely on the edifice of ethnic exclusivity. To put it another way, "race is a fact of life" in Fiji, but only one of the many facts of life. Gender inequality, poverty and social deprivation, mismanagement and corruption, abuse of public trust, and the impinging forces of globalization are others.

The inescapable truth is that using race as a scapegoat will lead Fiji nowhere. Indo-Fijians do not threaten the foundations of Fijian culture and traditional society, modernity does. According to Asesela Ravuvu, "the new political system emphasises equal opportunity and individual rights, which diminish the status and authority of chiefs. Equal opportunities in education and equal treatment under the law have further diminished the privileges which chiefs enjoyed under colonial rule and traditional life before....Although village chiefs are still the focus of many ceremonial functions and communal village activities, their roles and positions are increasingly of a ritualistic nature" (Ravuvu 1988:171). Sitiveni Rabuka said, "I believe that the dominance of customary chiefs in government is coming to an end and that the role of merit chiefs will eventually overcome those of traditional chiefs: the replacement of traditional aristocracy with meritocracy" (*Fiji Times,* 29 August 1991).

And so it goes. One can turn back the hands of the clock, but it will not do the clock any good, as the distinguished humanist Oscar Spate used to say. To reclaim the potential that is surely hers, Fiji will have to reject the exhausted orthodoxies of the past, old ways of thinking and doing things. There is no alternative coexistence. A past unexorcised of its demons will continue to haunt the country's future.

Notes

1. This chapter is a reflection, not a conventional research piece. For that reason, I have not used extensive documentation, but the main sources from which I have drawn are indicated.

2. Indo-Fijian members on the committee were Joe Singh, Ben Bhagwan, Fred Achari, and Joseph Kanhaiya Lal Maharaj, all Christians when the overwhelming majority of the Indo-Fijian population was (and is) Hindu and Muslim.

3. For instance, the Minister of Women and Social Welfare, Asenata Caucau, likened Indo-Fijians to "noxious weeds" and refused to retract her words.

References

Adams, R. McC.

1966   *The Evolution of Urban Society.* Chicago: Aldine.

Alatas, S. H.

1977   *The Myth of the Lazy Native.* London: Frank Cass.

Ali, A.

1977   *Fiji: From Colony to Independence, 1874–1970.* School of Social and Economic Development Monograph. Suva: University of the South Pacific.

2001   Sweeping Victory. *The Review* (August–September):10–15.

Andaya, L. Y.

1996   From American-Filipino to Filipino-American. *Social Process in Hawaii* 37:99–112.

Anderson, B. R. O'G.

1972   The Idea of Power in Javanese Culture. In *Culture and Politics in Indonesia,* edited by C. Holt, pp. 1–69. Ithaca, NY: Cornell University Press.

Austin, J.

[1832]   *The Province of Jurisprudence Determined.* London: Weidenfeld and Nicolson.
1954

Bakhtin, M. M.

1981   *The Dialogic Imagination: Four Essays,* edited by M. Holquist and translated by C. Emerson and M. Holquist. Austin: University of Texas Press.

REFERENCES

Bayly, C. A.
1991   Maine and Change in Nineteenth-Century India. In *The Victorian Achievement of Sir Henry Maine: A Centennial Reappraisal,* edited by A. Diamond, pp. 389–397. New York: Cambridge University Press.

Beckwith, M.
1940   *Hawaiian Mythology.* Reprint, Honolulu: University of Hawai'i Press, 1970.

Bedford, R.
1989   Out of Fiji: A Perspective on Emigration after the Coups. *Pacific Viewpoint* 30:142–153.

Beechert, E. D.
1985   *Working in Hawaii: A Labor History.* Honolulu: University of Hawai'i Press.

Belshaw, C. S.
1964   *Under the Ivi Tree: Society and Economic Growth in Rural Fiji.* London: Routledge and Kegan Paul.

Benton, R. A.
1987   *The Appalling Merciless Weight of Responsibility: Organizing and Administering Māori-English Bilingual Education in New Zealand.* Te Wahanga Māori Occasional Paper No. 22. Wellington: New Zealand Council for Educational Research.

Bohman, J.
1991   *New Philosophy of Social Science: Problems of Indeterminacy.* Cambridge: Polity Press.

Bourdieu, P.
1977   *Outline of a Theory of Practice,* translated by R. Nice. Cambridge: Cambridge University Press.

Brenneis, D.
1986   Shared Territory: Audience, Indirection and Meaning. *Text* 6 (3):339–347.

Brewster, A. B. (aka A. B. Joske)
1922   *The Hill Tribes of Fiji.* London: Seeley, Service and Co., Ltd. Reprint, New York: Johnson Reprint Corporation, 1967.

Brown, S. G., director, and D. Boyland, associate
1977   Interviews with George Ariyoshi. John A. Burns Oral History Project, University of Hawai'i, Honolulu. Typescript on file with author and probably in University of Hawai'i Library.

Burgess, H. F. (also known as Poka Laenui)
1992   *Collection of Papers on Hawaiian Sovereignty and Self-Determination.* Wai'anae, Hawai'i: Institute for the Advancement of Hawaiian Affairs.

Burridge, K.
1969   *New Heaven, New Earth.* Oxford: Basil Blackwell.

Bush, J. E., and S. Pa'aluhi
1893   Ka Mo'olelo o Hiiakaikapoliopele. In *Ka Leo o Ka Lahui,* 5 January–July 12.

Butler, J.

1990   *Gender Trouble: Feminism and the Subversion of Identity.* New York: Routledge.

Cahill, E.

1996   *The Shipmans of East Hawai'i.* Honolulu: University of Hawai'i Press.

Calvert, Rev. J.

[1858]   *Fiji and the Fijians: Volume II, Mission History.* Suva: Fiji Museum.
1983

Chang, J.

1996   Lessons of Tolerance: Americanism and the Filipino Affirmative Action Movement in Hawai'i. *Social Process in Hawaii* 37:112–147.

Chapman, J. K.

1964   *The Career of Arthur Hamilton Gordon, First Lord Stanmore, 1829–1912.* Toronto: University of Toronto Press.

Charlot, J.

1987   *The Kamapua'a Literature: The Classical Traditions of the Hawaiian Pig God as a Body of Literature.* Monograph Series, No. 6. Lā'ie, Hawai'i: The Institute for Polynesian Studies, Brigham Young University, Hawai'i Campus.

1998   Pele and Hi'iaka: The Hawaiian-Language Newspaper Series. *Anthropos* 93:55–75.

2001   History of Hawaiian Education. Unpublished paper. Department of Religion, University of Hawai'i.

Chinen, J. J.

1958   *The Great Mahele: Hawaii's Land Division of 1848.* Honolulu: University of Hawaii Press.

Clammer, J.

1975   Colonialism and the Perception of Tradition in Fiji. In *Anthropology and the Colonial Encounter,* edited by T. Asad, pp. 199–220. London: Ithaca Press.

Coffman, T.

1998   *Nation Within: The Story of America's Annexation of the Nation of Hawai'i.* Honolulu: Epicenter Press.

Cohn, B.

1989   Law and the Colonial State in India. In *History and Power in the Study of Law,* edited by J. Starr and J. F. Collier, pp. 131–152. Ithaca, NY: Cornell University Press.

Cohn, B. S.

1987   The Census, Social Structure and Objectification in South Asia. In *An Anthropologist Among the Historians and Other Essays,* pp. 224–254. Delhi: Oxford University Press.

Collier, J., W. Maurer, and S. Suarez-Navaz

1995   Introduction to special issue on sanctioned identities. *Identities: Global Studies in Culture and Power* 2:1–29.

Collier, J. F.

1973　*Law and Social Change in Zinacantan.* Stanford, Calif.: Stanford University Press.

Collier, J. F., and M. Z. Rosaldo

1981　Politics and Gender in "Simple" Societies. In *Sexual Meanings,* edited by S. Ortner, pp. 275–329. New York: Cambridge University Press.

Coman, K.

1903　The History of Contract Labor in the Hawaiian Islands. *Publications of the American Economic Association* IV (3):1–67.

Comaroff, J., and J. Comaroff

1991　Of Revelation and Revolution. In *Christianity, Colonialism and Consciousness in Southern Africa,* vol. 1. Chicago: University of Chicago Press.

Comaroff, J., and S. Roberts

1981　*Rules and Processes: The Cultural Logic of Dispute in an African Context.* Chicago: University of Chicago Press.

Comaroff, J. L.

1978　Rules and Rulers: Political Processes in a Tswana Chiefdom. *Man* (n.s.) 13:1–20.

Cooper, G., and G. Daws

1990　*Land and Power in Hawaii.* Honolulu: University of Hawai'i Press.

Cottrell, J., ed.

2000　*Educating for Multiculturalism.* Suva, Fiji: Citizens Constitutional Forum.

Crozier, D.

1958　The Establishment of the Central Archives of Fiji and the Western Pacific High Commission. *Transactions and Proceedings of the Fiji Society* 5:91–106.

1959　Archives and Administrative Efficiency. *Transactions and Proceedings of the Fiji Society* 6:144–152.

Dakuvula, J.

1992　Chiefs and Commoners: The Indigenous Dilemma. In *Tu Galala: Social Change in the Pacific,* edited by D. Robie, pp. 70–79. Wellington: Bridget William Books.

Dakuvula, J., and V. Naidu

2002　The Politics of Land and Sugar: How to Ensure the Survival of the Industry. *The Review* (June):10–17.

Danziger, E.

1996　Parts and Their Counterparts: Spatial and Social Relationships in Mopan Maya. *Journal of the Royal Anthropological Institute* (n.s.) 2 (1):67–82.

Davis, N. Z.

1987　*Fiction in the Archives: Pardon Tales and Their Tellers in Sixteenth-Century France.* Stanford, Calif.: Stanford University Press.

Dean, E., and S. Ritova
1988   *Rabuka: No Other Way.* Melbourne: Doubleday.

De Cambra, H., ed.
1993   *He Alo A He Alo Voices on Hawaiian Sovereignty.* Honolulu: American Friends Service Committee.

Derrick, R. A.
1943   The Removal of the Capital to Suva, Fiji. In *Transactions and Proceedings of the Fiji Society of Science and Industry for Years 1940 to 1944,* pp. 203–209. Suva, Fiji: Fiji Society of Science and Industry.
1950   *A History of Fiji.* Vol. 1. Suva, Fiji: The Government Press.

Dewey, C.
1991   The Influence of Sir Henry Maine on Agrarian Policy in India. In *The Victorian Achievement of Sir Henry Maine: A Centennial Reappraisal,* edited by A. Diamond, pp. 353–375. New York: Cambridge University Press.

Diamond, A. I.
1978   The Development of the Central Archives of Fiji and the Western Pacific High Commission. *Transactions and Proceedings of the Fiji Society* 12:69–78.

Di Leonardo, M.
1998   *Exotics at Home: Anthropologies, Others, American Modernity.* Chicago: University of Chicago Press.

Dirks, N. B.
2001   *Castes of Mind: Colonialism and the Making of Modern India.* Princeton, NJ: Princeton University Press.

Douglas, M.
1966   *Purity and Danger: An Analysis of Concepts of Pollution and Taboo.* New York: Praeger.

Dowson, E., and V. L. O. Sheppard
1956   *Land Registration.* Colonial Research Publications, no. 13. 2d ed. London: HMSO.

Earle, T., ed.
1991   *Chiefdoms: Power, Economy, and Ideology.* New York: Cambridge University Press.

Ellis, W.
1969   *Polynesian Researches: Hawaii.* Rutland, Vt., and Tokyo: Charles E. Tuttle Co.

Emerson, N. B.
[1909]   *Unwritten Literature of Hawaii: The Sacred Songs of the Hula.* Rutland, Vt.:
1965   Tuttle.

[1915]   *Pele and Hi'iaka: A Myth from Hawaii.* Rutland, Vt.: Tuttle.
1978

Fallers, L. A.

1969   *Law Without Precedent: Legal Ideas in Action in the Courts of Colonial Busoga.* Chicago: The University of Chicago Press.

Faludi, S. C. T.

1991   Broken Promise: Hawaiians Wait in Vain for Their Lands. *The Wall Street Journal,* 9 September, A1.

Ferguson, K. E., and P. Turnbull

1999   *Oh, Say, Can You See? The Semiotics of the Military in Hawai'i.* Minneapolis: University of Minnesota Press.

Fieldhouse, D. K.

1984   *Economics and Empire, 1830–1914.* London: Macmillan.

Fiji Bureau of Statistics

1989   *Report on the Fiji Population Census 1986.* Suva, Fiji: Government Printer.

2001   "Fiji Census 1996"; available from www.statsfiji.gov.fj.

Fiji Daily Post

2000   "Vinaka Fiji Water," 18 November, editorial; available from fijilive.net/extras/editorial/16_11.htm.

Fijilive (Website)

2000   "New PM Addresses Nation," July.

Firth, S.

1989   The Contemporary History of Fiji: A Review Article. *Journal of Pacific History* 24:242–246.

Fitzpatrick, P.

1992   *The Mythology of Modern Law.* London: Routledge.

Foucault, M.

1991a   Governmentality. In *The Foucault Effect: Studies in Governmentality,* edited by G. Burchell, C. Gordon, and P. Miller, pp. 87–104. London: Harvester Wheatsheaf.

1991b   *Discipline and Punish: The Birth of the Prison,* translated by A. Sheridan. New York: Penguin Books.

Fox, J. J., and C. Sather, eds.

1996   *Origins, Ancestry and Alliance: Explorations in Austronesian Ethnography.* Canberra: Department of Anthropology, Australian National University.

France, P.

1969   *The Charter of the Land: Custom and Colonization in Fiji.* Melbourne: Oxford University Press.

Fried, M.

1967   *The Evolution of Political Society: An Essay in Political Economy.* New York: Random House.

Fuchs, L. H.

1961   *Hawaii Pono: An Ethnic and Political History.* Honolulu: Bess Press.

[1983 preface]

Fujikane, C.

2000   Introduction: Asian Settler Colonialism in Hawai'i. *Amerasia Journal* 26 (2):xv–xxii.

Fuller, L.

1941   Consideration and Form. *Columbia Law Review* 41:799–824.

Gani, A.

2000   Some Dimensions of Fiji's Recent Emigration. *Pacific Economic Bulletin* 15:1, 94–103.

Garrett, J.

1982   *To Live Among the Stars: Christian Origins in Oceania.* Geneva, Switzerland and Suva, Fiji: World Council of Churches in association with the Institute of Pacific Studies, University of the South Pacific.

1992   *Footsteps in the Sea: Christianity in Oceania to World War II.* Suva, Fiji and Geneva, Switzerland: World Council of Churches in association with the Institute of Pacific Studies, University of the South Pacific.

Geertz, C.

1973   *The Interpretation of Culture.* New York: Basic Books.

1980   *Negara: The Theatre State in Nineteenth-Century Bali.* Princeton, NJ: Princeton University Press.

1983   *Local Knowledge: Further Essays in Interpretive Anthropology.* New York: Basic Books.

Ghai, Y.

2000   The Implementation of the Fiji Islands Constitution. In *Confronting Fiji Futures,* edited by H. Akram-Lodhi, pp. 21–49. Canberra: Asia Pacific Press.

Gillion, K. L.

1962   *Fiji's Indian Migrants.* Melbourne: Oxford University Press.

1977   *The Fiji Indians: Challenge to European Dominance, 1920–1946.* Canberra: Australian National University Press.

Gluckman, M.

1955   *The Judicial Process among the Barotse of Northern Rhodesia.* Manchester: Manchester University Press.

1965a   *Politics, Law and Ritual in Tribal Societies.* Chicago: Aldine.

1965b   *The Ideas in Barotse Jurisprudence.* New Haven, Conn.: Yale University Press.

Goldman, I.

1970   *Ancient Polynesian Society.* Chicago: University of Chicago Press.

REFERENCES

Goldman, L.

1993   *The Culture of Coincidence: Accident and Absolute Liability in Huli.* Oxford: Clarendon Press.

Goodhue, K. P., and D. K. Sai

2000   *The Polynesian* XXI, 2 October, pp. 1, 3.

Goody, E. N.

1978   Towards a Theory of Questions. In *Questions and Politeness: Strategies in Social Interaction,* edited by E. N. Goody, pp. 17–43. Cambridge: Cambridge University Press.

Gordon, A.

1879   The System of Taxation in Force in Fiji. Paper read before the Royal Colonial Institute. London: Harrison and Sons.

1897   (See Stanmore.)

Griffin, A., ed.

2001   *Election Watch II: A Citizens Review of the Fiji Islands General Election 2001.* Suva, Fiji: Citizens Constitutional Forum.

Guha, R.

1981   *A Rule of Property for Bengal.* Delhi: Orient Longman.

Haas, M.

1992   *Institutional Racism: The Case of Hawai‘i.* Westport, Conn.: Praeger.

Hanks, W. F.

2000   *Intertexts: Writings on Language, Utterance, and Context.* Lanham, Md.: Rowman & Littlefield Publishers, Inc.

Hann, C. M.

1998   The Embeddedness of Property. Introduction to *Property Relations: Renewing the Anthropological Tradition,* pp. 1–47. Cambridge: Cambridge University Press.

Harvey, E. J.

1910   *Land Law and Registration of Title: A Comparison of the Old and New Methods of Transferring Land.* London: Longmans, Green & Co.

Harvey-Elder, C.

1910   Looking Ahead in Hawaii: The Japanese and the Census—A Suggestion for Government. *Sunset Magazine* 24:183–184.

Hasager, U., and J. Friedman, eds.

1994   *Hawai‘i: Return to Nationhood.* Document No. 75. Copenhagen, Denmark: International Work Group for Indigenous Affairs.

Hawai‘i

1896   Republic of Hawaii. Session Laws.

Hayek, F. A.

[1948]   *Individualism and Economic Order.* Chicago: University of Chicago Press.
1980

Higham, J.
1955   *Strangers in the Land: Patterns of American Nativism, 1860–1925.* Reprint, New York: Atheneum, 1970.

Hocart, A. M.
[1936]   *Kings and Councillors.* Chicago: University of Chicago Press.
1970

Hogg, J. E.
1920   *Registration of Title to Land Throughout the Empire.* Toronto: The Carswell Company.

Hooulumahiehie-i-ka-oni-malie-a-pua-lilia-lana-i-ka-wai (cited as *Hoʻoulumāhiehie*)
1909–   Ka Moolelo Hiwahiwa o Kawelo. In *Kuokoa Home Rula* (newspaper).
1910

Howard, A.
1990   Cultural Paradigms, History, and the Search for Identity in Oceania. In *Cultural Identity and Ethnicity in the Pacific,* edited by J. Linnekin and L. Poyer, pp. 259–281. Honolulu: University of Hawaiʻi Press.

Hurley, Sister B.
2000   Interfaith Search, Fiji. In *Educating for Multiculturalism,* edited by J. Cottrell, pp. 92–97. Suva, Fiji: Citizens Constitutional Forum.

J. S. E. [John S. Emerson]
1861   Letter to *Ka Hoku Loa.* (November):20.

Kaeppler, A. L.
1993   Hula Pahu: Hawaiian Drum Dances. Vol. 1. Haʻa and Hula Pahu: Sacred Movements. *Bishop Museum Bulletin in Anthropology* 3. Honolulu: Bishop Museum.

Ka Hae Hawaii (newspaper)
1856–1861

Kahn, J.
2000   The Mahogany King's Brief Reign. *The New York Times,* 14 September, C1 and C8.

Ka Hoku o ka Pakipika (newspaper)
1861–1862

Ka Lāhui Hawaiʻi
1993   *The Sovereign Nation of Hawaiʻi: A Compilation of Materials for Educational Workshops on Ka Lāhui Hawaiʻi.* Honolulu: Ka Lāhui Hawaiʻi.

Kamakau, S. M.
1961   *Ruling Chiefs of Hawaii.* Honolulu: Kamehameha Schools Press.

Kameʻeleihiwa, L.
1992   *Native Land and Foreign Desires—Pehea Lā e Pono Ai?* Honolulu: Bishop Museum Press.

References

Kamikamica, J.

1997   Fijian Native Land: Issues and Challenges. In *Fiji in Transition*, edited by B. V. Lal and T. Vakatora, pp. 259–290. Vol. 1. Research Papers of the Fiji Constitution Review Commission. Suva, Fiji: School of Social and Economic Development, University of the South Pacific.

Kanahele, P. K., and D. K. Wise

n.d.   Ka Honua Ola (The Living Earth): An Introduction to Pele and Hiʻiaka with Annotated Bibliography. Photocopy manuscript. University of Hawaiʻi Hamilton Library.

Kānepuʻu, J. H.

1862   Letter to the editor. *Ka Hoku o ka Pakipika*, 30 October.

Kapihenui, M. J.

1861–   He Moolelo no Hiiakaikapoliopele. In *Ka Hoku o ka Pakipika*, December
1862   1861 to July 1862.

Kaplan, M.

1988   Land and Sea and the New White Men: A Reconsideration of the Fijian Tuka Movement. Ph.D. diss., Department of Anthropology, University of Chicago.

1989a   Luve ni wai as the British Saw It: Constructions of Custom and Disorder in Colonial Fiji. *Ethnohistory* 36 (4):349–371.

1989b   The Dangerous and Disaffected Native in Fiji: British Colonial Constructions of the Tuka Movement. *Social Analysis* 26:20–45.

1990   Christianity, People of the Land, and Chiefs in Fiji. In *Christianity in Oceania: Ethnographic Perspectives*. Association for Social Anthropology in Oceania Monograph No. 12, edited by J. Barker, pp. 127–147. Lanham, Md.: University Press of America.

1991   Meaning, Agency and Colonial History: Navosavakadua and the Tuka Movement in Fiji. *American Ethnologist* 17:3–22.

1995   *Neither Cargo Nor Cult: Ritual Politics and the Colonial Imagination in Fiji.* Durham, NC: Duke University Press.

1998   When 8,870-850 = 1: Discourses Against Democracy in Fiji, Past and Present. In *Making Majorities: Constituting the Nation in Japan, Korea, China, Malaysia, Fiji, Turkey, and the United States*, edited by D. C. Gladney, pp. 198–214. Stanford, Calif.: Stanford University Press.

n.d.   The Hau of Other Peoples' Gifts. Unpublished manuscript.

Kaplan, M., and J. D. Kelly

1994   Rethinking Resistance: Dialogics of Disaffection in Colonial Fiji. *American Ethnologist* 21 (1):123–151.

1999   On Discourse and Power: "Cults" and "Orientals" in Colonial Fiji. *American Ethnologist* 26 (4):843–863.

n.d.   *Laws Like Bullets.* Durham, NC: Duke University Press, forthcoming.

Kauanui, J. K.

2002   The Politics of Blood and Sovereignty in *Rice* v. *Cayetano. Polar: Political and Legal Anthropology Review* 25 (1):110–128.

Kaukaliu, K. H.

1861   No ka Heluhelu ana i na Moolelo (On Reading Stories/Histories). In *Ka Hoku o ka Pakipika,* 17 October.

Keane, W.

1997   *Signs of Recognition: Powers and Hazards of Representation in an Indonesian Society.* Berkeley: University of California Press.

Kelly, J. D.

1988   Fiji Indians and Political Discourse in Fiji: From the Pacific Romance to the Coups. *Journal of Historical Sociology* 1 (4):399–422.

1989   Fear of Culture: British Regulation of Indian Marriage in Post-Indenture Fiji. *Ethnohistory* 36 (4):372–391.

1991   *A Politics of Virtue: Hinduism, Sexuality, and Countercolonial Discourse in Fiji.* Chicago: University of Chicago Press.

1995a   Threats to Difference in Colonial Fiji. *Cultural Anthropology* 10 (1):64–84.

1995b   *Bhakti* and Post-Colonial Politics: Hindu Missions to Fiji. In *Nation and Migration: The Politics of Space in the South Asian Diaspora,* edited by P. van der Veer, pp. 43–72. Philadelphia: The University of Pennsylvania Press.

1997   Gaze and Grasp: Plantations, Desires, Indentured Indians, and Colonial Law in Fiji. In *Sites of Desire, Economies of Pleasure: Sexualities in Asia and the Pacific,* pp. 72–99. Chicago: University of Chicago Press.

1998   Aspiring to Minority and Other Tactics Against Violence in Fiji. In *Making Majorities: Constituting the Nation in Japan, Korea, China, Malaysia, Fiji, Turkey, and the United States,* edited by D. Gladney, pp. 173–197. Palo Alto, Calif.: Stanford University Press.

1999   The Other Leviathans: Corporate Investment and the Construction of a Sugar Colony. In *White and Deadly: Sugar and Colonialism,* edited by P. Ahluwalia, B. Ashcroft, and R. Knight, pp. 95–134. Commack, NY: Nova Press.

2000a   Nature, Natives, and Nations: Glorification and Asymmetries in Museum Representation, Fiji and Hawaii. *Ethnos* 65:2, pp. 195–216.

2000b   Fiji's Fifth Veda: Exile, Sanatan Dharm, and Countercolonial Initiatives in Diaspora. In *Questioning Ramayanas: A South Asian Tradition,* edited by P. Richman. Delhi: Oxford University Press; Berkeley: University of California Press.

Kelly, J. D., and M. Kaplan

2001   *Represented Communities: Fiji and World Decolonization.* Chicago: University of Chicago Press.

Kelly, M.

1980   Land Tenure in Hawaii. *Amerasia Journal* 7:57–73.

REFERENCES

Kent, N. J.
1983   *Hawai'i: Islands Under the Influence.* New York: Monthly Review Press.

Kerkvliet, M. T.
1996   Interpreting Pablo Manlapit. *Social Process in Hawaii* 37:1–26.

Kingdom of Hawai'i
1845   Legislative Records, State Archives of Hawai'i.

Kuykendall, R. S.
1938   *The Hawaiian Kingdom, Volume I: 1778–1854, Foundation and Transformation.* Honolulu: University of Hawai'i Press.

Lal, B. V.
1986   Politics Since Independence: Continuity and Change, 1970–1982. In *Politics in Fiji: Studies in Contemporary History,* edited by B. V. Lal, pp. 74–106. Honolulu: Institute for Polynesian Studies, Brigham Young University, Hawaii campus, distributed by the University of Hawaii Press.

1988   *Power and Prejudice: The Making of the Fiji Crisis.* Wellington: New Zealand Institute of International Affairs.

1992   *Broken Waves: A History of the Fiji Islands in the Twentieth Century.* Honolulu: University of Hawai'i Press.

1997   *A Vision for Change: AD Patel and the Politics of Fiji.* Canberra: National Centre for Development Studies.

1998   *Another Way: The Politics of Constitutional Reform in Post-Coup Fiji.* Canberra: Asia Pacific Press.

2000a   *Chalo Jahaji: On a Journey of Indenture through Fiji.* Suva, Fiji: Fiji Museum; Canberra: Division of Pacific and Asian History, The Research School of Pacific and Asian History, Australian National University.

2000b   Madness in May: George Speight and the Unmaking of Modern Fiji. In *Fiji Before the Storm: Elections and the Politics of Development,* edited by B. V. Lal, pp. 175–194. Canberra: Asia Pacific Press at the Australian National University.

2002a   Making History, Becoming History: Reflections on Fijian Coups and Constitutions. *The Contemporary Pacific* 14 (1):148–168.

2002b   In George Speight's Shadow: Fiji General Elections of 2001. *Journal of Pacific History* 37:1, pp. 87–101.

Lal, B. V., ed.
1986   *Politics in Fiji: Studies in Contemporary History.* Laie, Hawai'i: Brigham Young University.

2000   *Fiji Before the Storm: Elections and the Politics of Development.* Canberra: Asia Pacific Press.

Lam, M.
1985   The Imposition of Anglo-American Land Tenure Law on Hawaiians. *Journal of Legal Pluralism* 23:103–129.

Latour, B.

1988   *The Pasteurization of France.* Cambridge, Mass.: Harvard University Press.

1993   *We Have Never Been Modern,* translated by H. Wheatsheaf and the President and Fellows of Harvard College. Cambridge, Mass.: Harvard University Press. (Original 1991: *Nous n'avons jamais été modernes: Essais d'antropologie symmétrique.* Paris: La Découverte.)

1996   *Aramis, or, The Love of Technology,* translated by K. Porter. Cambridge, Mass.: Harvard University Press.

Law, J.

1994   *Organizing Modernity.* Oxford: Blackwell.

Legge, J. D.

1958   *Britain in Fiji, 1858–1880.* London: Macmillan.

Lind, A. W.

1938   *An Island Community: Ecological Succession in Hawaii.* Chicago: University of Chicago Press.

1980   *Hawaii's People.* Honolulu: University of Hawai'i Press.

Linnekin, J., and L. Poyer

1990   Introduction to *Cultural Identity and Ethnicity in the Pacific,* edited by J. Linnekin and L. Poyer, pp. 1–17. Honolulu: University of Hawai'i Press.

Lloyd, D. T.

1968   A Brief Historical Review of the Land Boundaries in Fiji. *Transactions and Proceedings of the Fiji Society* 9:3–25.

Lucas, P. F. N.

2000   *E Ola Mau Kākou I Ka 'Ōlelo Makuahine:* Hawaiian Language Policy and the Courts. *Hawaiian Journal of History* 34:1–28.

Macaulay, T. B.

[1833]   Government of India. A speech delivered in the House of Commons, July
1910   10, 1833, in *The Miscellaneous Works,* vol.19 of *The Complete Works of Lord Macaulay,* pp. 146–93. Philadelphia: The University Library Association.

Macnaught, T.

1982   *The Fijian Colonial Experience: A Study of the Neotraditional Order under British Colonial Rule Prior to World War II.* Pacific Research Monograph 7. Canberra: Australian National University.

Madraiwiwi, R. J.

2002   Parkinson Memorial Lecture in *Good Governance in the South Pacific,* edited by K. Gravelle, pp. 7–15. Suva, Fiji: University of the South Pacific.

Mageo, J. M.

2001   On Memory Genres: Tendencies in Cultural Remembering. In *Cultural Memory: Reconfiguring History and Identity in the Postcolonial Pacific,* edited by J. M. Mageo. Honolulu: University of Hawai'i Press.

Maine, H.

1861   *Ancient Law: Its Connection with the Early History of Society and Its Relation to Modern Ideas.* London: Murray. Reprint, Tuscon: University of Arizona Press. 1st American ed. New York: Scribner, 1988.

1866   Mr. Prinsep's Panjab Theories: a Minute Paper. In Grant Duff, M. E., *Sir Henry Maine: A Brief Memoir of his Life...With Some of his Indian Speeches and Minutes,* edited by W. Stokes, pp. 335–340. London: Murray, 1892. Reprint, New York: Harper and Row, 1969.

1869   Trial of European British Subjects Under Jurisdiction Assumed by Native States: a Minute Paper. In Grant Duff, M. E., *Sir Henry Maine: A Brief Memoir of his Life...With Some of his Indian Speeches and Minutes,* edited by W. Stokes, pp. 400–401. London: Murray, 1892. Reprint, New York: Harper and Row, 1969.

1871   *Village Communities in the East & West.* London: Murray.

1987   *Lectures on the Early History of Institutions.* Buffalo, NY: William S. Hein and
(1875)   Sons.

Malinowski, B.

1966   *Crime and Custom in Savage Society.* London: Routledge.

Malo, D.

1839   On the Decrease of Population in the Hawaiian Islands, translated by L. Andrews. *The Hawaiian Spectator* 11, no. 2 (April):122–124.

Mamdani, M.

1996   *Citizen and Subject: Contemporary Africa and the Legacy of Late Colonialism.* Princeton, NJ: Princeton University Press.

Mara, Ratu Sir K.

1997   *The Pacific Way: A Memoir.* Honolulu: University of Hawaii Press.

Marcus, G.

1992   *Lives in Trust: The Fortunes of Dynastic Families in Late Twentieth-Century America,* with P. D. Hall. Boulder, Col.: Westview.

Maurer, B.

1997   *Recharting the Caribbean: Land, Law and Citizenship in the British Virgin Islands.* Ann Arbor: University of Michigan Press.

2002   Anthropological and Accounting Knowledge in Islamic Banking and Finance: Rethinking Critical Accounts. *Journal of the Royal Anthropological Institute* (n.s.) 8 (4):645–667.

Mayer, A. C.

1973   *Peasants in the Pacific: A Study of Fiji Indian Rural Society.* 2d ed. Berkeley, Los Angeles: University of California Press.

McCormack, J. L.

1992   Torrens and Recording: Land Title Assurance in the Computer Age. *William Mitchell Law Review* 18 (1):61–129.

Meek, C. K.

1949   *Land Law and Custom in the Colonies.* London: Oxford University Press.

Merry, S. E.

1997   Legal Vernacularization and Transnational Culture: The Ka
         Ho'okolokolonui Kanaka Maoli, Hawai'i 1993. In *Human Rights, Culture
         and Context: Anthropological Perspectives,* edited by R. Wilson, pp. 28–49.
         London: Pluto Press.

2000   *Colonizing Hawai'i: The Cultural Power of Law.* Princeton, NJ: Princeton
         University Press.

Meyer, M.

1998   Native Hawaiian Epistemology: Contemporary Narratives. D.Ed. diss.,
         Harvard University, Cambridge, Mass.

Miyazaki, H.

2000a   Faith and Its Fulfillment: Agency, Exchange and the Fijian Aesthetics of
         Completion. *American Ethnologist* 27 (1):31–51.

2000b   The Limits of Politics. *People and Culture in Oceania* 16:109–122.

n.d.a   Documenting the Present. In *Documents: Artifacts of Modern Knowledge,*
         edited by A. Riles. Durham, NC: Duke University Press, in press.

n.d.b   The Method of Hope. Stanford, Calif.: Stanford University Press, in press.

Mohanty, M.

2002   Contemporary Emigration from Fiji: Some Trends and Issues in the Post-
         Independence Era. Unpublished paper in the author's possession.

Money, J. W. B.

1861a   *Java; or, How to Manage A Colony, Showing A Practical Solution of the Questions
         Now Affecting British India.* Vol. 1. London: Hurst and Blackett.

1861b   *Java; or, How to Manage A Colony, Showing A Practical Solution of the Questions
         Now Affecting British India.* Vol. 2. London: Hurst and Blackett.

Moore, S. F.

1978   *Law as Process: An Anthropological Approach.* London: Routledge & K. Paul.

1992   Treating Law as Knowledge: Telling Colonial Officers What to Say to
         Africans about Running "Their Own" Native Courts. *Law & Society Review*
         26 (1):11–46.

Morgan, T.

1948   *Hawaii: A Century of Economic Change 1778–1876.* Cambridge, Mass.:
         Harvard University Press.

Moynagh, M.

1981   *Brown or White? A History of the Fiji Sugar Industry, 1873–1973.* Pacific
         Research Monograph 5. Canberra: Australian National University.

Murayama, M.

1959   *All I Asking For Is My Body.* Reprint, Honolulu: University of Hawai'i Press,
         1988.

REFERENCES

Nader, L.
2000   Anthropology Distinguished Lecture, 99th Annual Meeting of the
        American Anthropological Association, San Francisco, November.

Naidu, V.
2000   Evaluating Our Past and Moulding Our Future. In *Educating for
        Multiculturalism*, edited by J. Cottrell, pp. 59–64. Suva, Fiji: Citizens
        Constitutional Forum.

Narube, S.
1997   *Fijian Participation in Commerce in Fiji in Transition: Research Papers of the Fiji
        Constitution Review Commission*, edited by B. V. Lal and T. R. Vakatora,
        pp. 226–246. Suva, Fiji: School of Social and Economic Development,
        University of the South Pacific.

Nayacakalou, R. R.
1965   The Bifurcation and Amalgamation of Fijian Lineages over a Period
        of 50 Years. *Transactions and Proceedings of the Fiji Society* 8:122–133.
1971   Fiji: Manipulating the System. In *Land Tenure in the Pacific*, edited by
        R. Crocombe, pp. 206–226. Melbourne: Oxford University Press.

Niukula, P.
1997   Religion and the State in Fiji. In *Fiji in Transition: Research Papers of the Fiji
        Constitution Review Commission*, edited by B. V. Lal and T. R. Vakatora,
        pp. 53–79. Suva, Fiji: School of Social and Economic Development,
        University of the South Pacific.

Norton, R.
1990   *Race and Politics in Fiji*. 2d ed. St. Lucia: University of Queensland Press.
1999   Chiefs for the Nation: Containing Ethnonationalism and Bridging the
        Ethnic Divide in Fiji. *Pacific Studies* 22:1, 21–50.

Okamura, J. Y.
1996   Writing the Filipino Diaspora: Roman R. Cariaga's *The Filipinos in Hawai'i*.
        Social Process in Hawaii 37:36–57.
1998   The Illusion of Paradise: Privileging Multiculturalism in Hawai'i. In
        *Making Majorities: Constituting the Nation in Japan, Korea, China, Malaysia,
        Fiji, Turkey, and the United States*, edited by D. C. Gladney, pp. 264–284.
        Stanford, Calif.: Stanford University Press.
2000   Race Relations in Hawai'i during World War II: The Non-internment of
        Japanese Americans. *Amerasia Journal* 26 (2):117–142.

Okihiro, G.
1991   *Cane Fires*. Philadelphia: Temple University Press.

Ortner, S.
1981   Gender and Sexuality in Hierarchical Societies: The Case of Polynesia and
        Some Comparative Implications. In *Sexual Meanings*, edited by S. Ortner,
        pp. 359–409. New York: Cambridge University Press.

Osorio, J. K. K.

2001   What Kine Hawaiian Are You? *Journal of the Contemporary Pacific,* special edition (August).

2002   *Dismembering Lāhui: A History of the Hawaiian Nation to 1887.* Honolulu: University of Hawai'i Press.

Overton, J., ed.

1988   *Rural Fiji.* Suva, Fiji: Institute of Pacific Studies.

Parks, N.

1999   Notice of Arbitration to Initiate Recourse to Arbitral Proceedings in Compliance with the Permanent Court of Arbitration Optional Rules for Arbitrating Disputes Between Two Parties of Which Only One Is a State.

Parmentier, R. J.

1987   *The Sacred Remains: Myth, History and Polity in Belau.* Chicago: University of Chicago Press.

Pickering, A.

1997   Concepts and the Mangle of Practice: Constructing Quaternions. In *Mathematics, Science, and Postclassical Theory,* edited by B. H. Smith and A. Plotnitsky, pp. 40–82. Durham, NC: Duke University Press.

Posner, R.

2003   *Economic Analysis of Law.* New York: Aspen Publishers.

Povinelli, E. A.

1993   'Might Be Something': The Language of Indeterminacy in Australian Aboriginal Land Use. *Man* (n.s.) 28 (4):679–704.

Prasad, S., J. Dakuvula, and D. Snell

2001   Economic Development, Democracy and Ethnic Conflict in the Fiji Islands. Private paper in the authors' possession.

Pukui, M. K.

1980   Notes from a Kumu Hula. In *Hula: Historical Perspectives.* Pacific Anthropology Records No. 30, edited by D. Barrère, M. K. Pukui, and M. Kelly, pp. 69–93. Honolulu: Bernice Pauahi Bishop Museum.

n.d.   A Hawaiian Legend of a Terrible War between Pele-of-the-Eternal-Fires and Waka-of-the-Shadowy-Waters. Translation of Ke Kaua Nui Weliweli Ma Waena o Pelekeahialoa me Wakakeakaikawai by Tone-Iahuanu-Tahuria-Iarafai E (Moses Manu) in *Ka Loea Kalaiaina May 13 to December 30, 1899.* Hawaiian Ethnological Notes, vol. II, pp. 942–1008, Bishop Museum Archives.

Pukui, M. K., and S. H. Elbert

1986   *Hawaiian Dictionary.* Rev. ed. Honolulu: University of Hawai'i Press.

Rappaport, J.

1994   *Cumbe Reborn: An Andean Ethnography of History.* Chicago: University of Chicago Press.

Ratuva, S.

2002   *Participation for Peace: A Study of Inter-ethnic and Inter-religious Perception in Fiji.* Suva, Fiji: Ecumenical Council for Research, Education and Advocacy.

Ravuvu, A.

1985   *Vaka I Taukei. The Fijian Way of Life.* Suva, Fiji: Institute of Pacific Studies.

1988   *Development or Dependence: The Pattern of Change in a Fijian Village.* Suva, Fiji: Institute of Pacific Studies.

1992   *The Façade of Democracy: Fijian Struggle for Political Control, 1830–1987.* Suva, Fiji: Readers Publishing House.

Reeves, Sir P., T. R.Vakatora, and B. V. Lal

1996   *Towards a United Future: Report of the Fiji Constitution Review Commission.* Suva, Fiji: Government of Fiji.

The Review

2000a   "Tailor-Made for Small Businesses," October/November, pp. 28–29.

2000b   "The Thin Line," December, pp. 12–14.

Revilla, L. A.

1996   "Pineapples," "Hawayanos," and "Loyal Americans": Local Boys in the First Filipino Infantry Regiment, US Army. *Social Process in Hawaii* 37:57–74.

Riles, A.

1995   The View from the International Plane: Perspective and Scale in the Architecture of Colonial International Law. *Law and Critique* 6:39–54.

1997a   Part-Europeans and Fijians. In *Fiji in Transition,* vol. 1 of *Fiji Constitutional Review Commission Research Papers,* edited by B. V. Lal and T. R. Vakatora, pp.105–129. Suva, Fiji: School of Social and Economic Development, University of the South Pacific.

1997b   Part-Europeans and Fijians: Some Problems in the Conceptualisation of a Relationship. In *Fiji in Transition,* edited by B. V. Lal and T. R. Vakatora, pp. 105–129. Suva, Fiji: University of the South Pacific.

1998   Division within the Boundaries. *Journal of the Royal Anthropological Institute* (n.s.) 4 (3):409–424.

2000   *The Network Inside Out.* Ann Arbor: University of Michigan Press.

2004   The Empty Place: Legal Formalities and the Cultural State. In *The Place of Law,* edited by A. Sarat. Ann Arbor, Mich.: University of Michigan Press.

Roberts, R., and K. Mann

1991   Law in Colonial Africa. In *Law in Colonial Africa,* edited by K. Mann and R. Roberts, pp. 3–61. Portsmouth, NH: Heinemann.

Robertson, R. T.

1998   *Multiculturalism and Reconciliation in an Indulgent Republic.* Suva, Fiji: Fiji Institute of Applied Studies.

Robertson, R. T., and A. Tamanisau

1988   *Fiji-Shattered Coups.* Sydney, Australia: Pluto Press.

Rosa, J. P.
2000 Local Story: The Massie Case Narrative and the Cultural Production of Local Identity in Hawai'i. *Amerasia Journal* 26 (2):93–116.

Rumble, W.
1988 John Austin and His Nineteenth-Century Critics: The Case of Sir Henry Sumner Maine. *Northern Ireland Legal Quarterly* 39 (2):119–149.

Ruoff, T. B. F.
1957 *An Englishman Looks at the Torrens System.* Sydney, Australia: The Law Book Co. of Australasia.

Rutz, H., and E. M. Balkan
1992 Never on Sunday: Time Discipline and Political Crisis in Fiji. In *The Politics of Time,* edited by H. Rutz, pp. 62–85. Washington, D.C.: American Anthropological Association.

Rutz, H. J.
1978 Fijian Land Tenure and Agricultural Growth. *Oceania* 49 (1):20–34.
1995 Occupying the Headwaters of Tradition: Rhetorical Strategies of Nation Making in Fiji. In *Nation Making: Emergent Identities in Postcolonial Melanesia,* edited by R. J. Foster, pp. 71–93. Ann Arbor, Mich.: University of Michigan Press.

Sahlins, M.
1985 *Islands of History.* Chicago: University of Chicago Press.
1991 The Return of the Event, Again. In *Clio in Oceania: Toward a Historical Anthropology,* edited by A. Biersack, pp. 37–99. Washington, D.C.: Smithsonian Institution Press.
1992 Historical Ethnography. Vol. I of *Anahulu: The Anthropology of History in the Kingdom of Hawaii,* edited by P. Kirch and M. Sahlins. Chicago: University of Chicago Press.

Sai, D. K., P. U. Sai, G. V. Dubin, and K. P. Goodhue
2000 Memorial of the Hawaiian Kingdom Government to The Permanent Court of Arbitration at The Hague, Netherlands. Honolulu: Council of Regency. Available from www.alohaquest.org.

Sanadhya, T.
1991 *My Twenty-One Years in the Fiji Islands,* translated by U. Singh and J. Kelly. Suva, Fiji: Fiji Museum.

Scarr, D.
1973 *I, the Very Bayonet.* Canberra: Australian National University.
1980 *Viceroy of the Pacific: The Majesty of Colour, A Life of Sir John Bates Thurston.* Canberra: Australian National University.
1984 *Fiji: A Short History.* Laie, Hawai'i: Brigham Young University.
1988 *Fiji: The Politics of Illusion. The Military Coups in Fiji.* Kensington, Australia: University of New South Wales.

REFERENCES

Service, E.

1975   *Origins of the State and Civilization: The Process of Cultural Evolution.* New York: Norton.

Sharma, S.

2000   "Water Plant Seized," *Fiji Daily Post,* 12 July.

Silva, N. K.

1997   *Kū'ē!* Hawaiian Women's Resistance to the Annexation. *Social Process in Hawai'i* 38:2–16.

1999   *Ke Kū'ē Kūpa'a Loa Nei Mākou:* Kanaka Maoli Resistance to Colonization. Ph.D. diss., Department of Political Science, University of Hawai'i.

2000   *"He Kanawai E Hoopau I Na Hula Kuolo Hawaii":* The Political Economy of Banning the Hula. *Hawaiian Journal of History* 34:29–48.

Silva, N. K., and N. Minton

1998   *Kū'ē:* The *Hui Aloha 'Āina* Anti-Annexation Petitions 1897–1898. Honolulu: manuscript published by the authors.

Simpson, S. R.

1976   *Land Law and Registration.* Cambridge: Cambridge University Press.

Sinclair, M.

1969   Princess Nahienaena. *Hawaiian Journal of History* 3:3–31.

Singh, Sir V. R.

1995   Opening address in *Protecting Fijian Interests and Building a Democratic Fiji: A Consultation on Fiji's Constitution Review,* pp. 9–14. Suva, Fiji: Citizens Constitutional Forum.

Smith, A.

[1776]   *An Inquiry into the Nature and Causes of the Wealth of Nations.* Vol. 2. London:
1961   Metheun.

Sokonibogi, F. W.

1999   Letter to the Editor, *Fiji Daily Post,* 11 January.

Spate, O. H. K.

1959   *Fijian People: Economic Problems and Prospects.* Legislative Council Paper no. 13. Suva, Fiji: Government of Fiji.

Stanmore, A. H. G.

1912   *Fiji, Records of Private and of Public Life, 1875–1880.* Vol. I. Edinburgh: privately printed. Microfilm, University of Chicago Library, DU600.S68.

Stannard, D.

1989   *Before the Horror: The Population of Hawai'i on the Eve of Western Contact.* Honolulu: Social Sciences Research Institute and University of Hawai'i Press.

Stein, B.

1989   *Thomas Munro: The Origins of the Colonial State and His Vision of Empire.* Delhi, India: Oxford University Press.

Stillman, A. K.

2001   Re-membering the Cultural History of Hawaiian Hula. In *Cultural Memory: Re-Configuring History and Identity in the Pacific,* edited by J. M. Mageo, pp. 187–204. Honolulu: University of Hawai'i Press.

2002   Resurrecting Archival Poetic Repertoire for Hawaiian Hula. In *Handle with Care: Ownership and Control of Ethnographic Materials,* edited by S. Jaarsma, pp. 130–147. Pittsburgh: University of Pittsburgh Press.

Stoler, A.

1995   "Mixed Bloods" and the Cultural Politics of European Identity in Colonial Southeast Asia. In *The Decolonization of Imagination: Culture, Knowledge, and Power,* edited by J. P. N. Pieterse and B. Parekh, pp. 128–148. London: Zed Books.

Strathern, M.

1988   *The Gender of the Gift: Problems with Women and Problems with Society in Melanesia.* Berkeley: University of California Press.

1991   *Partial Connections.* Sabage, Md.: Rowman & Littlefield Publishers.

1992   Parts and Wholes: Refiguring Relationships in a Post-Plural World. In *Conceptualizing Society,* edited by A. Kuper, pp. 75–104. London: Routledge.

1996   Cutting the Network. *Journal of the Royal Anthropological Institute* (n.s.) 2 (3):517–535.

Sukuna, Ratu Sir L.

[1950]   *Fiji: The Three-Legged Stool: Selected Writings of Ratu Sir Lala Sukuna,* edited
1983   by D. Scarr. London, Basingstoke, England: Macmillan Education.

Suleri, S.

1992   *The Rhetoric of English India.* Chicago: University of Chicago Press.

Sullivan, L. R.

1923   The Labor Crisis in Hawaii. *Asia Magazine* 23:511–534.

Sutherland, W.

1992   *Beyond the Politics of Race: An Alternative History of Fiji to 1992.* Social and Political Change Monograph. Canberra: Australian National University.

Takaki, R.

1983   *Pau Hana: Plantation Life and Labor in Hawaii, 1835–1920.* Honolulu: University of Hawai'i Press.

1989   *Strangers from a Different Shore: A History of Asian Americans.* Boston: Little, Brown.

Tamura, E.

2000   Using the Past to Inform the Future: An Historiography of Hawai'i's Asian and Pacific Islander Americans. *Amerasia Journal* 26 (1):55–86.

Thomas, N.

1991   *Entangled Objects: Exchange, Material Culture and Colonialism in the Pacific.* Cambridge, Mass.: Harvard University Press.

REFERENCES

1992   The Inversion of Tradition. *American Ethnologist* 19 (2):213–232.

1994   *Colonialism's Culture: Anthropology, Travel and Government.* Princeton, NJ: Princeton University Press.

1997   *In Oceania: Visions, Artifacts, Histories.* Durham, NC: Duke University Press.

Toren, C.

1988   Making the Present, Revealing the Past: The Mutablility and Continuity of Tradition as Process. *Man* (n.s.) 23 (4):696–717.

Trask, H.

1993   *From a Native Daughter: Colonialism and Sovereignty in Hawai'i.* Monroe, Maine: Common Courage Press. Rev. ed. Honolulu: University of Hawai'i Press

1999   *From a Native Daughter: Colonialism and Sovereignty in Hawai'i.* Rev. ed. Honolulu: University of Hawai'i Press.

2000   Settlers of Color and "Immigrant" Hegemony: "Locals" in Hawai'i. *Amerasia Journal* 26 (2):1–24.

Trask, M. B.

2000a   Hawai'i and the United Nations. *Amerasia Journal* 26 (2):27–30.

2000b   Hawaiian Sovereignty. *Amerasia Journal* 26 (2):31–36.

Trautmann, T.

1997   *The Aryans and British India.* Berkeley, Calif.: University of California Press.

Vakatale, T.

2000   The Constraints and Challenges to Building Multiculturalism in Fiji. In *Educating for Multiculturalism,* edited by J. Cottrell, pp. 13–23. Suva, Fiji: Citizens Constitutional Forum.

Valeri, V.

1985   *Kingship and Sacrifice: Ritual and Society in Ancient Hawaii.* Chicago: University of Chicago Press.

Wagner, R.

1981   *The Invention of Culture.* 2d ed. Chicago: University of Chicago Press.

1986   *Symbols That Stand for Themselves.* Chicago: University of Chicago Press.

Wall, C.

1920   Sketches in Fijian History. In *Transactions of the Fijian Society for the Year 1919.* Suva, Fiji: The Fijian Society.

Wallerstein, E.

1974   *The Modern World-System I.* New York: Academic Press.

Ward, R. G.

1969   Land Use and Land Alienation in Fiji to 1885. *The Journal of Pacific History* 4:3–25.

1987   Native Fijian Village: A Questionable Future? In *Fiji: Future Imperfect,* edited by M. Taylor, pp. 33–45. North Sydney, Australia: Allen and Unwin.

Waterhouse, Rev. J.

1866   *The King and People of Fiji.* Reprint, Honolulu: University of Hawai'i Press, 1997.

Watters, R. F.

1969   *Koro: Economic Development and Social Change in Fiji.* Oxford: Oxford University Press.

Weber, M.

1947   *The Theory of Social and Economic Organization,* translated by A. M. Henderson and T. Parsons. New York: The Free Press.

Williams, Rev. T.

1858   *Fiji and the Fijians, Volume II: The Islands and Their Inhabitants.* Reprint, Suva, Fiji: Fiji Museum, 1982.

Wise, J. H.

1933   The History of Land Ownership in Hawaii. In *Ancient Hawaiian Civilization: A Series of Lectures Delivered at the Kamehameha Schools by Handy, Emory, Bryan, Buck, Wise, and Others,* pp. 77–91. Honolulu: The Kamehameha Schools.

Wittgenstein, L.

1953   *Philosophical Investigations,* translated by G. E. M. Anscombe. Oxford: Blackwell.

Wolf, E.

1982   *Europe and the People Without History.* Berkeley, Calif.: University of California Press.

Worsley, P.

1968   *The Trumpet Shall Sound.* New York: Schocken Books.

Yaqara Pastoral Company

1981   *Annual Report.* Fiji.

Yoshinaga, I., and E. Kosasa

2000   Local Japanese Women for Justice (LJWJ) Speak Out Against Daniel Inouye and the JACL. *Amerasia Journal* 26 (2):143–157.

Zerner, C., ed.

2003   *Culture and the Question of Rights: Forests, Coasts, and Seas in Southeast Asia.* Durham, NC: Duke University Press.

Index

School of American Research
Advanced Seminar Series

PUBLISHED BY SAR PRESS

CHACO & HOHOKAM: PREHISTORIC
REGIONAL SYSTEMS IN THE AMERICAN
SOUTHWEST
   Patricia L. Crown &
   W. James Judge, eds.

RECAPTURING ANTHROPOLOGY:
WORKING IN THE PRESENT
   Richard G. Fox, ed.

WAR IN THE TRIBAL ZONE: EXPANDING
STATES AND INDIGENOUS WARFARE
   R. Brian Ferguson &
   Neil L. Whitehead, eds.

IDEOLOGY AND PRE-COLUMBIAN
CIVILIZATIONS
   Arthur A. Demarest &
   Geoffrey W. Conrad, eds.

DREAMING: ANTHROPOLOGICAL AND
PSYCHOLOGICAL INTERPRETATIONS
   Barbara Tedlock, ed.

HISTORICAL ECOLOGY: CULTURAL
KNOWLEDGE AND CHANGING
LANDSCAPES
   Carole L. Crumley, ed.

THEMES IN SOUTHWEST PREHISTORY
   George J. Gumerman, ed.

MEMORY, HISTORY, AND OPPOSITION
UNDER STATE SOCIALISM
   Rubie S. Watson, ed.

OTHER INTENTIONS: CULTURAL
CONTEXTS AND THE ATTRIBUTION
OF INNER STATES
   Lawrence Rosen, ed.

LAST HUNTERS–FIRST FARMERS: NEW
PERSPECTIVES ON THE PREHISTORIC
TRANSITION TO AGRICULTURE
   T. Douglas Price &
   Anne Birgitte Gebauer, eds.

MAKING ALTERNATIVE HISTORIES:
THE PRACTICE OF ARCHAEOLOGY AND
HISTORY IN NON-WESTERN SETTINGS
   Peter R. Schmidt &
   Thomas C. Patterson, eds.

SENSES OF PLACE
   Steven Feld & Keith H. Basso, eds.

CYBORGS & CITADELS:
ANTHROPOLOGICAL INTERVENTIONS IN
EMERGING SCIENCES AND TECHNOLOGIES
   Gary Lee Downey & Joseph Dumit, eds.

ARCHAIC STATES
   Gary M. Feinman & Joyce Marcus, eds.

CRITICAL ANTHROPOLOGY NOW:
UNEXPECTED CONTEXTS, SHIFTING
CONSTITUENCIES, CHANGING AGENDAS
   George E. Marcus, ed.

THE ORIGINS OF LANGUAGE: WHAT
NONHUMAN PRIMATES CAN TELL US
   Barbara J. King, ed.

REGIMES OF LANGUAGE: IDEOLOGIES,
POLITIES, AND IDENTITIES
   Paul V. Kroskrity, ed.

BIOLOGY, BRAINS, AND BEHAVIOR: THE
EVOLUTION OF HUMAN DEVELOPMENT
   Sue Taylor Parker, Jonas Langer, &
   Michael L. McKinney, eds.

WOMEN & MEN IN THE PREHISPANIC
SOUTHWEST: LABOR, POWER, & PRESTIGE
   Patricia L. Crown, ed.

HISTORY IN PERSON: ENDURING
STRUGGLES, CONTENTIOUS PRACTICE,
INTIMATE IDENTITIES
   Dorothy Holland & Jean Lave, eds.

THE EMPIRE OF THINGS: REGIMES OF
VALUE AND MATERIAL CULTURE
   Fred R. Myers, ed.

Participants in the School of American Research advanced
seminar "Law and Empire in the Pacific: Intersections of
Culture and Legality," Santa Fe, New Mexico, March 18–22, 2001.
From left: Donald Brenneis, Sally Engle Merry, John D. Kelly,
Annelise Riles, Hirokazu Miyazaki, Martha Kaplan,
Jonathan Kamakawiwoʻole Osorio, and Jane F. Collier.
Not pictured: Brij V. Lal and Noenoe K. Silva